For Liberty

For Liberty

Larry B. Bramble

Copyright © 2011, Larry B. Bramble
Paperback ISBN: 978-1-257-97600-3
Hardcover ISBN: 978-1-257-97599-0

Preface to the Story

<u>Liberty</u>: the quality or state of being free:
    a: **The power to do as one pleases**
    b: **Freedom from physical restraint**
    c: **Freedom from arbitrary or domestic control**
    d: **The enjoyment of various social, political, or economic rights and privileges**
    e: **The power of choice**

As defined in the 1971 edition of *Webster's Seventh New College Dictionary*[1]

    As we look back upon the history of the United States, it appears that the one thing we all have in common is that all of our families have immigrated here from another part of the world. For any person seeking a better way of life will follow that desire no matter how far it may take them. Under the rule of kings, queens, monarchs, dictators, potentiates and the like, every facet of life is controlled by those in power; the idea that common people may do as they choose is greatly diminished, as their liberty is tied by the restraints of their dictators' desires. The answer to the question, "Why did these people choose to come here?" is therefore obvious: for liberty! The United States was established as a republic where the supreme power rests in all the citizens entitled to vote and those elected responsible to them and there will and not just a democracy where those elected feel more entitled to use their own judgment, which may conflict with the will of the

---

[1] *Webster's Seventh New College Dictionary*, (PAGE 486) (Company, 1971)

people. The United States offered immigrants the opportunity to create the kind of life they had always wanted for themselves and their families.

So it is not surprising that during the decades preceding the outbreak of the Civil War, there was a great influx of immigrants who sought security and opportunity here in America. Between 1820 and 1860, approximately 4,000,000 people immigrated to this still new republic we call the United States. Many of these hearty souls quickly sought to adapt to their new country, seeking citizenship, sending their children to school, and attempting to learn English.

When hostilities broke out in 1861, the patriotism of these new arrivals moved them to quickly respond to Lincoln's call for troops in a stirring fashion. Many regiments were initially formed by men from the same backgrounds, who swiftly organized and banded together in the states where they had settled. The overwhelming majority of those foreign-born soldiers, who made up better than one-third of the army, served the United States, their new home country, loyally and well throughout the war and for the rest of their lives. Their valiant efforts helped to ensure a united country and to secure the future of the nation. By their deeds, they proved their devotion to the Union; in fact, without their considerable contribution, it is doubtful whether the Union could have been preserved at all. America is a land of great diversity, and there is nothing more diverse than the multitude of origins of its people; it is a true immigrant nation, whose ancestors saw opportunity in a new homeland.

Table of Contents

Chapter 1. In the Beginning 1
Chapter 2. To the Battle of Springfield 11
Chapter 3. To the Battle of Antietam 31
Chapter 4. To the Second Battle of Winchester 83
Chapter 5. To the Battle of Fort Sanders, Knoxville 111
Chapter 6. To the Battle of the Wilderness 149
Chapter 7. To Bermuda Hundred 165
Chapter 8. To the End of the War 193
Chapter 9. In Their Hearts, They Were Americans! 225

Chapter 1

In the Beginning

I'm not a writer by trade, nor am I a historian. And though all my life I knew my maternal great-great-grandfathers had fought in the Civil War, it wasn't until later in life that I became interested in history and started investigating my genealogy. Not surprisingly, the more I learned, the more interested I became, especially considering the current state of immigration in our country. Better understanding of immigration to this country today can be found in the roots of all our forefathers who came to this country to escape repression and begin a new life, so I decided to put this story together to follow their movements during the war.

My goal is to tell the story of my great-great-grandfathers as accurately as possible as they crisscross the country as well as some of what they saw and experienced during this time in history. The characters in this book are all immigrants in my family who came over before or during the Civil War.

We knew that Tougart Snyder, whose original name was Trougott Schneider,[2] had received his citizenship for service during the Civil War.[3] As I dug back into my family's history and explored all the various names attached to my family, I found the Lenderking branch on my father's side. Philip

---

[2] Names of immigrants are sometimes spelled differently than they were born with, which complicates the research of genealogy.
[3] There is documentation that proves this.

Lenderking, another great-great-grandfather, and his four brothers also served in different regiments during the Civil War.

Initially I found research already completed by Ruth Lenderking Wormelle, who had put together a summary of the Lenderking family's history that was very helpful. This collection includes more than sixty letters and documents dated from the birth of Christopher Theodore Lenderking in 1796.

According to a manuscript genealogy of the Lenderking family, the father of my great-great-grandfather, Christopher Theodore Lenderking, was the second of five children of Gottfried and Mary Lenderking. By the time Christopher Theodore entered his teens, Napoleon had already succeeded against great odds, driving the Austrian army out of Italy at the helm of Italy's army. The rising power of Napoleon and his successful campaign in Egypt would likely have been a prominent subject of conversation among Christopher Theodore's father and the men in his regiment.[4] As the army swept into and captured Westphalia, threatening Hesse, Theodore was also ready to take his part in defending his country. While he served in the artillery corps 1814–1815, the efforts and sacrifices of his regiment were successful in repelling the invasion. The citation he received for his part follows:

"…that the Constable Theodore Lenderking formerly attached to the Artillery Corps, born at Homburg, territory Homburg, in accordance with the highest order of March 14, 1821, given all those warriors and subjects of the electorate of Hesse, who during the year 1814 and 1815 participated [in] and supported Germany's fight for independence, herewith receives the favorable appointed Memorial and Medal of Honor, forged of captured artillery, by the power of the undersigned authority, and accordingly is true bearer of this citation, for which this document is received, giving the rights of legitimate post session of all honors mentioned herein."

---

[4] Wormelle, *The Lenderking Family*, (PAGE 2) (Wormelle, 1969)

Christopher Theodore was married January 27, 1827, in Hersfeld, to Friedricke Karoline Marie Philippine Sunkel, of the same town; he was employed there as a sergeant major and continued in that capacity until 1834. His first child and only daughter, Martha Barbara, was born in Hersfeld March 20, 1833. He was later transferred to Netra where four sons were born: Georg Frederick, March 27, 1835; Carl Jacob, April 1, 1837; Georg Heinrich, June 10, 1839; and Rudolph Theodore, June 10, 1841.

In 1842 Theodore took his family to Heiligestock (between Nassau and Frankfurt), where he became a road tariff collector. It was here that Philip Heinrich was born, June 17, 1843. The family made their last home in Fritzlar, beginning in 1846. Ludwig (Louis) was born there July 7 of the same year. Six months later, on February 11, 1847, their mother Philippine died, followed by Christopher Theodore Lenderking in October 1855.[5]

The brothers and sister continued to live in the house for two years, but there were changes in the family circle. A few months later, the three of the eldest sons, Rudolph, George and Frederick departed for Detroit, Michigan. Philip was confirmed the following spring, in Fritzlar, on April 19, 1858. In the spring of the following year, June 8, he applied for permission to emigrate to America which he quickly received. Philip sailed with his aunt Maria Lenderking, arriving in Baltimore on September 11, 1857. Ludwig (Louis) went to live with the Schlotthauers,[6] whom I believe were friends of the family.

At the time of Christopher Theodore Lenderking's death, a daughter of his sister, Maria, was living in Michigan. Her name was Martha Andrass, and she was married to Theodore Eglof. The Eglofs owned a farm on the northern peninsula in Michigan.[7] Mr. Eglof did a small amount of mining in

---

[5] Wormelle, *The Lenderking Family*, 2 (Wormelle, 1969p.2)
[6] Ibid., 2–3 (Wormelle, 1969pp.2-3)
[7] Ibid., 5 (Wormelle, 1969, p.5)

addition to running his farm in Marquette County. It was to this place that the Eglof family welcomed the two younger Lenderking boys, George and Rudolph, in 1856.

Rudolph was to be given one hundred dollars, meals, and laundry for three years to help with the mining and farming. But after a disagreement, he left the Eglofs in June to stay with his brother Fritz (Frederick) and found a job tending horses for six dollars a month. Then Peter Wieber, a friend of the family from Fritzlar who was also in America by that time, asked him to apprentice as a blacksmith and offered to pay the same three-year arrangement as the Eglof's and even added fifteen dollars.

Maria and Philip Lenderking spent about six months in Baltimore after their arrival in America. Martha Eglof expressed that it would be to their benefit to come to Michigan and live with them. Philip chose to stay behind, but Maria continued out west, building visions of a happy family, succeeding in their ventures in this new country and eventually settling in Michigan as Maria had suggested.

Philip, who had remained in Baltimore, took residence in the southern Baltimore area. There were a large number of German settlers in that city at the time, and he had managed to establish a place among them.

Rudolph was anxious to hear from Phillip but was greatly disappointed to receive no word from him. He wrote Philip asking if he had learned yet how to speak and write English.

"If not you had better not hold on to the few shillings but go to night school or Sunday school to learn it… If you cannot read this I will write in German in my next letter."

In February of 1858, Rudolph wrote to Philip who apparently was considering a trip to Michigan,

"if you would come here at first it would have been much cheaper since immigrant fares are cheaper. Victuals are very reasonable here (Detroit). One can buy a bushel of potatoes for $.24-$.35; good apples for $.50; flour 300 cents for Rye and 375 cents for superfine; eggs for $.13 a dozen; $.15 from butter, etc."

Reading the correspondence between the Lenderkings, one feels the Ditmars of Baltimore may have been friends of theirs in Germany, perhaps godparents to Philip. This may have been the reason he remained in Baltimore rather than proceeding to Detroit.[8] Phillip lived with them from his arrival until the late spring of 1858, the duration of his apprenticeship in the tinsmith trade. Both Maria and Rudolph seem familiar with the family, mentioning them in their correspondence. His sister, Martha, wrote saying,

"... You wrote that you became a tinsmith but did not mention how you did so... Best wishes to you and Ditmar and the children."

If the Lenderkings came to America in the late 1850s to escape turmoil and bloodshed in Europe, they were not to find peace for long. Unrest prevailed in Maryland and Virginia, and Baltimore was not without its problems either.[9] October 16, 1859, was marked by John Brown's abolitionist raid, whose intent was to start an armed slave revolt by seizing a United States arsenal at Harper's Ferry, Virginia. His plan failed, and he was hung for his traitorous efforts.

The Republican Party that first arrived on the scene in 1854 was still in its infancy. With a strict opposition to slavery, the Grand Old Party grew rapidly as it opposed the expansion of slavery into the Western territories. Its members believed strongly in the idea of life, liberty, and the pursuit of happiness. As the party further believed that slavery hampered the ability of the free man to make a living, it was evident that slavery was an affront to all men's liberty. Even in the South, only about twenty-four percent of the families owned slaves, the cheapest form of labor, which restricted the ability of the rest of the southern population to grow in their own prosperity.

Political unrest continued into the 1860s as the presidential election heated up. In Baltimore, the chosen

---

[8] Wormelle, *The Lenderking Family*, 6–7 (Wormelle, 1969, pp.6-7)
[9] Ibid., 7 (Wormelle, 1969, p.7)

home of Martha, Philip and now Louis (Ludwig), many citizens were strongly Southern in their convictions. Similar actions and reactions occurred in other border states with many Northern sympathizers enlisting in the armed forces. On November 6, 1860, Lincoln won the presidential election, raising the turmoil in the states to the boiling point.

Southerners in many respects felt closer to England than those living in the North. In fact, Southerners actually thought of themselves as purer than the Northerners who were mingling with the masses of immigrants from many other countries. So on December 20, South Carolina was the first state to secede from the Union. On January 9, 1861, supply ships containing reinforcements headed to Fort Sumter were repulsed by secessionist batteries. Local newspapers reported to the people, keeping them informed as the country continued to heat up like a pressure cooker about to explode. The inauguration of Abraham Lincoln on March 4, 1861 added fuel to the already treacherous fire brewing in the South, changing the exchange of harsh words to Cannon fire.

Bombardment of Fort Sumter

With more states seceding from the Union, Fort Sumter was fired upon April 12, and war officially began. By the fourteenth, the Union forces inside could no longer withstand the bombardment, so they lowered their countries flag and abandoned the fort.

The country was now in dire circumstances. Many of the good officers from the South serving in the American Army resigned their commissions to join their home Confederate States Army. The total U.S. Army, now deficient of officers, only consisted of ten regiments of infantry, four artillery, two cavalry, two dragoons, and one of mounted infantry. These ten army regiments, which contained approximately 197 companies, were scattered widely. Throughout the seventy-nine isolated posts in the West were only 179 companies, and east of the Mississippi about a mere eighteen, primarily located along the Canadian border and the Atlantic coast.[10]

On a somewhat different note was the case of Maryland, which had been involved in military conflict since the war of 1812. Now, its citizens were taking sides, with the majority favoring the South—a choice that would be particularly tragic for states that were still loyal to the Union but yet containing slave holders. The divide was so great in the state; it was even splitting families, with one brother choosing the Confederate Regiments, while another joined the Union Army. As a result, President Lincoln divided Maryland into three military districts that were to be secured by Federal troops. On April 15, Lincoln initiated a proclamation calling for Maryland to contribute several ninety-day Regiments of Maryland volunteers to serve in the Union Army.

---

10 Wikipedia, "Union Army" (PAGE 2) (http://en.wikipedia.org/wiki/Union_Army, 2011)

Baltimore Riots

As more states in the South seceded from the Union, President Abraham Lincoln found the U.S. Army had a drastic shortage of men. Also Washington D.C. was suddenly in a dangerous position, bordered by Virginia, a state in secession, and further surrounded by slave holding states. The 6th Massachusetts Regiment was the closest and possibly the best-equipped volunteer unit in the Bay-states at the time. It left for Washington on the very same day that Virginia seceded. They reached Baltimore (where Martha, Louis, and Philip Lenderking still lived) on April 19,. That city was greatly divided in its loyalty, with violent political gangs dominating Baltimore's streets. With no direct train route across the city of Baltimore, the 6th Massachusetts bound for Washington was forced to pass through its streets. A mob with secessionist sympathies had gathered to block them, and not surprisingly, the scene eventually turned hostile. The angry mob picked up stones and threw them at the soldiers, wounding a number of them, so they were forced to reply by firing their muskets. During the riot, four soldiers and twelve citizens were killed and dozens more injured on both sides.[11] As a result of this violence, Baltimore would require special attention throughout the period of political unrest. The 1st Maryland infantry was the only military unit in Maryland in the spring of 1861,[12] so as Northern regiments traveled through the state, the 1st Maryland was made responsible for maintaining law and order.

The Division of States during the Civil War

Lincoln called on the states to raise a force of seventy-five thousand men for a three-month period to put down this insurrection. Of course, this put more strong pressure on the bordering states to choose sides, which four did by joining the Confederacy. With the Confederacy now eleven states strong, the patriotic Northerners, abolitionists and immigrants were quick to respond to the president's call. Ten thousand

---

[11] Maryland Online Encyclopedia, "Riots, Baltimore, 1861" (PAGES 1-2) (mdoe.org, 2005 www.mdoe.org/riots_balt_1861.html)
[12] Author? "Maryland Regiments" (PAGE 1) (War, http://www.2ndmdinfantryus.org/sites.html)

Germans in New York and Pennsylvania immediately responded, as did the French patriots.[13]

Each regiment that was raised contained ten companies, each commanded by a captain and deployed according to their ranks of captains. As most regiments were primarily raised by a single state, they were generally known by the number and state, such as 2nd Michigan, 5th Maryland, etc.[14]

It is in the beginning of these trying times for the country that we will begin to follow the movements of my great-great-grandfather Philip Lenderking's immigrant family and my great-great-grandfather Tougart Snyder.

Encampment of Army of the Potomac at Cumberland Landing on Pamunkey River

---

[13] Wikipedia, "Union Army," 2 (http://en.wikipedia.org/wiki/Union_Army, 2011p.2)
[14] Ibid., 4 (http://en.wikipedia.org/wiki/Union_Army, 2011p.4)

Chapter 2
To the Battle of Springfield

2nd Michigan near Bull Run

Rudolph Lenderking
2nd Michigan Infantry Regiment

On April 13, 1861, President Lincoln presented the first proclamation, calling for seventy-five thousand volunteers of the organized militia of the states to serve three months. A number of militia quickly organized and were accepted into federal service as a three-month regiment. Subsequent orders from the war department caused the unit to be reorganized and re-enlisted as a three-year regiment. Those who desired to withdraw from federal service due to this extended tour of duty were allowed to do so. These uniformed companies were ordered to wait in their organized units at their home locations until needed.[15]

On April 25, the order came to rendezvous at Detroit for their acceptance into service. Moving swiftly to the call, all were in camp by the twenty-seventh. As they were not expected to arrive so quickly, the quarters they reported to were not properly prepared.

---

[15] Don & Lois Harvey, "2nd Regiment Michigan Volunteer Infantry "(PAGE 1) (War.org, michiganinthewar.org/infantry/2ndinf.htm)

During the organization process, the regiment was ordered to Fort Wayne, near Detroit, where its recruitment was completed. It was also at this time, that Rudolph Lenderking patriotically answered the president's call and enlisted in Company A as a private. He was a blacksmith by trade and stood five feet, eight and a half inches high, with a light complexion, blue eyes, and light hair.[16]

Soon after, the men found themselves marching and drilling as part of their daily routine. They drilled in squads and in company formations. These men had to get a accustomed to the orders and the formations such as marching in a column and in a "company front," how to face properly, dressed the line so the men were evenly spaced in formation, as well as interact with your fellow soldiers. For some, it was difficult at first to salute officers they had previously known as barbers or clerks from their own hometown. Getting used to the rigors and demands of army life was not easy, as discipline was of first and foremost importance, a concept some people found hard to understand.[17]

The infantryman had to learn the manual of arms in order to properly use his rifle-musket. The drill would be performed over and over again until he could do it instinctively. The infantry used tactics that hadn't changed much since the time of the American Revolution. The men were taught to move in

---

[16] The National Archives, "Rudolph Lenderking, Co. A, 2nd Michigan Infantry" (A.G.O. No. 45-First) (The National Archives, Record Group 94, Entry 534, Box1411)

[17] Service, The United States Dept. of the Interior, *"The Civil War soldier, what was life as a soldier like in 1863?",* 1-2 (Service, Gettysburg National Military Parkpp.1-2)

close knit formations of two rows of soldiers, with each man standing side-by-side, even shoulder to shoulder. These close ranks were considered a necessity because of the limitations of the musket. Although old-fashioned, the formations were still useful to insure the massing of continuous firepower that an individual soldier could not sustain. However, marksmanship on the rifle range was not considered as important, as the war department believed each man would shoot accurately when told to, and they did not wish to waste ammunition fired on random targets.[18]

The 2nd Michigan Infantry was mustered into federal service on May 25, 1861, with 1,013 officers and men on the rolls. This was the first of the three-year regiments to be raised in that state. At this time it was attached to Richardson's Brigade, Division of the Potomac. Private Lenderking was put on a special detached duty on Bk. Road that would last through August of 1861 by order of Gen. I. B. R[19] (General Israel Bush Richardson).

June 6, 1861, the Regiment moved from Fort Wayne to Washington D.C.; A few days later, on the tenth, they proceeded to Camp Winfield Scott on Washington Heights overlooking the "Chain Bridge," where they were quartered.[20]

The regiment was serving in General Tyler's division. With Col. Richardson in command of the brigade and Lt. Col. Chipman a captain in the regular army,[21] the regiment was now under the command of Maj. Williams. Under this

---

[18] Service, The United States Dept. of the Interior, *The Civil War soldier, what was life as a soldier like in 1863?*, 2 (Service, Gettysburg National Military Parkp.2)
[19] The National Archives, "Rudolph Lenderking, Co. A, 2nd Michigan Infantry" (Company Muster Roll , May 25th to August (The National Archives, Record Group 94, Entry 534,Box1411)
[20] Harvey "2nd Regiment Michigan Volunteer Infantry" (PAGE 1) (War.org, michiganinthewar.org/infantry/2ndinf.htm)
[21] Civilwarintheeast.com, "2nd Regiment Michigan Volunteer Infantry" (PAGE 1) (East, civilwarintheeast.com/USA/MI/2MI.php)

command structure, the 2nd Michigan occupied the Fairfax Courthouse on July 17, 1861

The following day, July 18, they marched out toward Blackburn's Ford on the Bull Run. The creek itself was not impressive as far as width or depth but its banks were steep and its crossings few. In the lead was the 1st Maine and half of the 12th New York, followed by the 2nd Michigan, which was flanked by the other half of the 12th New York on the left and the 3rd Michigan to their right. The forward observer detected a Confederate battery across the Run, but no significant infantry could be seen. As the light Battalion went forward, Union parrot rifles opened fire around noon. There was no appreciable response, so the rest of the brigade sent out skirmishers to a forward position and advanced toward the thick woods. The Union skirmishers soon encountered scattered resistance from Confederates guarding the approach to Manassas at Blackburn's Ford. As the line continued to press forward, the Confederate line erupted with approximately five thousand muskets fired at once. Heavy volleys of musketry rained into and around the Union line. The Federals were heavily engaged when some of the 12th New York fell back in confusion, leaving only sixty men total in the front line. With much heavy fighting, artillery was used to cover the withdrawal from the battle. This sharp firefight at Blackburn's Ford was the 2nd Michigan's first engagement with only a small loss of two wounded. It also gave the Federals valuable information on the Confederate position along this stretcher of Bull Run.[22]

(Note: Picture of 2nd Michigan in the field covering the retreat top of page 12.)

---

[22] Elliott, *Blue & Gray, 150th Anniversary* (PAGES 19-20) (Elliott, 2011)

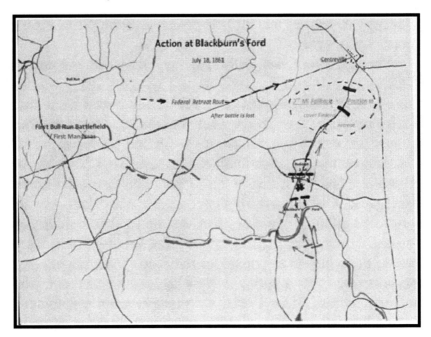

On July 21, the regiment was not engaged directly at the Battle of Bull Run, which was taking place just upstream to their right. As they stood in their battle line, they could easily hear the roar of the fighting, especially the thundering of cannons. When the battle was finally lost and the sound of the battle grew closer, they stood ready, along with the 3rd Michigan, to cover the retreat of Union forces as they made their way back to Washington. They kept the Confederates coming across Blackburn's Ford from advancing and cutting off the Federal retreat. Also complicating the matter, many civilians came out to watch the spectacle, which they thought would be a triumph for the North. When the battle went badly for the Federals, many of the fleeing civilians became an obstacle to the retreating troops headed back to Washington. By the end of the day, one man was wounded and another was missing.[23]

---

[23] History Data System, Inc, "2nd MI Infantry (3-years)" (PAGE 1) (History Data System, P.O. Box 35, Duxbury, MA 02331)

During the month of August, the 2nd Michigan was again doing duty in the defenses of Washington. One man was wounded on September 4, and another on October 15. On September 16, Capt. Orlando Poe of the United States engineers was appointed Col. of the Regiment. In October of 1861, the regiment was shifted to Richardson's Brigade, Heintzelman's Division, Army of the Potomac.[24]

From October 21 to 24, the regiment moved out on a reconnaissance mission to Occoquan, about twenty miles southwest of Washington. Again from November 12 to 14, they moved out in reconnaissance to Pohick's Church, Virginia, which is about fifteen miles southwest of D.C.[25]

Fremont's Bodyguard, Missouri Cavalry
Frederick Lenderking

Frederick (Fritz) Lenderking was the oldest brother of the Lenderking family living in the United States. He had blue eyes, auburn hair, a dark complexion, and stood about five feet eight inches tall. Frederick came to this country with George and Rudolph, his two other brothers, and had been living in Michigan, only recently moving to Cincinnati, Ohio.[26][27] With Rudolph already in the service of the United States since late May, Frederick traveled to St. Louis, Missouri after hearing of the need for cavalrymen in that state. On August 12, 1861 he joined Fremont's Bodyguard, Missouri Cavalry for a three-year term.[28] Frederick must have considered himself lucky as

---

[24] Civilwarintheeast.com, "2nd Michigan Infantry Regiment" (PAGE 1) (East, civilwarintheeast.com/USA/MI/2MI.php)

[25] Ibid., (PAGE 1) (East, civilwarintheeast.com/USA/MI/2MI.php)

[26] Wormelle, *The Lenderking Family* (PAGE 5) (Wormelle, 1969)

[27] National Archives and Record Service "Frederick Lenderking" (PAGE 3) (National Archives and Record Service, Microcopy number 405, role 293, Fremont Bodyguard, Cavalry)

[28] National Archives and Record Service, "Frederick Lenderking" (PAGE 3) (National Archives and Record Service, Microcopy number 405, role 293, Fremont Bodyguard, Cavalry)

Fremont's Bodyguard was selected from a host of applicants. They were selected for their high intelligence, fine physique, and manifest aptitude for military service.[29] It consisted of ardent young Americans, mainly from Ohio and Kentucky, including only thirteen foreigners. Some considered it without question to be one of the finest bodies of cavalry ever seen in the United States service.

The 5th Maryland Infantry Regiment
Phillip Lenderking

With the continued civil unrest in the country, Philip was pondering his next step. He and his family had arrived here seeking a better life, but having come from a country where one's liberties were suppressed, the desire and need to take action was ever building. Then, just prior to the departure of Rudolph's regiment from Michigan for the "front," he wrote to his brother Philip from Detroit, May 28, 1861.

> Dear Brother,
>
> I have intended not to write anything about my plan to join the Army, but as I have three years now ahead of me, I should inform you about it. Address any letter to me to Peter Katus. Most likely we'll get away from here during the next few days. Give all my love to our sister, Martchan and our brother, Louis. I remain your loving brother,
>
> R. Lenderking

In the same letter, the address of brother George was given as," Minnesota Mines, Lake Superior, Michigan." Rudolf wrote most of the letters that have survived. Rudolph's letters to Martha and the younger brothers, while serving in

---

[29] Stevens, "Fremont Body Guard, Ohio, Civil War" (PAGE 1) (Larry Stevens, 1997, www.ohiocivilwar.com/fremont.html)

the Washington-Alexandria area, are all written on stationery showing scenes of the Capitol in Washington, or patriotic symbols (a small American flag in the upper left-hand corner with a couplet of the "Star Spangled Banner"; a young woman—Columbia (a cymbal for the District of Columbia)—dressed in the striped skirt and bodice with stars balanced on a globe while waving and unfurled flag; the flag loosely guarded by the eagle with outspread wings and a ribbon below bearing the slogan," Union Forever"; the National Capital building etched across the top.) It was just a small detail but thoughtful of Rudolph to add a bright touch for the family in Baltimore. From the camp at Arlington Heights, August 14, 1861, Rudolph writes:[30]

Dear Brother,

I have arrived safely and without mishap. Overpowered by tiredness I went to sleep in the car. I was not asked for my passport 'till I went on the bridge where they let me pass without further delay. It rained yesterday and the night was so cold, we shivered in spite of the overcoats and blanket.

R. Lenderking

(Note: He obviously arrived in Washington by train explaining his sleeping in the car. The bridge he mentions is the Chain Bridge located near the northwest corner of Washington, D.C., which was heavily guarded. The barracks where he stayed at that location in the Federal fortifications also overlooked that same chain bridge.)

He also asked about "Martchan's health (I believe one of the family they were living with) and how Lewis was getting along with his boss. A footnote to his letter reads," The bottle of whiskey didn't live to see Monday night."[31]

---

[30] Wormelle, *The Lenderking Family* (PAGE 8) (Wormelle, 1969)
[31] Ibid. (PAGE 8) (Wormelle, 1969)

In the meantime, the 5th Maryland was organizing in Baltimore in September of 1861. With his two brothers Rudolph and Frederick already enlisted, Philip decided that now was the time for him to help preserve the Union as well. On September 19, 1861, Philip mustered into Company G, Public Guard, Maryland Infantry for three years of service. He quickly organized his affairs and reported to duty September 30, as a private.[32]

(Note: It might be mentioned that despite the rigors of army life there were times when a soldier could relax. Much of this leisure time would have been spent writing letters home. Soldiers during the Civil War were prolific writers and used every opportunity to keep in contact with their families by mail. Thrifty soldiers would even support their families by sending home any portion of their pay they were able to save. When mail arrived in the camp it was always a cause for celebration among the men. If the mail was late there would be much grumbling, a sign of the importance with which soldiers regarded such contact. The letters they received from home were treasures that would be kept safe and read over and over again. Families would also send packages to the soldiers to contain baked goods, new socks or shirts, underwear, and other necessities such as soap, towels, combs and toothbrushes.)[33]

Frederick Lenderking

Fremont's Bodyguard, Missouri Cavalry

Maj. Gen. John C. Fremont had been put in charge of the Western department, which was headquartered in St. Louis. After two significant Union defeats in Missouri, the Lincoln

---

[32] National Archives and Record Service, "Philip Lenderking" (Dec. 31, 1861 Company Muster-in Roll) (National Archives and Record Service, Microcopy No. 384, roll 142, Fifth Infantry, Ke – Li)

[33] Service, The United States Dept. of the Interior, *The Civil War soldier, what was life as a soldier like in 1863?*, 3 (Service, Gettysburg National Military Parkp.3)

administration was prodding him to take decisive action to eliminate the threat posed by the Missouri State Guard. The Union garrison of 3,500 men at Lexington, along the Missouri River, was captured after a three day siege, and forced Fremont to act. On October 7, Fremont left St. Louis and gathered more than twenty thousand troops.[34] His mounted forces numbered five thousand men including Major Frank J. White's Prairie Scouts, Fremont's Bodyguards commanded by Maj. Charles Zagonyi, a foreign-born officer, along with other cavalry units.

The units under Major Zagonyi operated in front of Fremont's army to gather intelligence. As Fremont neared Springfield, the Local State Guard commander, Col. Julian Frazier, sent out requests to nearby localities for additional troops. By late October, Fremont stopped to make camp on the Pomme de Terre River, about fifty miles from Springfield. It was believed at this time that no more than five hundred State Guardsmen occupied the town of Springfield.[35]

Major Zagonyi and his men had been ridiculed in St. Louis for their fine uniforms and their easy duty protecting the general, so Zagonyi, sensing an excellent opportunity to prove the reliability of his troops and demonstrate they were more than" kid gloves soldiers," asked Fremont for the chance to capture Springfield. Fremont agreed but ordered him to unite his three companies with three other cavalry companies. Those companies that joined him were the two company "Prairie Scouts" of Major Frank J. White, and the "Irish Dragoons" led by Capt. Patrick Naughton. Major White's Prairie Scouts eventually were turned over to Major Zagonyi when White later fell ill.

---

[34] Wikipedia, "First Battle of Springfield" (PAGE 1) (Wikipedia.org, ... wikipedia.org/.../First_Battle_of_Spring...)
[35] Ibid. (PAGE 1) (Wikipedia.org, ... wikipedia.org/.../First_Battle_of_Spring...)

(Note: Charles Zagonyi was born in Szatmar, Hungary in 1826. He served in the war of independence under General Bem. Following the defeat, he immigrated to England and then to the United States in 1851. Upon the outbreak of the Civil War, he joined General Fremont in Missouri who gave Zagonyi permission to organize and command the body of guard cavalry unit to be known as Fremont's Guard. He immediately put himself to the task of personally selecting the horses and designing the uniforms to be used by the guard.)[36]

Zagonyi and his men, including my great-great-grandfather's brother Frederick, set out again about 9:00 p.m. on October 24. The 172 members of the Bodyguard he commanded soon joined Major White and his 154 Prairie Scouts and the Irish Dragoons, who acted as rearguard of their column. Along the way, pro-Union citizens told him the enemy around Springfield was in-experienced and would likely run at the approach of the Bodyguard. Zagonyi also discovered important information about Springfield's layout and the roads leading in and out of town.

The column had reached about eight miles north of Springfield when the sun was just starting to rise in the sky. Ahead of them they found a foraging party of about a dozen men from the Rebel State Guard, who were taking wheat from a barn in Robberson Township.[37] They were quickly charged and captured with only a few escaping into the woods behind the barn. Zagonyi quickly learned that there were about 1,800 to 1,900 men in Springfield, when only five hundred were expected. Still, Zagonyi's column, continued on to Springfield.[38]

Zagonyi decided to leave the Bolivar Road north of Springfield about 2:30 p.m. and make a five mile detour

---

[36] Clevelandmemory.org, "Hungarians and Their Communities in Cleveland, chapter 2" (PAGE 5) (clevelandmemory.org, clevelandmemory.org/.../pg089.htm)

[37] Tuck, "Past and Present of Greene County, Missouri" (PAGE 5) (Tuck, thelibrary.org/lochist/.../ch11pt5.html, Chapter 11, Part 5)

[38] Schilling/Sellmeyer "Zagonyi's Charge (Battle of Springfield)," 2 (>>Zag..., 2009 www.ozarkscivilwar.org/archives/354p.2)

around to the west side of town, guided by a local farmer. In one report I found, it stated at this time, the men had marched for approximately 105 miles in a forty-eight- hour period and had only one meal, principally of salt beef.[39] Zagonyi received word that the enemy, about two thousand strong, were awaiting him ahead, already drawn up in line of battle.[40] So around 4:30 p.m., he halted the column on the Mount Vernon Road and made a dramatic speech to his men before riding into action. He informed the men of the enemy's strength but promised them victory. As he reached the conclusion of his speech, he gave the Bodyguard a battle cry: "Your watchword shall be, Fremont and the Union!" Then he drew his saber and ordered his column forward.[41]

Loyal to the Confederate cause, Fraser up ahead had been alerted earlier to their approach and set an ambush along the road on which Zagonyi traveled. Armed mostly with shotguns, hunting rifles, and revolvers, the State Guardsmen enjoyed the advantage of position. The main body of these Rebels were drawn up in line of battle, facing southeast, conforming to the outline of the dense woods that protected their rear and both flanks. It was a dense forest of oak, thick with underbrush, and with an abundance of wild grapevine making it impenetrable to men on horseback. It also offered them refuge should they be forced to retreat. The Rebel Guard Officers stationed themselves at the entrance to the woods on the lower side of the road to make their main stand. Skirmishers were scattered throughout the woods on both sides of the road where a high "stake and rider" fence enclosed the road.[42]

---

[39] Stevens, "Fremont Body Guard, Ohio, Civil War" (PAGE 1 is) (Larry Stevens, 1997, www.ohiocivilwar.com/fremont.html)
[40] Tuck and Edwin, "Past and Present of Greene County, Missouri "(PAGE 6) (Tuck, thelibrary.org/lochist/.../ch11pt5.html, Chapter 11, Part 5)
[41] Schilling/Sellmeyer " Zagonyi's Charge (Battle of Springfield)," 3 (>>Zag..., 2009 www.ozarkscivilwar.org/archives/354p.3)
[42] Schilling/Sellmeyer "Zagonyi's Charge (Battle of Springfield)," 3 (>>Zag..., 2009 www.ozarkscivilwar.org/archives/354p.3)

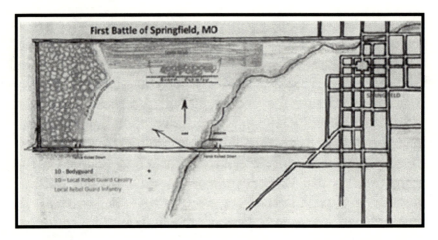

For a short time, the Bodyguard trotted down the Mount Vernon Road with little trouble. They soon started to pass through that same stand of timber where the Rebel Guardsmen were hiding. Up ahead, beyond the woods, they could see the white tents of the enemy camp.[43] The front of the column was close to reaching the clear space where Springfield was coming into sight. Suddenly, a murderous small arms fire opened on the front of the Union column from both sides of the road. The situation quickly became critical as the front of the column recoiled back and horses reared. Maj. Zagonyi realized quickly that their best chance of escaping the enemy fire was to forge ahead. He quickly led two of his companies at a quick pace through the gauntlet of fire, down the gradually sloped road. The sudden volley from the left of the thousand rifles exploded, opening holes in the line as a number of the Bodyguard were felled from their horses.[44] After a short distance, the road dropped off more abruptly for about 150 yards to Jordan Creek. Upon reaching the creek he dismounted his men, knocked the

---

[43] Tuck and Edwin, "Past and Present of Greene County, Missouri" (PAGES 6-7) (Tuck, thelibrary.org/lochist/.../ch11pt5.html, Chapter 11, Part 5)
[44] Rule, "Fremont's Hundred Days in Missouri "(PAGE 6) (Rule, 2004)

fence down and took shelter in the brambles and briars behind a bluff north of the road.[45]

Further back in the column, the companies of Maj. White's Prairie Scouts had become separated from Major Zagonyi and the Irish Dragoons. Approaching the scene of the battle, they were given orders by an unknown officer who was located approximately one hundred yards[46] ahead to take his men down a nearby farm lane on his left and cut off the retreat of a number of Rebels. As ordered, Fairbanks and the Prairie Scouts made several attacks on detached parties of the Rebel State Guardsmen in the rear of the Rebel attackers.[47]

Capt. James Foley, an officer leading one of Zagonyi's companies, was still up the road with the rest of the Bodyguard taking murderous fire. Thinking he could strike the State Guardsmen in the flank, he had ordered several men to knock down a whole in the fence on the north side of the road. But seeing the thick underbrush, he had second thoughts about the plan and abandoned it.[48] [49] [50] He looked up and saw Zagonyi some distance ahead, dismounted and frantically waved his saber, summoning them to join him. He immediately remounted his horse and led his men through the gauntlet of bullets to join the rest of the Bodyguard at the creek.[51]

The last company in the column was the Irish Dragoons under Capt. Naughton. They galloped up intending to go down the lane as well but found themselves separated with no Federals

---

[45] Schilling/Sellmeyer "Zagonyi's Charge (Battle of Springfield)," 4 (>>Zag..., 2009 www.ozarkscivilwar.org/archives/354p.4)
[46] Rule, "Fremont's Hundred Days in Missouri " (PAGES 6-7) (Rule, 2004)
[47] Schilling/Sellmeyer "Zagonyi's Charge (Battle of Springfield)," 4 (>>Zag..., 2009 www.ozarkscivilwar.org/archives/354p.4)
[48] Tuck and Fairbanks, "Past and Present of Greene County, Missouri" (PAGE 7) (Tuck, thelibrary.org/lochist/.../ch11pt5.html, Chapter 11, Part 5)
[49] Rule, "Fremont's Hundred Days in Missouri "(PAGE 7) (Rule, 2004)
[50] (Missouri Civil War Sesquicentennial) Springfield, First Battle of (Zagonyi's Charge) (PAGE #?) (Sp..., mocivilwar150.com/history/battle/185)
[51] Schilling/Sellmeyer "Zagonyi's Charge (Battle of Springfield)," 4 (>>Zag..., 2009 www.ozarkscivilwar.org/archives/354p.4)

in sight. Finding a hole in the fence that was knocked down previously, they falsely assumed that this was where Zagonyi had gone. In an attempt to catch up, they passed through the hole in the fence and into the thick underbrush.[52] They were met with a murderous fire from the Rebel State Guard. Thirteen of them were cut down quickly, including Naughton who was shot in the arm. Lieutenant Patrick Conley also received two bullets in the leg and one in the left shoulder. The Irish Dragoons retreated, with most of the surviving members of the company joining Fairbanks, where they stayed for the remainder of the fight. Only one company led by a sergeant tried to fight their way down the road to link up with the Bodyguard. Unfortunately, only five of the Dragoons that tried, managed to brave their way through the gauntlet to Zagonyi's position.[53]

The enemy line was beginning to reform from the woods to the open field. Zagonyi ordered his troops to remount and prepared to advance forward. At first, he observed carefully the enemy atop the hill awaiting their arrival. He gathered his soldiers together and told them that any man wishing to turn back had his permission to do so, but not a man flinched. He then ordered Lieut. Maythenyi to take a small detachment of thirty men and attacked the cavalry.[54][55] Without hesitation, the line of horses and men advanced as one body in a zealous charge up the gentle, grassy slope toward the seven hundred Guardsmen Cavalry. With battle cries of victory on their lips, a dogged determination in their hearts and on hooves of speed, they rode forward gallantly, determined to win the day. So great was the site of this line of moving horses and thirty riders in such perfect determined unison, it unnerved many of the Rebel Guardsmen. So much so, the Guard shattered their

---

[52] Rule, "Fremont's Hundred Days in Missouri" (PAGE 7) (Rule, 2004)
[53] Schilling/Sellmeyer "Zagonyi's Charge (Battle of Springfield)," 4 (>>Zag..., 2009 www.ozarkscivilwar.org/archives/354p.4)
[54] Tuch and Fairbanks, "Past and Present of Greene County, Missouri" (PAGE 7) (Tuck, thelibrary.org/lochist/.../ch11pt5.html, Chapter 11, Part 5)
[55] Rule,, "Fremont's Hundred Days in Missouri" (PAGE #?) (Rule, 2004)

center, without any consideration of their superior numbers. Without waiting for orders, the Rebel Cavalry suddenly broke rank and fled in all directions,[56] many back into the cornfield behind their position with the Bodyguard close behind. So hasty and sudden was their retreat that horses reared and banged together, causing a number of Rebels to fall from their horses to the ground. Those men, now dismounted, were forced to take cover wherever they could find it. Some ran into a nearby cornfield and others into an adjacent wooded area.

Zagonyi rallied the remainder of the men and ordered a second charge. With his sword pointed up the hill, the order was given to move forward. He confidently led the remainder of the Bodyguard, about 130 men, up the hill, and they were instantly met with a fierce fire from all sides by Rebels hidden in the underbrush.[57] The Local Guardsmen had strategically formed in lines between the Bodyguard and the town of Springfield like a wall. Zagonyi's cavalry moved decisively and with machinelike precision, spread out like a fan. They continued to advance as the Rebel Guardsmen battle line aimed and fired their muskets, shotguns, and rifles.

The Rebels could only hold their line for a short time with the Bodyguard quickly bearing down on them. Finally the Local Guardsmen's line wavered, broke, and scattered for cover. The Bodyguard line wheeled right and then left, like a giant broom, determined to completely sweep the enemy from the field. The fighting then spread out into a series of smaller individual encounters scattered about the battlefield. Some of the Rebel Guardsmen fled into the woods and hid behind trees and bushes, continuing a fierce resistance and deadly fire into the Bodyguard ranks.[58] [59] The State Guardsmen fired their weapons from

---

[56] Schilling/Sellmeyer "Zagonyi's Charge (Battle of Springfield)," 4 (>>Zag..., 2009 www.ozarkscivilwar.org/archives/354p.4)
[57] Tuck and Fairbanks, "Past and Present of Greene County, Missouri" (PAGE 7) (Tuck, thelibrary.org/lochist/.../ch11pt5.html, Chapter 11, Part 5)
[58] Tuck and Fairbanks, "Past and Present of Greene County, Missouri" (PAGE 7) (Tuck, thelibrary.org/lochist/.../ch11pt5.html, Chapter 11, Part 5)

behind trees, fences, and thick underbrush. Federal pistols cracked with smoke. Sabers clanged and cut to the bone. The battle was violent and fast-moving. Many of the Local Rebel Guard lost hope and retreated along the edge of the woods and over fences back to the protection of Springfield.[60]

The Federals, not losing their momentum, continued their pursuit of the State Guardsmen through the streets of the town.[61] In groups of threes and fours, the Bodyguard pursued the Rebel Guardsmen having made some twenty charges through the town.[62] Some Union prisoners were found and freed. The Confederate loss was 106 men killed, a number wounded, and twenty-seven captured. Also captured were sixty stands of arms and over $4,000 in gold. In less than a half-hour, the main battle was over. It was now growing dark, and Zagonyi rode into the town square and sounded assembly. Only around eighty men answered the call who were still mounted. They faced the possibility of a Confederate counterattack. Around 9:00 p.m., he ordered the majority of the Union troops to ride back to rejoin Fremont's main body.[63] The wounded had been carried to the courthouse / hospital and the twenty-four dismounted troopers were placed in charge to guard them.[64] Dr. Hughes, of the Prairie Scouts and Dr. Melcher, with the help of local citizens, cared for the wounded throughout the night.[65]

---

[59] ,Ibid., 7 (Rule, 2004p.7)
[60] Ibid. (Rule, 2004p.7)
[61] Summaries, CWSAC Battle, "Springfield" (PAGE 1) (Summaries, Reference # Mooo8, Pres. Pri. IV.2 (Class D))
[62] Tuck and Fairbanks, "Past and Present of Greene County, Missouri" (PAGE 8) (Tuck, thelibrary.org/lochist/.../ch11pt5.html, Chapter 11, Part 5) (Rule, 2004)
[63] Historical Data Systems, "Battle History, Springfield, Missouri, October 25, 1861"(PAGES 1-2 (Historical Data Systems, source: the union Army, volume 6,P.O. Box 35,Duxbury, MA 02331)
[64] Rule, "Fremont's Hundred Days in Missouri," 8 (Rule, 2004p.8)
[65] Tuck and Fairbanks, "Past and Present of Greene County, Missouri" (PAGE 9) (Tuck, thelibrary.org/lochist/.../ch11pt5.html, Chapter 11, Part 5)

Out of Zagonyi's three companies, a total of sixteen were killed, with an estimated thirty-three men and forty-five horses[66] lost overall in the battle. Four officers out of nine were wounded along with twenty-two other men. This first Battle of Springfield, or as some would call it, Zagonyi's Charge, was the only Union victory in Southwest Missouri in 1861.

The records of Private Frederick Lenderking show he was wounded twice in this battle. A ball entered the outside of the right leg near and below the knee, lodging in the canalized structure of the head of the tibia.[67] (This bullet was never removed.) This injury could have been received at any time during the battle. A second wound was to the left-hand: a bullet cut off the first two joints of the little finger, wounding the finger next to it, entered the palm of the hand and passed out the back of the wrist, shattering the metacarpal bone of the palm and rendering the thumb about useless.[68] This wound would cause him to be considered 50 percent disabled. The positioning of the wound and the fact that the left-hand is primarily used for

---

[66] (Missouri Civil War Sesquicentennial) "Springfield, First Battle of (Zagonyi's Charge)" (PAGE 2) (Sp..., mocivilwar150.com/history/battle/185)
[67] Federal Pension File, The National Archives, "Frederick Lenderking" (PAGES 5-6 (Federal Pension File, 1861)
[68] Ibid., (PAGES 5-6 (Federal Pension File, 1861)

the steering of the horse leads me to believe this wound came at the point of the charge where the fight had come down to man-to-man combat. The guardsmen that shot Private Lenderking in the hand would have to have been very close to his horse on the left-hand side, as the horse was possibly being turned left around a tree or some other obstacle or building as they chased Rebels through the fields or town. Any other position, or distance, would have resulted in another part of his body being struck. They had to have been at very close quarters at the time the shot was fired.

When the wounded were finally removed from the battlefield, they were first taken into the town of Springfield, where they spent the night. Upon the arrival of the reinforcements, they were taken to the St. Louis, Missouri Hospital. There, Private Lenderking remained until February 12, 1862, when he was discharged from service due to his disability. He then traveled to Cincinnati, Ohio, where he remained for several years.[69]

---

[69] Federal Pension File, The National Archives, "Frederick Lenderking" (PAGE 6) (Federal Pension File, 1861)

Chapter 3
To the Battle of Antietam

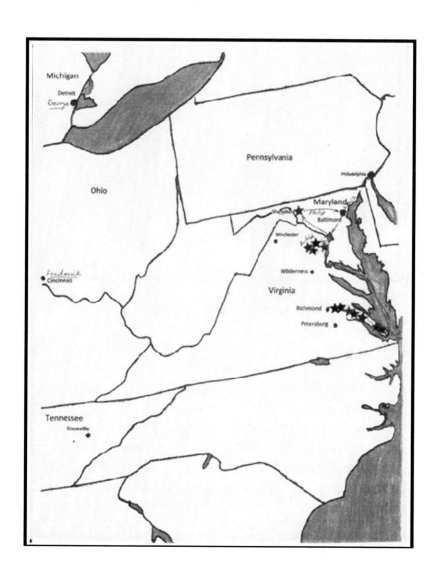

Rudolph Lenderking
2nd Michigan Infantry Regiment

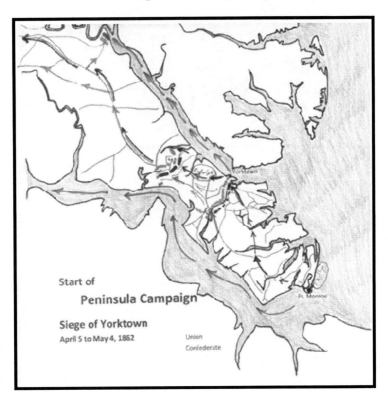

During March of 1862, the 2nd Michigan was shifted into the 3rd Brigade, 3rd Division, 3rd Army Corps, Army of the Potomac. On March 6, Maj. Williams was promoted to Lt. Col. and Capt. Lewis Dillman promoted to Major. By March 17, preparations had been completed and they moved out to the Virginia Peninsula.[70] Private Rudolph of the 2nd Michigan, along with the rest of the Army of the Potomac, boarded 389 vessels and were transported to Fort Munro. There were 121,500 men that made the voyage, along with forty-four artillery batteries, 1,150 wagons, 15,000 plus horses and tons

---

[70] Civil War in the East (website from earlier?), "2nd Michigan Infantry Regiment" (PAGE 1) (East, civilwarintheeast.com/USA/MI/2MI.php)

of equipment and supplies,[71] and started their way up the neck of land in the direction of Richmond. This was the beginning of what would be called The Peninsula Campaign.

By April 4, 1862, the Union Army had already pushed through the initial Confederate line of defense with little difficulty. But the exact disposition of the Confederate forces were difficult to determine due to the nature of the terrain in this area. On April 5, the 9th Corps made the initial contact with a second Confederate line's right flank at Lee's Mill. This was an area in which McClellan expected to pass his troops with little to no resistance. The 7th Main Infantry Regiment deployed as skirmishers approximately 1,000 yards before the Confederate fortifications. They were soon joined by another brigade and artillery.[72]

Both sides engaged in an artillery duel for several hours, as reconnaissance of the area was ordered. The 6th Maine Infantry and the 5th Wisconsin Infantry performed the reconnaissance around Dam Number One, where the Confederate forces had created a nearby water obstacle. They quickly drove off the Confederate pickets and took some prisoners. The conditions around the area led the Federals to the belief that there was a considerable Confederate force dug

---

[71] Wikipedia, "Peninsula Campaign," 5 (Wikipediap.5)
[72] Wikipedia, Siege of Yorktown (1862)," 2 (Wikipediap.2)

in there. McClellan decided to order the construction of siege fortifications and brought his heavy siege guns to the front.[73] [74]

For the next ten days, McClellan's men dug in and set in place fifteen batteries with more than seventy heavy guns. These placements, including two 200-pounder Parrots and twelve 100-pound Parrots, with the rest of the rifled pieces divided between twenty-pounder and thirty-pounder Parrot's and 4 1/2 inch Rodman siege rifles. These batteries were also augmented by forty-one other mortars ranging in size from eight inches to thirteen-inch seacoast mortars, which weighed over ten tons and fired shells weighing 220 pounds.[75] If fired in unison, 7,000 pounds of ordnance would rain down onto the enemy position with each volley.[76] During this same time, the Confederates reinforced their line to the strength of 35,000 men. On April 6, one of the men on picket duty from the 2nd Michigan was taken captive by the Confederates.[77]

Union Morters at Battery, No. 4   *Union Baloon Intrepid*

As these positions were being dug in, the Union Army Balloon Corps used two balloons, the Constitution and the

---

[73] Wikipedia, "Peninsula Campaign" 5 (Wikipediap.5)
[74] Wikipedia, "Siege of Yorktown (1862)," 2 (Wikipediap.2)
[75] Ibid., 3 (Wikipediap.3)
[76] Wikipedia, "Peninsula Campaign," 6 (Wikipediap.6)
[77] History Data System, Inc., "2nd MI Infantry (3-years)" (PAGE 1) (History Data System, P.O. Box 35, Duxbury, MA 02331)

Intrepid, to perform an aerial observation. On April 11, the Intrepid carrying Brig. Gen. Porter, a Division Commander of the Third Corps, hit unexpected winds aloft, sending the balloon over enemy lines. The Union troops naturally had great concern as the Confederates were unsuccessfully trying to bring the balloon down. Luckily, the winds changed direction and returned the balloon with Brig. Gen. Porter back to safety.[78]

On April 16, 1862, Union forces probed the Confederate line at Dam Number One with a brief skirmish. It started with an artillery bombardment that ended around 8:00 a.m., at which time skirmishers were sent forward. When they had advanced close enough to the enemy line, they fired on the Confederate defenders positions. After exchanging several rounds of fire, the Federals felt the Confederates were in withdrawal; around 3:00 p.m., four companies of the 3rd Vermont Infantry crossed the Dam and routed the remaining defenders. The Confederates quickly rallied and a hail of bullets flew in both directions. The four Vermont companies, unable to obtain reinforcements, were forced to withdrawal and suffered casualties along their whole line of retreat.[79][80]

Farther downstream, the 6th Vermont was ordered to attack the Confederate positions while the 4th Vermont demonstrated at the Dam itself. The 6th Vermont came under heavy Confederate fire and were forced to withdraw, receiving a number of casualties. Unfortunately some of the wounded man drowned as they fell into the shallow pond behind the Dam, and another man was killed the same day in the 2nd Michigan.

Somehow amidst all this confusion of battle, Private Lenderking had to replace some of his equipment. He had

---

[78] Wikipedia, "Siege of Yorktown (1862)," 3 (Wikipediap.3)
[79] Wikipedia, "Peninsula Campaign," 6 (Wikipediap.6)
[80] Wikipedia, "Siege of Yorktown (1862)," 4 (Wikipediap.4)

sixty-nine cents deducted from his pay for the belt strap and another ten cents for the belt plate.[81] On May 4, Lieut. Col. Williams of the 2nd Michigan was lightly wounded in the daily sniping fire.[82] McClellan had planned a massive bombardment to commence the next day at daybreak, but the Confederate Army had already slipped away during the night toward Williamsburg.

On May 5 McClellan's Union forces were making slow progress on the muddy roads, yet still gaining ground on the Confederates. Trudging along in the mud with the 2nd Michigan, Rudolph knew there was another fight ahead. A skirmish took place as the Union cavalry overtook the rearguard of the Confederate forces, retreating from Yorktown. Hooker's 2nd Division of the 3rd Corps was the lead infantry in the Union Army advance, and they steadily approached the large earthen fortifications, Fort Magruder, straddling the Williamsburg Road. It contained Confederate infantry deliberately left behind to slow the Union advance.[83]

Hooker's 2nd Division formed up and attacked the Confederate entrenchments, but a Confederate counterattack threatened to overwhelm Hooker's Division, which has been contesting the ground since early morning. Hooker had expected Union reinforcements, which unfortunately had been halted more than a mile away from his position. Confederate defenders under Longstreet left their fortifications and attacked Hooker's Division, applying strong pressure to his line. Hookers division began to give way, and the Regimental band began to play," Yankee Doodle,"[84]

---

[81] The National Archives, "Rudolph Lenderking, Co. A, 2nd Michigan Infantry" (Company Muster Roll March & April) (The National Archives, Record Group 94, Entry 534,Box1411)
[82] Civilwarintheeast.com, "2nd Michigan Infantry Regiment" (PAGE 1) (East, civilwarintheeast.com/USA/MI/2MI.php)
[83] Wikipedia, "Peninsula Campaign," 7 (Wikipediap.7)
[84] Wikipedia, "Battle of Williamsburg," 2 (Wikipedia(Will)p.2)

rallying the men long enough for reinforcements to arrive. At about this same time, 2:00 p.m., the 1st division of the Union's Ninth Corps arrived to support and extend the right of Hooker's line, having been pushed back some 600 to 1,000 yards from the Confederate fortifications. Their arrival on the field came at a critical moment, allowing his brigade, which was on the verge of retreat, to recover their over-run artillery battery and stabilize their line.

Kearny's 3rd Division of the Union's Third Corps, containing Rudolph and his regiment, advanced forward around.2:30 p.m. Kearny openly rode his horse before his advancing picket lines to reconnoiter and urged his men forward by flashing his saber with his only arm (The other had been amputated due to injury).[85] A sharp firefight ensued as the Confederates were pushed off Lee's Mill Road, back into the woods and after more heavy fighting, finally back into their defensive positions. Hooker continued to confront the Confederate forces in front of Fort Magruder, as Smith's. division now joined the fight, bombarding Longstreet's left flank around noon.

At this time, 1,200 Confederate attackers emerged from the woods to attack the Union lines. They quickly found themselves facing Hancock's 3,400 infantrymen and eight artillery pieces which significantly outnumber them.[86] In the hard fighting that commenced, the Confederates lost 810 men while Union losses were only about one hundred. In total, McClellan lost a total of 2,283 men while the Confederates losses were only 1,682 men.[87] The battle of Fort Magruder, also known as the Battle of Williamsburg, cost the 2nd Michigan, seventeen men killed, thirty-eight wounded and five missing.[88] Lieut. Wallace was among those killed while

---

[85] Wikipedia, "Peninsula Campaign," 7 (Wikipediap.7)
[86] Wikipedia, "Battle of Williamsburg," 3 (Wikipedia(Will)p.3)
[87] Wikipedia, "Peninsula Campaign," 7 (Wikipediap.7)
[88] Michigan.org, "2nd Michigan Volunteer Infantry, "E" Company 1861–1865," 3 (Michigan.orgp.3)

Lieut. Col. Williams was again wounded. Lieut. Dobson was also wounded.[89]

Private Rudolph in the 2nd Michigan, along with about 42,000 Union troops under McClelland's command, were about seven miles east of Richmond, Virginia.[90] McClellan had three cores on the North side of the Chickahominy River and two on the side toward Richmond. On the night of the thirtieth, a severe thunderstorm turned the treacherous and already high Chickahominy river into a torrent, increasing the danger of the divided Union Army. The roads were deep in mud, causing great difficulty in moving artillery. It was sometime after noon when the Confederates attacked with vigor, causing the Federals to quickly lose ground. Standing at attention on the other side of the river, Gen. Sumner marched his two Union divisions across the two bridges near his position and came to their aid,[91] preserving the Union left wing from a rout. The Southern army suffered a grievous loss in the severe wounding of General Johnston, who was knocked from his horse by a fragment of a shell near the end of the fight. On June 1, 1862, the Confederates attached in force once more but after much hard fighting were repulsed to within four miles of Richmond.[92] They were not pursued. The Union soldiers, having no further orders, returned to their lines that they occupied before the battle.

---

[89] Civilwarintheast.com, "2nd Michigan Infantry Regiment" (PAGE 1) (East, civilwarintheeast.com/USA/MI/2MI.php)
[90] How Stuff Works, "Battle of Fair Oaks" (PAGE 1) (Works)
[91] Rhodes, *History of the Civil War* (PAGE 1) (Rhodes, 1917)
[92] Rhodes, *History of the Civil War* (PAGE 1) (Rhodes, 1917)

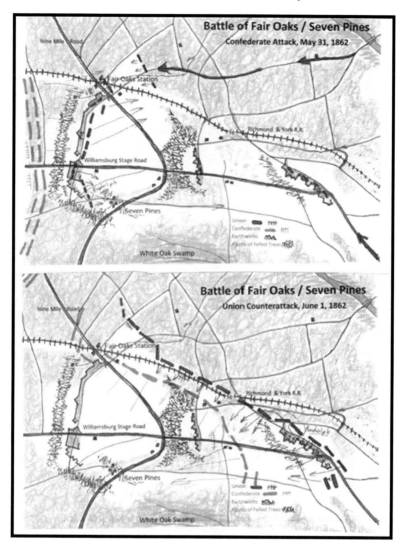

Union losses totaled about 5,000 men while the Confederate lost about 6,000 men. In this battle of Fair Oaks, or Seven Pines, the 2nd Michigan Regiment saw ten men killed and forty-seven wounded along with Lieut. Col. Williams. The 2nd Michigan was conspicuously marked for bravery for its conduct during this action.[93]

---

[93] Michiganinthewar.org, "2nd Regiment Michigan Volunteer Infantry" (PAGE 2) (War.org, michiganinthewar.org/infantry/2ndinf.htm)

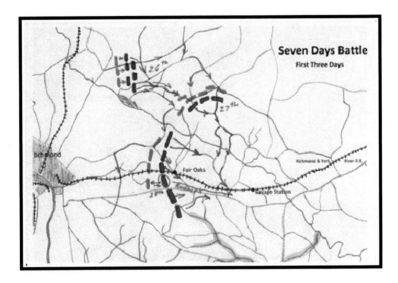

After the battle and well into the next day, the 2nd Michigan moved out in reconnaissance beyond Seven Pines. During this month of June, Col. Poe and Lieut. Col. Williams took a leave of absence, leaving Major Lewis Dillman in command.[94] During other actions around Richmond, two additional men were killed and another nineteen men wounded.[95]

The Regiment continued to push forward with McClellan, and by June 25, the 2nd Michigan Regiment

---

[94] Civilwarintheeast.com, "2nd Michigan Infantry Regiment" (PAGE 1) (East, civilwarintheeast.com/USA/MI/2MI.php)
[95] Michiganinthewar.org, "2nd Regiment Michigan Volunteer Infantry," 2 (War.org, michiganinthewar.org/infantry/2ndinf.htmp.2)

had made its way to Oak Grove. General McClellan had advanced his lines along the Williamsburg road with the objective of placing his siege guns within the range of Richmond. Rudolph, along with the 2nd Michigan and other regiments, made their advance over swampy ground but made little progress. The harsh fighting in the swamp was concluded as the light faded into darkness.[96] During this period, the Confederates managed to wound two more of the 2nd Michigan and one at a time, captured another four men.[97] It was with this Union attack that the seven days battle is said to have begun. General Lee launched a Confederate attack the very next day, June 25, and was determined to push the Union forces away from Richmond. McClellan quickly lost the initiative and began their retreat down the Virginian Peninsula toward the James River. The Confederates launched another attack to the Union rear on the twenty-sixth to keep the Union forces from regrouping and digging in.

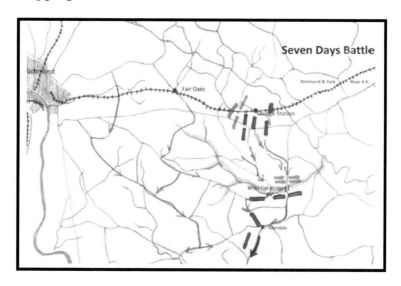

---

[96] Summaries, CWSAC Battle, "Oak Grove" (PAGE 1) (Summaries, #VA015)
[97] History Data System, Inc., "2nd MI Infantry (3-years)" (PAGE 1) (History Data System, P.O. Box 35, Duxbury, MA 02331)

By June 29, the 2nd Michigan had reached Savage station where there was a Confederate attack on the rearguard.[98] McClellan continued to push his Army of the Potomac down the peninsula in retreat of the enemy.

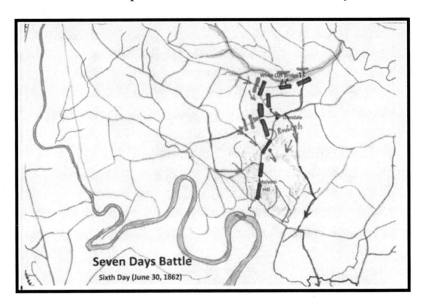

By noon of June 30, most elements of McClellan's Army had been able to cross the White Oak Swamp Creek. About one-third of the Army had reached the James River, but the remainder was still marching between Oak Creek Swamp and Glendale. The 2nd Michigan, containing Rudolph, was just reaching Glendale and Charles City Crossroads.[99] This was not a strategically safe area, as it contained an inadequate road setup that was a natural bottleneck to the Union forces.

---

[98] Civilwarintheeast.com, "2nd Michigan Infantry Regiment" (PAGE 1) (East, civilwarintheeast.com/USA/MI/2MI.php)
[99] Civilwarintheeast.com, "2nd Michigan Infantry Regiment" (PAGE 1) (East, civilwarintheeast.com/USA/MI/2MI.php)

The Confederate men under Jackson marched south on the White Oak Road particularly slowly as they were accompanied by thousands of wounded Union prisoners and many of the provisions that they obtained at Savage Station. They found that the single bridge over the swamp had been burned two hours earlier. They kept themselves low and out of sight but could clearly see the Union soldiers on the other side of the river.[100]

Union soldiers on the other hand did not see the Confederates and at 2:00 p.m. were caught by surprise, as seven Confederate batteries of thirty-one guns opened fire. Totally unprepared for this attack, the Union soldiers abandoned a number of guns where they stood and quickly scrambled into a makeshift defensive position, set up what artillery they could, and fired on Confederate positions. Confederate engineers were preparing to build a pontoon bridge, while other Confederate men and horses waded through water that was belly deep and foul with debris in an attempt to cross to the other side. Jackson and Maj. Gen. D.H. Hill also made the crossing to perform a personal reconnaissance. A Union cannon greeted them with a shell that exploded only a few feet away from the two generals mounted on horseback. Neither was injured, but they did manage

---

[100] Wikipedia, "Battle of White Oak Swamp," 2 (wikipedia-WAS, 2010p.2)

to catch a number of the Federal defenses being put in place. At the same time, Union sharpshooters were preparing to fire on the engineers attempting to build the pontoon bridge. There was no infantry action, but an artillery duel began and lasted for over an hour. As the Union forces moved on, they took axes and felled trees to obstruct the Confederate regiments from following them. The Confederate losses in the Battle of White Oak Swamp were three artillerymen killed and twelve wounded. There are no accurate records of Union casualties for this engagement, but estimates are as high as one hundred men killed or wounded.[101]

Later that same day, McClellan's forces, still in retreat down the Peninsula, were again converged upon near Glendale, or Frayser's Farm. McClellan himself had moved on ahead but had failed to name a second-in-command. As a result, the Union's Fifth Corps under Brig. Gen. Porter moved to occupy Malvern Hill, while the remaining cores of the Army of the Potomac essentially operated independently in their fighting withdrawals.[102] Long-range Union artillery was directed at Confederate troops before them around 2:00 p.m.. Unbeknownst to them at the time, the visiting Confederate president Jefferson Davis was conferring on horseback with Lee and Longstreet. The heavy artillery fire wounded two men and killed three horses near them. Longstreet attempted to silence the six batteries of Federal guns firing in his direction, but his long-range artillery fire proved to be insufficient and fell short of its target.[103]

Around 4:00 p.m., an attack was launched by Lee's Confederate troops to knock out some of the Union long-range artillery. Their strong assault was launched toward the Turkey Bridge and Malvern Hill. With the aid of Federal gunboats Galena and Aroostook, located on the James River, the attack was repulsed. Then Longstreet and Hill launched

---

[101] Wikipedia, "Battle of White Oak Swamp," 3 (wikipedia-WAS, 2010p.3)
[102] Wikipedia, "Battle of Glendale," 1–2 (Wikipedia-BoGpp.1-2)
[103] Ibid., 2–3 (Wikipedia-BoGpp.2-3)

another Confederate attack of 20,000 men in a piecemeal fashion over the course of two hours. Subsequently, a line of Confederate soldiers charged through the thick woods and emerged in front of five batteries of Union artillery. This inexperienced brigade from Virginia conducted a disorderly but enthusiastic assault, which carried them through the guns, capturing two artillery batteries, and braking through the Union lines. The Union defenses in this location near Willis Church contained some 40,000 men but was at least two miles long, in a disjointed ark.[104]

The Confederate brigades met stiff resistance and the bitter fighting turned hand-to-hand. Men were violently stabbing one another with bayonets and using rifles as clubs in a desperate life-and-death struggle that left many men dead or dying on the field.[105] Officers even took to using their normally ornamental swords as weapons, slashing and stabbing the Confederate attackers. In this barbaric brawl, one of the artillery batteries was retaken. The Union launched counterattacks with three brigades of men that managed to seal the break and save their line of retreat along the Willis Church Road. Confederates again attempted to attack the Union left flank at Turkey Bridge but were driven back. The Confederate attack on the southern flank was also thrown back, but the fighting continued. The heavy, bitter struggle proceeded until about 8:30 p.m. when all Confederate resources were exhausted. Of the Federal forces, 297 men were killed, along with 1,804 missing or captured. Confederate losses were almost equal in overall numbers but broke down into 638 men killed, 2,814 wounded, and 221 missing.[106] By this time, two more men were killed in the 2nd Michigan.[107] Later that night, the Union Army established a strong position on Malvern Hill.

---

[104] Wikipedia, "Seven Days Battle," 11 (Wikipedia-SDBp.11)
[105] Wikipedia, "Battle of Glendale," 3 (Wikipedia-BoGp.3)
[106] Ibid. (Wikipedia-BoGp.3)
[107] History Data Systems, Inc., "2nd MI Infantry (3-years)" (PAGE 1) (History Data System, P.O. Box 35, Duxbury, MA 02331)

On July 1, 1862, the final day of the Seven Days Battle, the Union forces were well dug in at Malvern Hill. Except for one division of the Ninth Corps that had proceeded on to Harrison's Landing, the entire Army of the Potomac occupied the hill. The slopes were cleared of timber, providing great visibility of the open fields to the north. Two hundred and fifty guns, under the charge of Col. Hunt, were placed in positions that could easily sweep those fields with deadly fire. Three gunboats were now on the James River: the USS Galena, USS Jacob Bell, and the USS Aroostook, which added even more firepower.[108] Beyond the open fields to the north, the terrain was swampy and thickly wooded. The Federal line extended in a vast semicircle from Harrison's Landing on the extreme right, to the geographical advantageous ground on the northwestern slopes of the hill. Just to the right of the center of that line was Heintzelman's 3rd Corps, containing Rudolph and the 2nd Michigan.[109]

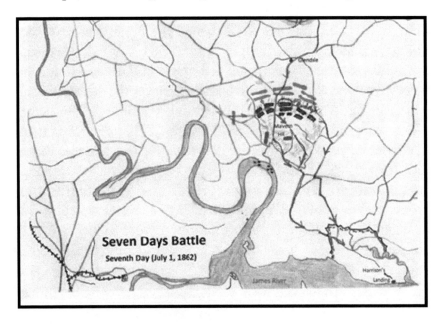

---

[108] Wikipedia, "Battle of Malvern Hill" (PAGE 1) (Wikipedia-BoMH, 2010)
[109] Ibid., 2 (Wikipedia-BoMH, 2010p.2)

The chief of artillery Col. Hunt viewed the Confederates massing for attack and open fired his Federal batteries around 1:00 p.m., and continued on until 2:30 p.m.. It is said that this was one of the greatest artillery barrages of the Civil War. The Union gunners possessed superior equipment and with great expertise, disabled most of the Confederate batteries concentrated on the hill, approximately 1,200 yards to the north of the Crew House and at Poindexter's farm to the northeast.[110]

The Confederate infantry columns advanced towards the Union line on the hill around 3:30 p.m. but were blasted to pieces. The three gunboats on the James River also pounded the field with fifty-pound shells, causing great damage. By 4:00 p.m., Confederate reinforcements arrived and moved in to support the Confederate advance, but the attack was piecemeal and poorly organized. Another division launched an attack along the Quaker Road just past the Willis Church, Against determined resistance, the Confederate troops reached only within 200 yards of the Union center and were repulsed by nightfall with heavy losses.[111] As the sun was beginning to set,

---

[110] Wikipedia, "Battle of Malvern Hill," 2–3 (Wikipedia-BoMH, 2010pp.2-3)
[111] Ibid., 3 (Wikipedia-BoMH, 2010p.3)

another Confederate column began to move forward but soon halted as the battle was already lost. During this day the Union casualties and losses were 3,214 men, while the Confederate casualties and losses numbered 5,355 men.[112] The 2nd Michigan Regiment had another eleven men wounded this day, four taken prisoner and three missing.[113] After the battle, McClellan's Army continued its withdrawal to Harrison's Landing on the James River, where the army entrenched itself and was protected by gunboats, ending the Peninsula Campaign.

From July 2 through August 15, the regiment continued full duty at Harrison's Landing, where daily gunfire wounded two more men. On July 26 Lieut. Col. Williams transferred as Col. to the 20th Michigan infantry. At this same time, Major Dillman was promoted to Lt. Col. and Capt. Cornelius Byington to Major.[114][115]

In August of 1862, the Regiment was shifted to 3rd Brigade, 1st Division, Third Army Corps, Army of the Potomac. On August 15, the Regiment moved out once again, this time in the direction of Williamsburg. The root of march took them by way of Charles City, in the direction of Williamsburg, reaching their destination on the 18th. The next day they marched to Yorktown,[116] (maybe to Fortress Monroe[117]), from where they embarked on a steamer for Alexandria the following day. They reached Alexandria about August 21 and waited there two days for a train. The train took them on to Warrington Junction, from where the

---

[112] Wikipedia, "Seven Days Battle," 12 (Wikipedia-SDBp.12)
[113] History Data Systems, Inc., "2nd MI Infantry (3-years)" (PAGE 1)_ (History Data System, P.O. Box 35, Duxbury, MA 02331)
[114] Civilwarintheeast.com, "2nd Michigan Infantry Regiment" (PAGE 1)) (East, civilwarintheeast.com/USA/MI/2MI.php)
[115] Michigan.org, "2nd Michigan Volunteer Infantry, "E" Company 1861–1865," 3 (Michigan.orgp.3)
[116] Michiganinthewar.org, "2nd Regiment Michigan Volunteer Infantry," 2 (War.org, michiganinthewar.org/infantry/2ndinf.htmp.2)
[117] Civilwarintheeast.com, "2nd Michigan Infantry Regiment" (PAGE 1)_ (East, civilwarintheeast.com/USA/MI/2MI.php)

regiment marched to Manassas, arriving on August 28 at noon.[118]

At 3:00 p.m., Heintzelman's men containing the 2nd Michigan Regiment left for Centreville, Virginia., Upon reaching Blackburn's Ford along their way, they met and engaged the Confederate cavalry and repulsed them. The regiment reformed and continued their march, reaching Centreville at 6:00 p.m. that same day.[119]

Earlier that day, to the southwest of Centreville, another Federal column marching eastward to concentrate with the rest of Popes Army now at Centreville was under Jackson's observation. Jackson commenced by displaying himself openly to the Union troops, but his presence was unnoticed. He reentered the woods, and within a very short time, the Confederate line began to emerge from the forest. At about 6:30 p.m., the Confederate artillery began shelling the position of the Federal column to their front. Union artillery was quickly set up, and an artillery battle commenced, halting the center of the Confederate advance. That part of the Union column which had already passed the point of the attack was not endangered, but those in the rear of the column immediately sought cover.[120]

---

[118] Michiganinthewar.org, "2nd Regiment Michigan Volunteer Infantry," 2 (War.org, michiganinthewar.org/infantry/2ndinf.htmp.2)
[119] Michigan.org, "2nd Michigan Volunteer Infantry, "E" Company 1861–1865," 3 (Michigan.orgp.3)
[120] Wikipedia, "Second Battle of Bull Run," 4 (Wikipedia-SBoBRp.4)

The Union commands of Gibbon and Doubleday were left to respond to Jackson's attack. The 14th Brooklyn Zouaves were sent out to reconnoiter (or scout for) the enemy's position. It was falsely assumed that this was merely horse artillery cannons from Jeb Stuart's cavalry. Other brigades were called on for reinforcements and the capture of the Confederate artillery up the rise. The 2nd Wisconsin answered the call and advanced obliquely back through the woods that the Union column was passing through. Upon emerging from the woods, the 430 men quickly formed up and advanced further up the hill. Reaching the plateau, they deployed skirmishers and continued their advance, driving back the Confederate line. Their ill-conceived advance was suddenly rewarded by a volley, blasted into their right flank by eight hundred Confederates, who were positioned approximately 150 yards away.[121] The 2nd Wisconsin did not waver from the devastating volley, but quickly replied with its own to the Confederate line. Still closing on the Union regiment, upon reaching the point some eighty yards away, the Confederates released another destructive volley. The Union men loaded and fired with the energy of mad men as fast as a man could load and shoot, which stopped the rush of the enemy.[122]

Out in this open field, there was little cover, and both sides were reinforced for this up close exchange of massive volleys for over two hours. The fighting was fierce, accompanied by much bloodshed and carnage. Three Georgia regiments were sent in to join the fight, endangering the Union lines, so even more reinforcements entered the battlefield. The 56th Pennsylvania and the 76th New York advanced through the woods, checking for any new Confederate advancement as darkness covered the battlefield. In the strobe-like flash of muskets, the assaults became uncoordinated. The day's engagement ended at last around

---

[121] Ibid. (Wikipedia-SBoBRp.4)
[122] Ibid. (Wikipedia-SBoBRp.4)

9:00 p.m., with Gibbon's men slowly retreating backwards to the edge of the woods, still firing their weapons. Doubleday's Regiment likewise retired in an orderly fashion, back to the Turnpike. The Union's losses that day were 1,150 men, while the Confederates' casualties reached 1,250.[123] In this battle were few tactics and little maneuvering were applied; tragically, an average of every three men engaged was shot.

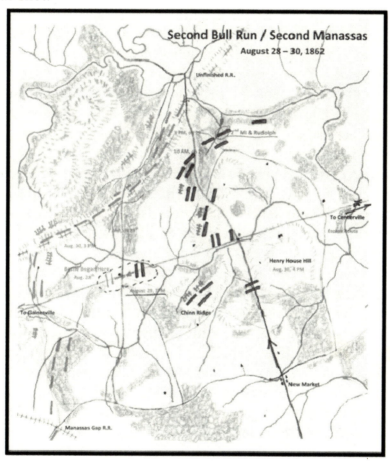

Maj. Gen. John Pope was unaware that Lee's army, commanded by Maj. Gen. Longstreet, had broke through the

---

[123] Wikipedia, "Second Battle of Bull Run," 5 (Wikipedia-SBoBRp.5)

light Union resistance at Thoroughfare Gap and was rapidly approaching the battlefield. He was convinced he had Jackson trapped with his back to Stony Ridge. Jackson spent the night reorganizing his defense in anticipation of an attack. He organized his men along the Manassas–Sudley road and behind the unfinished railroad grade near Sudley Church to his left. Meanwhile, Pope planed his attack against Jackson on both flanks.

On August 29, Heintzelman's Federal Third Corps, containing the 2nd Michigan under the command of Lt. Col. Dillman (in place of Col. Poe who was now in command of the brigade), came up across Bull Run and positioned itself on the Union's right flank with Kearny's division on the far right, up against the stream.[124] The 2nd was again deployed as skirmishers as they cautiously moved up the watercourse.[125] Repositioned north on the Manassas-Sudley Road, the two brigades under Schurz were the first to come into contact with Jackson's men at about 7:00 a.m., and a heavy firefight immediately commenced. The skirmishing was intense with both sides committing their forces in a piecemeal fashion. With the fighting begun, two more regiments were sent in to assist. Some success was achieved as the 82nd Ohio breached Confederate lines in the ground depression known as the Dump, but eventually were repulsed.[126] At the same time a little farther to the east, the 2nd Michigan was engaged with a number of artillery batteries; shrapnel from their shells exploded in their midst, and the regiment was forced to withdraw across the stream under a heavy fire.[127]

On the opposite side of the battlefield, the Union forces had advanced to Gainesville and attacked what they

---

[124] Hyslop, *Atlas of the Civil War,* (94, 96 maps) (Hyslop, 2011p.94 & 96 Maps)
[125] Michigan.org, 2nd Michigan Volunteer Infantry, "E" Company 1861–1865," 3. (Michigan.orgp.3)
[126] Wikipedia, "Second Battle of Bull Run," 6 (Wikipedia-SBoBRp.6)
[127] Michigan.org, "2nd Michigan Volunteer Infantry, "E" Company 1861–1865," 3 (Michigan.orgp.3)

mistakenly considered to be the Confederate right flank. Unsure of Jackson's disposition, the Union advance was strung out along a broad front and subject to a heavy artillery barrage. Union batteries answered with counter fire but the infantry was unable to advance any further.

Schurz ordered another Union assault against the hill around 10:00 a.m. on the Union right. He had assumed that Kearny's division, containing the 2nd Michigan, was poised to support him, but Kearny did not move forward in the second assault.[128] After much hard fighting, the Union assault failed., Having been delayed by a brief firefight with Stuart's cavalry that temporarily halted the Union column, Maj. Gen. Pope arrived on the battlefield with Federal reinforcements by 1:00 p.m.[129]

While Union forces were reorganizing, Stuart's cavalry tied tree branches behind a regiment of horses, causing a great cloud of dust that would simulate a large column of marching soldiers. At the same time, another report was received from the Gainesville area, announcing the arrival of what turned out to be Longstreet's seventeen regiments of infantry, one battery, and five hundred cavalry. The Union's progress was again halted to reassess the situation.[130]

Maj. Gen. Pope decided to attack Jackson's line in four different locations. The first attack was on the Union right, beginning around 3:00 p.m.. The Federal brigade surprisingly struck the Confederate defenses with a bayonet charge where a gap existed, thus allowing them to break through the line. Kearny's division was again expected to come in support of this attack, but once again it failed to move.[131] The Confederates rallied, and after some bloody fighting, pushed the Union brigade back.

---

[128] Wikipedia, "Second Battle of Bull Run," 6 (Wikipedia-SBoBRp.6)
[129] Ibid. (Wikipedia-SBoBRp.6)
[130] Ibid., 7 (Wikipedia-SBoBRp.7)
[131] Ibid. (Wikipedia-SBoBRp.7)

A brigade from the Union's Ninth Corps was ordered in to attack the center of Jackson's line, but they also were repulsed, meeting heavy resistance. At another point, a Union brigade attacked but only was able to advance as far as the railroad embankment. A Confederate counterattack not only restored their lines but pushed the Federals back into the open field; if not for the Union artillery barrage leveled at them, it would have pushed them even further. Unaware of how the battle was going, Pope ordered Kearny to attack Jackson's far left. At 5:00 p.m., for the first time in the battle, Kearny's men—10 regiments including the 2nd Michigan—surged forward.[132] [133] They struck A.P. Hill's depleted division and threatened to roll up Jackson's left flank. A Confederate counterattack immediately commenced. This combating turned quickly into the fiercest combat of the day, and after much bloodshed, repulsed the Union advance.

The Union 1st Corps was moving several divisions to the Henry House Hill and was confused as a Federal retreat by the Confederates. Therefore, Hood's division was sent forward as a reconnaissance in force to pursue them. Pope, believing the Confederates were retreating, sent a division

---

[132] Michiganinthewar.org, "2nd Regiment Michigan Volunteer Infantry," 2 (War.org, michiganinthewar.org/infantry/2ndinf.htmp.2)
[133] Wikipedia, "Second Battle of Bull Run," 8 (Wikipedia-SBoBRp.8)

west on the Turnpike in pursuit. The two opposing forces collided at the Groveton crossroads in a short but extremely violent confrontation that was ended by darkness. Both sides withdrew their weary troops to reorganize and rest.[134]

Early on the morning of August 30, 1862, a division of Confederates arrived on the battlefield, very fatigued, and halted on a ridge east of Groveton. By early dawn, they had realized that they were too close to the Union lines and fell back. Maj. Gen. Pope heard about their early-morning movement and believed this confirmed the Confederates were in retreat. He had also just received a report that Hood's troops had withdrawn the night before, which further reinforced his conviction. The Confederates were not retreating but digging in; Lee positioned eighteen artillery pieces on high ground northeast of the Brower farm. In that position, they were ideally situated to bombard the open fields in front of Jackson.[135]

It took the Union forces of 10,000 men under Porter two hours to prepare for the assault against Jackson's frontline. The Union men faced a formidable task as they had to cross six hundred yards of open pastureland, the final 150 yards of which were steeply uphill. At that point, the Confederates were well dug in behind the unfinished railroad bed. Because of positioning on the battlefield, one of the Union divisions had only three hundred yards to traverse, but was required to perform a complex right wheel maneuver while under fire from the enemy in order to hit the Confederate entrenchments squarely in the front. The Federal advance experienced devastating fire from the batteries and simultaneous, withering volleys from the Confederate infantry line. Still, they bravely pushed forward and fought their way through the Confederate lines, routing the 28th Virginia infantry. The Stonewall brigade rushed in to restore the line, but not

---

[134] Wikipedia, "Second Battle of Bull Run," 8 (Wikipedia-SBoBRp.8)
[135] Ibid., 9 (Wikipedia-SBoBRp.9)

without taking heavy casualties, including their own commanding officer. This was a brutish battle, in which the brigades fired so intensively that they ran out of ammunition. Some of the Confederate soldiers resorted to throwing large rocks at the 24th New York, which was obliged to throw them back, causing occasional damage. The Confederate line was about to falter. Longstreet's Rebel artillery was quickly added to the barrage against the Union reinforcements that were attempting to move in, which cut them to pieces. Porter called a halt to the assault, leaving the leading brigades, at great cost, to fight their own way out of this brawl with no further support. Some of the in frenzied Confederates attempted to carry on, but ran into Union troops covering their retreat along the Groveton-Sudley Road.[136]

Pope began to regroup his Union troops quickly and ordered a division from below the Turnpike to come up and reinforce Porter's position. This decision left only 2,200 Union troops south of the Turnpike. The 25,000 men in Longstreet's five Confederate divisions stretched out nearly a mile and a half at this point in the battle. Their ordered objective would be the Henry House Hill, which had been the key terrain in the First Battle of Bull Run. To reach the hill, they would have to traverse a mile and a half to two miles of ground containing ridges, streams, and some heavily wooded areas. He had to rely heavily on the initiative and drive of his own division commanders. Upon receiving their orders, they immediately started their advance.[137]

---

[136] Wikipedia, "Second Battle of Bull Run," 9-10 (Wikipedia-SBoBRpp.9-10).
[137] Wikipedia, "Second Battle of Bull Run," 10 (Wikipedia-SBoBRp.10).

There were only two brigades of Union defenders South of the Turnpike: Col. McLean's men from the First Corps, and Warren's from the 5th Corps. Warren was near Groveton, about eight hundred yards west of McLean, who held the Chinn Ridge. Hood's Confederate forces began the assault at 4:00 p.m., which immediately overwhelmed Warren's two Zouave regiments, the 5th New York and the 10th New York.

They held the line for ten precious long minutes of battle, during which the 5th New York suffered 120 men killed and another 180 wounded out of a total 500 men. This was considered the largest loss of life in a single infantry regiment in a single battle during the entire war. The dead from these two crushed Zouave regiments, with uniforms of bright red and blue, spread out across the field like a morbid field of flowers.[138]

(Note : There were roughly seventy Zouave regiments of mixed nationalities in the Union Army. Their dress was fashioned after the French North African Army some people refer to as the Foreign Legion. Their distinctive uniforms consisted of a Fez and turban, very baggy pants, a vest, a short jacket cut away from the top with a single button or clasp at the throat, and a sash. Their brightly colored uniforms were heavily trimmed with braid and/or many brass buttons and also, most times, leggings.)[139]

---

[138] Wikipedia, "Second Battle of Bull Run," 11 (Wikipedia-SBoBRp.11)
[139] 72nd PVI, Civil War Zouave History (PAGE 1) (72ndPVI)

Zouave Infantry with fixed bayonets

Maj. Gen. Pope and McDowell quickly realized the danger of their situation and moved Federal troops to occupy the Henry House Hill, but this would take some time to enact. Maclean's brigade on the Chinn Ridge was the only obstacle left to the Confederate advance. His four regiments of 1,200 Ohioans lined up facing west with one artillery battery in support. The first Confederate division advanced on their position on the ridge and after some bitter fighting was repulsed. It was quickly replaced with a second Confederate division that was also pushed back after much bloodshed. As a third Confederate assault commenced from the southern tip of the ridge, they were mistakenly taken for reinforcements, and Maclean's men withheld their fire. Realizing their mistake, a fierce firefight ensued for over ten minutes at virtually point-blank range. The Louisiana artillery battery also commenced firing on them, leading to the collapse of their line. Maclean's Ohio brigade gave Pope an additional thirty minutes to bring up reinforcements at the cost of 33 percent of his men.[140]

---

[140] Wikipedia, "Second Battle of Bull Run," 11 (Wikipedia-SBoBRp.11)

The first Union brigade attempting to reinforce the ridge was soon surrounded on three sides by attackers who quickly overwhelmed them, seriously wounding the commanding officer and capturing their artillery battery. The second brigade to advance on the field was likewise surprised by the arrival of two new Confederate brigades. Two more Union brigades poured into the battle from the 1st Corps but had no more success than their predecessors. The Union forces were in disorder, resulting in two brigades driven off the field. By 6:00 p.m., the Confederates had swept all Union resistance off the Chinn Ridge, but at a high cost in both men and time. With only an hour of daylight left, the Henry House Hill was still seven hundred yards away, with four Union brigades ready to defend the position.[141]

In spite of all, the Confederate lines marched toward the hill and commenced the attack. Lee sent in an additional three thousand men to assist them. This was the largest counterattack of the afternoon, but it was poorly coordinated and the attackers were tired. The four Union brigades fought hard and held their ground. Two more Confederate brigades were sent in, creating great pressure on the line in the open field, which was finally pushed back toward the Henry House. Still, the Federals remained in control of the hill.[142]

Stonewall Jackson was under orders from Lee to support the attack, so he pushed forward north of the Turnpike. As he had delayed in doing so before this, his effectiveness was greatly reduced. Pope had already ordered Federal units north of the Turnpike to withdraw. During this time, the 2nd Michigan (including Rudolph) on the far right flank above the Turnpike was being charged again and again by Confederate cavalry; they continually engaged in protecting the flank as

---

[141] Ibid. (Wikipedia-SBoBRp.11)
[142] Wikipedia, "Second Battle of Bull Run," 11–12 (Wikipedia-SBoBRpp.11-12)

they crossed the river and gallantly repulsed the Confederate attacks until they had withdrawn from the field.[143]

During this fierce assault, the Confederates were able to overrun a number of artillery batteries and infantry units; by 7:00 p.m., Pope had established a strong defensive line that aligned with the units on the Henry House Hill. Around 8:00 p.m., he ordered a general withdrawal of the Turnpike toward Centreville, which proved to be quiet and orderly. The Confederates were weary from battle and low on ammunition and decided not to continue on in darkness. The 2nd Michigan again reformed, having two men wounded, and marched up the Turnpike, reaching Centerfield about 11:00 p.m.[144] The casualties of this Second Battle of Bull Run, included ten thousand Union men killed and wounded, and approximately 1,300 Confederate men killed, with another seven thousand wounded.[145]

On September 1, 1862, Pope ordered one Union brigade north to reconnoiter while keeping his general movement in the direction of Washington. McDowell's Corps was sent out toward Jamestown where they could protect an important intersection for the army's continued retreat. But having received orders to attack the enemy, Pope sent two brigades from Reno's 9th Corps, placed under the command of Brig. Gen. Isaac Stevens, back toward the last known position of the Confederate Army. Maj. Gen. Philip Kearny's division followed later that afternoon.[146]

The two Federal brigades found a Confederate force poised upon Fox Hill, southeast of the Chantilly plantation around 3:00 p.m.. The Confederates may have been tired and hungry but they greatly outnumbered these two Union brigades. Still, Stevens chose to attack across the grassy field

---

[143] Michiganinthewar.org, "2nd Regiment Michigan Volunteer Infantry," 2 (War.org, michiganinthewar.org/infantry/2ndinf.htmp.2)

[144] Ibid. (War.org, michiganinthewar.org/infantry/2ndinf.htmp.2)

[145] Wikipedia, "Second Battle of Bull Run," 11–12 (Wikipedia-SBoBRp.12)

[146] Wikipedia, "Battle of Chantilly" (PAGE 2) (Wikipedia-Chan, 2010)

against the Confederate center. They promptly formed up and marched into the fight at around 4:00 p.m., which at first was successful in routing one Confederate brigade and the flank of another. The success was short-lived, as a counterattack of greater force soon drove them back. The brutal fighting continued, with no apparent advantage held by either side. Then around 5:00 p.m., during this vicious brawling, Stevens was killed by a shot through his temple.[147]

The 2nd Michigan, as part of Kearny's division, had broken camp earlier and marched out in the direction of the Fairfax Court House. They were about three miles from their destination when they arrived at the scene of battle, about the time of Stevens's death. Kearny quickly ordered the attack of his closest brigade on Stevens's left, which he did with haste. Kearny's other two brigades quickly followed suit to engage the enemy. During the melee, as the fighting had turned to hand-to-hand combat, the battle lines became blurred; Kearny mistakenly rode too far inside Confederate lines and was killed. The fighting continued on until dark, when the Union forces withdrew to the southern side of the battlefield.[148]

The 2nd Michigan continued on picket duty on the battlefield until the arrival of Longstreet's troops around 3:00 a.m.. The Union Army, fearing the renewal of the battle, withdrew to Germantown and Fairfax Court House, which was reached by around sunrise.[149] During this skirmish called the Battle of Chantilly, 1,300 of the Union's men were killed or wounded while only eight hundred men were killed or wounded of the Confederates.[150] From The 2nd Michigan, one man was dead, two wounded, and one taken prisoner.[151]

---

[147] Ibid., 2 (Wikipedia-Chan, 2010p.2)
[148] Wikipedia, "Battle of Chantilly," 2–3 (Wikipedia-Chan, 2010pp.2-3)
[149] Michiganinthewar.org, "2nd Regiment Michigan Volunteer Infantry," 3 (War.org, michiganinthewar.org/infantry/2ndinf.htmp.2) (War.org, michiganinthewar.org/infantry/2ndinf.htmp.3)
[150] Wikipedia, "Battle of Chantilly," 1 (Wikipedia-Chan, 2010p.1)
[151] History Data Systems, Inc., 2nd MI Infantry (3-years) (PAGE 1) (History Data System, P.O. Box 35, Duxbury, MA 02331)

Fearing the Union Army was in danger, Pope continued its retreat toward Washington. Still with the 2nd Michigan, Rudolph made several short marches during this retreat, finally reaching camp at Fort Ward. Following this, they marched to Upton's Hill. By September 3, the regiment was back in Washington, D.C on-duty in its customary role of defense.[152]

Having received another letter from Martha, Rudolph wrote her again from Alexandria, Virginia, on September 4, 1862, thanking her for the money and stamps. His regiment had been withdrawn from the field to allow the men to rest and replace the men who had been lost or wounded in heavy fighting. Another package that Martha said she had send had still not arrived, and he feared the food would be spoiled. He was disappointed, but he expected to be paid soon, so he would be able to buy some rations. He wrote another letter and mentioned,[153]

"You can learn more from the newspaper concerning our Regiment then I can write."

George Lenderking
27th Michigan Infantry Regiment

With the call for more troops, George Lenderking /Landerking (spelled both ways on Government Papers) followed Rudolph's lead and joined the Infantry. A twenty-three-year-old laborer, George had blue eyes, dark hair, fair complexion, and stood five feet, six and a half inches high. On August 15, 1862, he joined Company A, 27th Michigan Infantry as a 2 Corporal to serve his new country dressed in Union blue.[154]

---

[152] Civilwarintheeast.com, "2nd Michigan Infantry Regiment "(PAGE 1) (East, civilwarintheeast.com/USA/MI/2MI.php).
[153] Wormelle, *The Lenderking Family*, 8(Wormelle, 1969p.8)
[154] The National Archives, George Lenderking, Co. A, Michigan infantry (PAGES 2-3) (Archives, 1867)

The soldiers in the Union Army wore wool uniforms, a belt set that included cartridge box, cap box, bayonet, and scabbard. They also carried a haversack for rations, a canteen for water, and a blanket roll or knapsack, which contained a wool blanket, a shelter half (or small piece of canvas that could be combined with another to make a small tent for two) and perhaps a rubber blanket or poncho. Many would also wrap up a change of socks, toothbrush, comb, and other personal items: even paper, stamps, and envelopes, ink, and a pen. Each man would decide for himself what was important to take along, so personal items varied from soldier to soldier.[155]

Most infantryman carried a muzzle-loading rifle-musket that weighed approximately eight and a half pounds and fired a pointed-shaped bullet called the Mini Ball. Bullets were made of a very soft lead, which could cause horrible wounds and were difficult to heal. The bayonet was an important weapon that was placed on the muzzle, making it very imposing on the battlefield. The bayonet could also be used as a handy candleholder or for grinding coffee beans.[156]

Phillip Lenderking
5th Maryland Infantry Regiment

The family had informed Philip of Frederick's injury at the battle of Springfield, Missouri on October 25, but all were relieved that his wound was not life-threatening. He further realized that Frederick would have great difficulty continuing in his trade as a saddler, but being a family that was no stranger to war, the brothers were ready to perform their duty.

---

[155] Service, The United States Dept. of the Interior, "The Civil War soldier, what was life as a soldier like in 1863?", 2–3 (Service, Gettysburg National Military Parkpp.2-3)

[156] Service, The United States Dept. of the Interior, "The Civil War soldier, what was life as a soldier like in 1863?", 6 (Service, Gettysburg National Military Parkp.6)

Philip was promoted from private to corporal. on November 13, 1861, and on December 1, 1861 transferred into the band as a musician of Company G, now called the 5th Maryland Infantry Regiment.[157] The regiment continued at Baltimore and trained at Lafayette Square until March 11, 1862, where the men drilled, disciplined, and prepared for active service. It was not a surprise to the family to find that Philip had become a musician, because it was a family tradition, and both Philip and Lewis had previously played in local bands.[158]

(Note: Some people reading this may assume at this point that members of the band stayed behind the lines where it was safe. Some people today, on the other hand, may remember the heroic band on the Titanic, who gallantly continued to play as the ship sank. In general, however, most would think that playing in a band would keep one relatively out of harm's way, but this was not the case during the Civil War.

Infantry in parade formation

---

[157] National Archives and Record Service, "Philip Lenderking" (Field and Staff Muster Roll December 31, 1861) (National Archives and Record Service, Microcopy No. 384, roll 142, Fifth Infantry, Ke – Li)
[158] Wormelle, *The Lenderking Family*, 9 (Wormelle, 1969p.9)

Regimental bands served in many ways. For one thing they were a highly effective draw to attract new recruits. When hostilities first broke out, both sides were busy organizing volunteer units; military bands were in high demand, and many commanding officers would pay large sums of money to pick a good one for the regiment. Many bands were in communities where a regiment was recruited and would enlist as a complete unit along with the local militia.

A regimental band could also bolster morale. They could play lively quick steps or marches for the war-weary soldiers on the march, as well as patriotic songs to inspire the men just prior to going into battle. Many of the military bandsmen also served as medics, retrieving the wounded from the battlefield or assisting surgeons in the field. Sometimes, they had the grim task of burying the dead.[159]

The Civil War bands usually received fleeting references in the regimental histories, which did not reflect their true importance, or sometimes heroic efforts on the battlefield. For instance, the 24th Massachusetts Volunteer Infantry had a band that not only played in camp but followed the regiment into the field, and even into the heat of battle.[160] When they were not playing their music, most bandsmen would act as hospital corpsmen. It was also earlier mentioned in this chapter how the band playing of "Yankee doodle" rallied the men in Hooker's Division, which was taking heavy fire, long enough to be reinforced by the 1st Division of the Ninth Corps during the Peninsula campaign.[161]

On June 8, 1864, just after the battle of Cold Harbor, the 13th New Hampshire Regiment band went into the trenches and engaged in a competition concert, with the band playing across to the trenches of the enemy. The Confederate band would play "Dixie"," Bonnie Blue Flag," "My Maryland,"

---

[159] Elrod, *Civil War Bands* 1–2 (Elrodpp.1-2)
[160] Era, *The Civil War Bands*, 1 (Erap.1)
[161] Wikipedia ,"Battle of Williamsburg," 2 (Wikipedia(Will)p.2)

and other songs that were dear to the Southern cause. The Union band would counter with the songs "America," "The Star Spangled Banner," "Old John Brown," etc. After a period of time, this music jousting took a turn as the Confederate band changed the style of music to a tune the Union band felt it could play simultaneously. The Confederates were not amused and shot some rounds of grapeshot (a cluster of small iron balls shot from a cannon) from one of their Rebel batteries. Of course they wasted their ammunition while the Union band continued its playing all the more earnestly until the shelling had ceased.[162]

At the beginning of the war, some of the bands were large and became a great expense to the war effort. As hostilities continued, the War Department began to trim the number of regimental bands by forbidding their further enlistment. Congress finally passed an act, abolishing all regimental bands in the volunteer service with the provision that each brigade be entitled to a band at headquarters. Thereafter, if a man was to continue with the regiment as a musician, he had to either be supported entirely by the members of that regiment, or drawn from the musicians authorized as company fifers, buglers, and drummers. As Philip Lenderking was transferred from within his regiment to the band, he fell into this category.) [163]

On March 11, 1862, the 5th Maryland Regiment was ordered to Fortress Monroe, Virginia.[164] This fort had massive walls of a moated hexagonal shape, capable of holding two hundred heavy ordinance rifles. Since May of 1861, it was manned by nearly 4,500 officers and men. On August 6, 1861, Congress passed the First Confiscation Act, which stated that any enslaved person used for military purposes against the United States could be confiscated. In a very short

---

[162] Era, *The Civil War Bands*, 4 (Erap.4)
[163] Ibid. 3 (Erap.3)
[164] Civil War References (AUTHOR OK?), "Campbell's Station, November 16, 1863" (PAGES 1-2) (References)

time, there was a surge of African-American refugees seeking out what they called," Freedom's Fortress." Eventually, a policy of providing wages, food, and clothing for the former slaves in contraband camps was established by the Union Army. Fort Monroe was in many ways a staging ground for emancipation.[165]

When Phillip's regiment arrived at the Fort, it was at the same time that McClellan was preparing for the Virginia Peninsula Campaign. So Phillips Regiment, the 5th Maryland, and Rudolph's Regiment, the 2nd Michigan, would have been in the same flotilla (or fleet) of steamers that brought the troops from Washington down to the Fort Munro area. As the family kept in close contact with one another, it is highly probable that the two brothers got to see one another prior to the commencement of the Peninsula campaign. As Phillip's regiment was to remain at the Fort and act in a supportive role for the campaign, he would be paying close attention to any word from the front as the troops moved up into Virginia. As the grim news arrived about the battles, he would have worried greatly for his brother's safety.

In July of 1862, after the dismal failure of the Peninsula Campaign, the 5th Maryland Infantry Regiment was transferred to Suffolk and attached to Weber's Brigade, Division at Suffolk, Virginia, 7th Army Corps, Department of Virginia to September. They were again transferred to Virginia, and soon after were assigned to 3rd Brigade, 3rd Division, 2nd Corps, Army of the Potomac and marched back north to Washington, D.C. to fend off Lee's invasion of Maryland.[166]

On September 8, the 5th Maryland, along with McClellan's Army of the Potomac, started their march that would take them to Antietam. Along the long dusty march, women with friendly faces opened their doors and windows to greet them. They

---

[165] (Encyclopedia) Virginia Encyclopedia, "Fort Monroe During the Civil War" (PAGE 2)
[166] Civilwarintheeast.com, PAGE 1 (References) civilwarintheeast.com/USA/MD/5MD.php

handed them bread, butter, apples, peaches and preserves. Periodically, at the gates along the roadside, tubs of cold water and lemonade were placed by neighborhood people to quench the men's thirst. The younger recruits, wanting to make a good showing, kept up a good pace, yelling hurrah or other cheers at times, and occasionally even attempting to outrun one other. Phillip and the other men marching along the road in this long dusty column were in very high spirits at this time. By late evening of the 15th, they arrived just short of the town of Sharpsburg and a well-entrenched enemy.[167]

Up ahead, near the town of Sharpsburg, Lee was busy deploying his Rebel forces behind Antietam Creek and along a low ridge. It was an effective defensive position with terrain excellent for infantry to take cover. There were rail and stone fences, outcroppings of limestone ranging from sixty to one hundred feet wide. The Antietam Creek, although fordable, was crossed by three bridges, each a mile apart. The Potomac River to the rear of the Confederate position however, did make it a precarious position should they have need to withdraw from the battlefield.[168]

While Phillip and the rest of the men in the Army of the Potomac waited for McClellan to decide when to attack, the Confederates were taking extra precautions in preparing better defensive positions. It was not until the evening of September 16 that McClellan ordered Hooker's 1st Corps to cross the Antietam to probe the enemy positions. Cautiously, they attacked the Confederate positions near the East Woods. The infantry fighting continued until dark, but the artillery fire continued as a cover, as McClellan continued to position his troops.[169]

The bridge farthest to the South was dominated by Confederate positions on the bluff overlooking it. The middle bridge was covered by artillery placed on the heights near

---

[167] Wikipedia "Battle of Antietam," 5 (Wikipedia-BoAnp.5)
[168] Ibid., 4 (Wikipedia-BoAnp.4)
[169] Ibid., 5 (Wikipedia-BoAnp.5)

Sharpsburg, while the upper bridge was at least two miles east of the Confederate guns, making it safer to cross. So the Union forces were deployed with the intention of striking the Confederate far left flank. The battle commenced at dawn, about 5:30 a.m. on September 17. The Union 1st Corps under Maj. Gen. Joseph Hooker advanced down the Hagerstown Turnpike with approximately 8,600 men, while ahead, in a very secure position, Stonewall Jackson awaited them dug in with 7,700 Confederate defenders.[170][171]

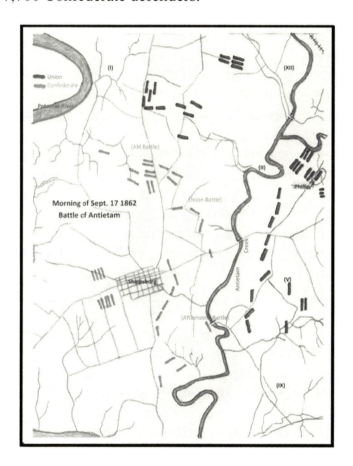

---

[170] Wikipedia, "Battle of Antietam,: 6 (Wikipedia-BoAnp.6)
[171] Sears, "Landscape Turned RED, The Battle of Antietam," 181 (Sears, 2003p.181)

At about the time that the first Union man emerged from the North Woods in front of the Confederate position and entered into the cornfield, an artillery duel suddenly commenced. The Confederates had at least five batteries on high ground across the Turnpike from the Dunker Church to the south, while the Union had nine batteries on the ridge behind the North Woods and four batteries of twenty-pounder Parrot rifles approximately two miles east of the Antietam Creek. Their results were deemed as "Artillery Hell," as the conflagration caused heavy casualties on both sides.[172]

Ahead of Hooker's advancing Union infantry, one could make out the glint of Confederate bayonets. The Union advance was halted and four batteries of artillery brought up, firing shell and canister over the heads of the Federal infantry and into the cornfield. Instantly, a savage battle began and chaos raged through the entire area. The conflict was heated and violent, creating a constant roar of muskets and cannons. Mounted on horseback, the officers yelled orders, cursed, and swore, but because the noise was so great, no one could hear them. The air was filled with a hail of bullets and shells, so much so that the barrels of the rifles became overheated from too much firing. With men beating each other over the heads with rifle butts and stabbing each other with bayonets, the fighting was brutal.[173]

Meade's 1st Brigade of Pennsylvanians began advancing through the East Woods and exchanging fire with the enemy. A heavy fire came down upon them, forcing the brigade to withdraw. Another Union division entered the cornfield, also to be turned back by the Confederate musketry and artillery. Brig. Gen. Abram Duryee's brigade marched directly into vicious Confederate fire, exchanging rounds from a range about 250 yards. He received no reinforcements because they

---

[172] Wikipedia "Battle of Antietam," 6–7 (Wikipedia-BoAnpp.6-7).
[173] Ibid., 7 (Wikipedia-BoAnp.7).

had difficulty reaching the scene, so there was no advantage gained and they also were ordered to withdraw.[174]

Again and again the Union line advanced into the cornfield, only to meet the same artillery and infantry fire from the enemy and be pushed back. The Confederates launched a counterattack by the Louisiana" Tiger" Brigade[175] that forced the Union men back into the East Woods, helping to cause the highest casualty rate of the day: 67 percent of the 12th Massachusetts infantry. The Federals quickly brought up a battery of three-inch ordnance rifles right into the cornfield. At point-blank range, they caused great slaughter to the Tigers, who were finally driven back after losing 323 of their five hundred men.[176]

Meanwhile, a few hundred yards to the west, the Iron Brigade began advancing down and astride the Turnpike into the cornfield and the West Woods. They continued to push the Confederates aside until finally halted by a charge of 1,150 men, which suddenly came to a stop and levied heavy fire from 30 yards away. The Iron Brigade returned the favor with their own fierce fire, finally causing a Confederate withdrawal. The Union advance resumed in the direction of the Dunker Church, cutting a large gap in the Confederate defensive lines.[177]

Around 7:00 a.m., Confederate reinforcements of approximately 2,300 men arrived through the West Woods and pushed the Union troops back through the cornfield again.[178] After two hours and 2,500 casualties, everyone was back where they started from. This cornfield, which measures about 250 yards deep and four hundred yards wide, was the scene of indescribable destruction. Fifteen times, it was

---

[174] Wikipedia "Battle of Antietam," 7 (Wikipedia-BoAnp.7)
[175] Sears, "Landscape Turned RED, The Battle of Antietam," 189 (Sears, 2003p.189)
[176] Wikipedia "Battle of Antietam," 7 (Wikipedia-BoAnp.7)
[177] Ibid. (Wikipedia-BoAnp.7)
[178] Sears, "Landscape Turned RED, The Battle of Antietam," 297–298 (Sears, 2003pp.297-298)

estimated, the field changed hands that morning, both sides paying a high price in casualties, yet nothing gained by either one. The battle had been so intense that every stalk of corn in the northern and greater part of the cornfield was cut close to the ground as if done deliberately with a knife. The Confederates lay on the ground in rows, precisely as they had stood in their ranks.[179]

The Union's 2nd Division of the 12th Corps under George Sears Greene saw an opportunity as the Confederate line pushed back into the West Woods to regroup. They were finally able to reach the Dunker Church, Hooker's original objective, where they were able to drive off the Confederate batteries. The Federal forces then held most of the ground to the East of the Turnpike.

Hooker, in the meantime, was attempting to gather his scattered regiments of the Federals 1st Corps to continue the assault when a Confederate sharpshooter took a shot at him, but only managed to hit him in the foot. Hooker was forced to leave the field; as his other senior subordinate was wounded as well, he left the command of the First Corps to General Meade. There seems to of been no further effort to rally the men of the 1st or the 12th Corps, so when Greene's men came under violent fire from the West Woods, they withdrew from the Dunker Church.[180]

At 7:20 a.m., two Union divisions of Sumner's Second Corps was ordered into the fight. The first division to ford the Antietam Creek was the 5,400 men under Maj. Gen. John Sedgwick.[181] After entering the East Woods, they became separated from Major General William H. French's division. At around 9:00 a.m., Maj. Gen. Edward Sumner, who was accompanying the division, used an unusual battle formation to launch the attack. He lined up the three brigades in three

---

[179] Wikipedia "Battle of Antietam," 8 (Wikipedia-BoAnp.8)
[180] Ibid. (Wikipedia-BoAnp.8)
[181] Sears, "Landscape Turned RED, The Battle of Antietam," 223 (Sears, 2003p.223)

long lines, the men side-by-side, with only fifty to seventy yards separating the lines. The Confederate artillery was the first to greet them, followed by a Confederate advance on three sides. In less than half an hour, Sedgwick's men received a devastating 2,200 casualties and were forced to retreat in a great disorderly fashion.[182]

At 10:00 a.m., two regiments of the 12th Corps advanced once again and were immediately confronted by a fresh Confederate division in the area between the cornfield and the West Woods. It was not long before two brigades of Greene's divisions marched in and drove the Rebels back. The Federal troops were able to seize some ground in the West Woods, but the fighting had caused thirteen thousand Union casualties, including two Union Corps commanders.[183]

Earlier in the morning, on the opposite side of Antietam Creek, Philip with the 5th Maryland had been waiting along with the rest of the men to be called into the battle they had been listening to from a distance. They anxiously awaited their first major battle and had full intentions of performing whatever they were called upon to execute. Their morale was high, their ammunition boxes full, and every man was in his place. It is not recorded, but many times the band would play patriotic songs to prepare the men's minds for battle, and it is likely that Philip and the rest of the band had been so engaged at this time. When they began to march in the front lines of the division, the regiment marched to the drums that beat their cadence.

Around 7:30 a.m. the 5th Maryland had forded the Antietam Creek with their division, marching in three columns of brigades. When the left flank had cleared the ford by a mile, the division faced left, forming three lines of battle adjacent to Sedgwick's, and immediately moved toward the front. The enemy that was in position in advance opened their batteries.[184][185]

---

[182] Wikipedia "Battle of Antietam," 9 (Wikipedia-BoAnp.9)

[183] Ibid., 9–10 (Wikipedia-BoAnpp.9-10)

[184] French, "Brig. Gen. William H. French's Official Report" (PAGE 1) (French, 1862)

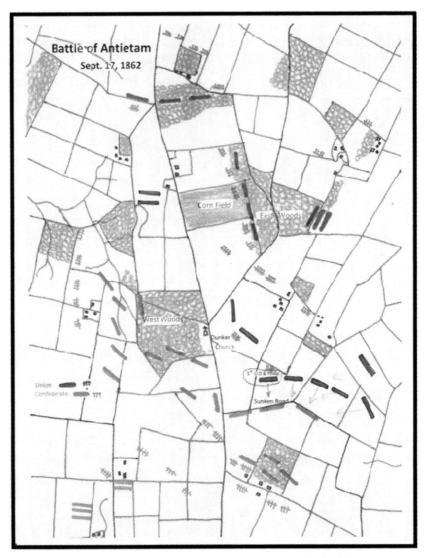

They steadily moved forward under fire until the first line encountered the enemy skirmishers. The order was given and they charged them briskly, then entered and cleared a group of houses the Confederates had used on the Roulette's farm. The enemy was driven back from their strong defensive

---

[185] Andrews, "Col. John W. Andrews Official Reports" (PAGE 1) (Andrews, 1864)

position after their line was broken. Weber's Brigade, containing the 5th Maryland, drove the enemy's front line steadily back, until a sudden and terrible fire opened up on their right by a group of Rebels that succeeded in breaking through the center division's line. At the same time, a heavy Confederate column endeavored to turn the Union's left.[186]

Battle of Antietam by Thulstrup

As the skirmishing temporarily subsided, Phillip's Union Regiment was prepared to march in and resume the fight. Maj. Gen. William H. French's 3rd Division, containing the 5th Maryland, had marched farther to the south than the rest of the 2nd Corps. They finally saw Sumner's aide (and son) quickly approaching them.[187] He hurriedly conveyed the activities of the morning, communicating that his right divisions were being severely handled, and orders were given to attack the Confederate center with all their might. French's 3rd Division was immediately given the order to move

---

[186] French, "Brig. Gen. William H. French's Official Report" (PAGE 1) (French, 1862)
[187] Wikipedia "Battle of Antietam," 10 (Wikipedia-BoAnp.10)

76   For Liberty

forward. There was some disorder in the line of march as they traversed through the woods, cornfield, and over fences, and the Division advanced forward.[188]

French pressed the line of his 5,700 Union men[189] forward to engage the enemy and swept over all obstacles until they crowned the crest of the hills on their left and right, flaunting the regimental banners in defiance of those Rebels daring to face them. The Confederate line ahead of them was in a strong, defensive position atop a gradual ridge. There were 2,500 Confederate men under D. H. Hill, posted in two lines of battle, in a road four feet below the surface of the adjoining field (the sunken road). The road had been worn down by years of wagon traffic forming a natural trench. There was a third line in the cornfield to the rear. The ground gradually rose so they could effectively fire over the heads of those in the road.[190]

Starting around 9:30 a.m., French launched a series a brigade-sized assaults against the Confederates' improvised breastworks.[191] The first brigade ordered to attack was the 3rd Brigade under Maj. Gen. Max Weber, which contained my great-great-grandfather Philip Lenderking and the 5th Maryland Infantry, many of whom were of German descent. Their color bearer was also of German descent and an enormous man over six feet tall, weighing three hundred pounds.[192] His march was measured and stately as he carried their flag proudly, but his shorter stride caused the center to advance slightly slower, causing the line to take a crescent shape. The 1st Delaware was on the right, the 5th Maryland in the center, and the 4th New York on the left. The whole command was excited by the gallantry and coolness of Major

---

[188] French, "Brig. Gen. William H. French's Official Report" (PAGE 1) (French, 1862)
[189] Wikipedia "Battle of Antietam," 10 (PAGE 10) (Wikipedia-BoAnp.10)
[190] Andrews, "Col. John W. Andrews Official Reports" (PAGE 1) (Andrews, 1864)
[191] Wikipedia "Battle of Antietam," 10 (Wikipedia-BoAnp.10)
[192] Sears, "Landscape Turned RED, The Battle of Antietam," 237 (Sears, 2003p.237)

General Max Weber as they continued to move forward over the plowed field that offered no cover to engage the enemy.[193]

With consummate skill and judgment, he ordered the men to fix bayonets as they neared the crest of the ridgeline. There seemed to be a hush over the battlefield as at last he gave the order to charge. They quickly found themselves only about twenty paces off the heavily engaged enemy.[194] The first Confederate volley knocked down 150 men of the 4th New York, giving the men the appearance of grain falling before the reaper.[195] The men in the front lines of the 1st Delaware and 5th Maryland likewise fell with one accord. Still, Weber commanded with much coolness and effect. He also soon became severely wounded and was forced to reluctantly leave the battlefield.[196] The Union troops he commanded were mostly inexperienced troops who had moved forward with the singular purpose to perform their duty. Many of them had been quickly cut down by heavy fire along with their commanding officer. Gradually they retreated to a less vulnerable position until relieved by the next line. The fighting became so heated at the sunken road that troops had to stop retrieving the wounded for fear of unnecessary losses of noncombatants.[197]

The second attack was made by the 2nd Brigade under Col. Dwight Morris and was also subject to the same exhaustive fire, which was also accompanied by a counterattack from an Alabama Brigade. As more and more dead and wounded dropped onto the battlefield, the more difficult it became to maneuver. While marching in line in close quarters, the soldiers had to be very conscious of the

---

[193] French, "Brig. Gen. William H. French's Official Report" (PAGE 1) (French, 1862)
[194] Andrews, "Col. John W. Andrews Official Reports" (PAGE 1) (Andrews, 1864)
[195] Sears, "Landscape Turned RED, The Battle of Antietam," 238 (Sears, 2003p.238)
[196] French, "Brig. Gen. William H. French's Official Report" (PAGE 1) (French, 1862)
[197] Andrews, "Col. John W. Andrews Official Reports," 2 (Andrews, 1864p.2)

men on the ground, stepping over or around their bodies. Some of the newer Union recruits in the second line got confused in the heat of battle and accidentally fired into the rear of the Union frontline before them. Despite the confusion and the suffering of heavy losses, they were still able to hold their ground and beat back the attacking Confederates. Running low on ammunition and having taken heavy casualties, they slowly backed away, firing to their front until they reached a safer position.[198]

The Union 1st Brigade under Brig. Gen. Nathan Kimball, which included three veteran regiments, pressed forward in the third attack and again many fell from the blistering fire issued from the sunken road. French's division suffered 1,817 killed, 1,614 wounded, and 203 missing[199] of his 5,700 men in under an hour. In the meantime, the surgeon general organized his division hospital only a short distance away while under fire.

By 10:30 a.m., reinforcements were entering the area on both sides. Around 3,400 men rushed in to bolster the Confederate lines, while 4,000 Union men in Maj. Gen. Israeli B. Richardson's Division simultaneously arrived on French's left.[200]

The Irish Brigade of Brig. Gen. Thomas F. Meagher led off the fourth attack against the sunken road. Father William Corby rode back and forth across the front of the formation shouting words of conditional absolution prescribed by the Roman Catholic Church for those who were about to die. With the emerald green flags snapping in the breeze, the troops pressed forward against the Confederate line and fought bravely under unrelenting volleys from the enemy. They unloaded some blistering volleys of their own into the Confederate line but

---

[198] Andrews, "Col. John W. Andrews Official Reports," 2 (Andrews, 1864 p.2)
[199] French, "Brig. Gen. William H. French's Official Report" (PAGE2) (French, 1862)
[200] Wikipedia, "Battle of Antietam," 10 (Wikipedia-BoAnp.10)

eventually were forced to withdraw, having lost 540 of their own men that were largely Irish immigrants.[201]

The next attack against the sunken road was Brig. Gen. John C. Caldwell's Brigade, (Caldwell being absent,) which was launched by Gen. Richardson personally. They tried to advance the brigade around the right flank of the Confederate's line with some success. The 350 men of the 61st and 64th New York spotted a weak spot in the Confederate line and seized the knoll commanding the Confederate line. They proceeded to unleash devastating enfilading volleys (gunfire from the flank that is directed along the length of the column or line of troops) into the sunken road, turning it into a death trap. In the confusion, the Confederates broke their line and moved swiftly toward the town. Richardson's men pursued them with great enthusiasm and deadly fire. The Confederates massed artillery fire, stopped their pursuit, and began to push them back. They were then struck by a counterattack of two hundred Confederates who had gotten around their left flank. The 5th New Hampshire charged fiercely into the attacking Confederates, breaking their momentum and driving them back. Due to lack of reinforcements, Richardson reluctantly ordered his division to fall back to a position north of the ridge facing the sunken road.[202]

His division lost about 1,000 men. The carnage that took place at the sunken road from 9:30 a.m. to 1 p.m. caused about 5,600 casualties, which gave it the name Bloody Lane. Along this eight hundred yard stretch of road, the Union casualties were numbered at three thousand men and the Confederate casualties at 2,600 men.[203] The 5th Maryland counted thirty-nine men killed and another 116 wounded, as

---

[201] Wikipedia, "Battle of Antietam," 10–11 (Wikipedia-BoAnpp.10-11)
[202] Wikipedia, "Battle of Antietam," 11 (Wikipedia-BoAnp.11)
[203] Wikipedia, "Battle of Antietam," 11 (Wikipedia-BoAnp.11)

well as two commanding officers, one man taken prisoner, and two men missing.[204]

As the battle again shifted to the most southern bridge, many man lay wounded on the battlefield. My great-great-grandfather Philip Lenderking was one of those casualties, struck across the left, back side of the head, across the parietal bone, by a projectile. The record says he was serving in the line of duty charging the enemy. The only explanation can be that he was trying to remove the wounded from the battlefield and got struck during his attempt. As the battle shifted farther to the south and away from the sunken road, he was taken to the field hospital. His wound was cared for as best they could on the battlefield, but as soon as feasibly possible, he and many of the other wounded were transferred back to Baltimore, Maryland. Philip stayed at the National Hotel Hospital in Baltimore until he recovered from his wound; on January 2, 1863, he was finally able to return to duty and rejoined his regiment.[205]

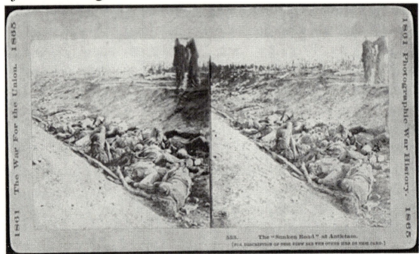

---

[204] Historical Data System, Inc.," 5th Maryland Infantry" (PAGE 2) (Historical Data System)
[205] National Archives and Record Service, "Philip Lenderking" (Company Muster Roll Sept. & Oct., 1862) (National Archives and Record Service, Microcopy No. 384, roll 142, Fifth Infantry, Ke – Li)

The Sunken Road at Antietam

Bodies in front of the Dunker Church

Bodies in Confederate rifle pit at Antietam

Chapter 4
To the Second Battle of Winchester

Rudolph Lenderking
2nd Michigan Infantry Regiment

By early October, Rudolph would have been informed of his brother Philip's injury at Antietam. He would have been relieved to know that his wound was not life-threatening, but the nature of the wound would have given him some concern. But he was still a soldier and had his own orders to follow. On October 11, 1862, the regiment again marched out of Washington on a reconnaissance mission up the Potomac as far as Edwards Ferry, Maryland. After breaking camp, they marched in the direction of the Chain Bridge and crossed it. Their line of march took them through Tannytown, Rockville, and Darnstown, where they bivouac for the night. Their march was resumed early the next morning and before noon formed a line of battle, where they expected to meet Stuart's Cavalry. In the afternoon, they proceeded on to Edwards Ferry, arriving around 7:00 p.m., where they encamped for the night. They remained here on picket duty along the canal until the twenty-eighth, when they resumed their march in the direction of White's Ford, via Poolesville. The column then crossed over into Virginia and marched on to Leesburg, arriving there on the thirty-first. On October 9, 1862, [206] [207] Private Lenderking was promoted to corporal.[208]

On November 1, the march continued, reaching Millville on the third and Waterloo on the eighth. On the 15 of November, 1862, the 2nd Michigan was transferred into 1st Brigade, 1st Division, 9th Army Corps, Army of the Potomac, and proceeded on to White Sulphur Springs that same day. On the sixteenth, they marched on to Bealton Station, on the

---

[206] Michiganinthewar.org, "2nd Regiment Michigan Volunteer Infantry," (PAGE 3) (War.org, michiganinthewar.org/infantry/2ndinf.htmp.3)
[207] Michigan.org, "2nd Michigan Volunteer Infantry, "E" Company 1861–1865," 4 (Michigan.orgp.4)
[208] (The National Archives, Record Group 94, Entry 534,Box1411)(Company Muster Roll Sept. & Oct.)

Orange and Alexandria Railroad. They continued to march on to Warrington Junction and on the seventeenth they marched toward Fredericksburg, arriving opposite that city on the nineteenth. Once there, they were placed on picket duty. They went into temporary camp near Falmouth, then on the twenty-ninth were sent to a point in front of Fredericksburg, where they were placed on duty supporting an artillery battery.[209]

On December 12, the first day of the battle of Fredericksburg, the regiment crossed the Rappahannock River where they were held in reserve during the engagement. Although not directly engaged in that battle, the Confederates shelled their position, killing one man and wounding two others.[210] On the fourteenth, they re-crossed the river and continued to stand by. After the battle was over, by the sixteenth, they returned to camp. During the battle of Fredericksburg, there were 1,284 Union troops killed, 9,600 wounded, and 1,769 men captured or missing; the Confederate losses numbered 608 men killed, 4,116 wounded, and 653 men captured or missing.[211]

Back at the Rappahannock River, desertion rose dramatically in the Union regiments. With supplies short, the quartermaster had difficulty in meeting the men's daily ration requirements. Many of the uniforms had not been replaced, and roll calls were answered for the most part in tattered rags. Payment for the men was also in arrears. Not surprisingly, morale of the men under Burnside, including Rudolph's Regiment, was suffering greatly.[212]

(Note : Normally in the field, Union soldiers would receive a variety of things to eat. The men usually received

---

[209] Michigan.org, "2nd Michigan Volunteer Infantry, "E" Company 1861–1865," 5 (Michigan.orgp.5)
[210] Michiganinthewar.org, "2nd Regiment Michigan Volunteer Infantry," 3 (War.org, michiganinthewar.org/infantry/2ndinf.htmp.3)
[211] Wikipedia, "Battle of Fredericksburg" (PAGE 11) (Wikipedia, ...wikipedia.org/.../Battle_of_Fredericksb...)
[212] U.K. Greg Bayne (CHECK AUTHOR—SEE BIBLIOG.), "Burnside's Mud March" (UK, americancivilwar.org.uk/news_burnsides...p.1)

rations meant to last three days while on an active campaign. The basic ration was meat and bread. The meat usually came in the form of salt pork or, on rare occasions, fresh beef. Salt pork and the like did at times spoil due to improper packing. On the other hand, even if properly prepared, it would still be unpalatable in the condition the soldier received it. Many would try to remedy the problem by soaking it in a nearby stream overnight. By the time the pork was retrieved from the stream, it usually had shrunk in size and still was very salty. If one takes into account the number of men using this method up and down the stream near their encampments, it is not hard to see how those soldiers' meat downstream may have easily been contaminated by the many soldiers and horses located above their position. This may account for a number of those men who died from dysentery or other diseases. Still, these rations of pork or beef were boiled, broiled, or fried over an open campfire—they usually had to be cooked as soon as a soldier possibly could. Raw meat would spoil quickly in the field, while cooked meat could last several days, and a man could eat it during any short break.

    The soldiers' bread was a flour biscuit called hardtack, although the men renamed it, "tooth-dullers," "worm castles," and "sheet iron crackers." Hardtack could be eaten plain although most men preferred to roast them over an open fire, crumble them into soup, or crumble and fry them with their pork and bacon fat in a dish called "skillygalee." Other food items that they would receive included rice, peas, beans, dried fruit, potatoes, molasses, vinegar and salt. Baked beans were a northern favorite when the time could be taken to prepare them, and a cooking pot with lid could be obtained.[213]

    One of the main staples of the soldiers diet was coffee, which to many of the men was more important than anything

---

[213] Service,, *The United States Dept. of the Interior, The Civil War soldier, what was life as a soldier like in 1863?*, 4 (Service, Gettysburg National Military Parkp.4)

else. It was distributed to the men green, and as soon as possible, so it was up to the soldier to roast and grind the beans. A common method for distributing coffee to the men began by laying two blankets out on the ground. One blanket would contain the coffee as evenly divided as possible in small piles according to the number of men. Without scales, it was impossible to make completely accurate measurements, so one pile may have looked larger than another. The second blanket would contain an equal number of piles of sweetener. The distributing sergeant would simply turn his back on the blankets and randomly call one soldier up at a time to pick his allotment from each blanket. However, at this particular time during the war, all such things seemed to be in short supply.)[214]

Despite the lack of many provisions, there still was no shortage of Christmas spirit. Whiskey was easy to obtain and many took advantage of the winter break. Their festive spirit continued on through the New Year. But still the war did not cease. There were still patrols as well as guard duties. The lack of supplies also lead to the first post-Christmas skirmish, as soldiers were searching for food. It was rumored among the men that they would move out soon against the Confederates, but the action seemed to have been delayed.[215]

Burnside ordered scouting parties up and down the Rappahannock River. Everywhere they looked across, they could see Lee's troops digging deeper and throwing up earthen works with interlocking lanes of fire from muskets and artillery. Twenty-five miles of river line were amply covered by Lee's Confederate troops and well-guarded for at least twenty-five miles in each direction. Rudolph and the rest of Burnside's troops were put to the task of cutting down

---

[214] Service,, *The United States Dept. of the Interior, The Civil War soldier, what was life as a soldier like in 1863?*, 4 (Service, Gettysburg National Military Parkp.4)
[215] U.K. Greg Bayne, "Burnside's Mud March," 1 (UK, americancivilwar.org.uk/news_burnsides...p.1)

trees, building new roads, and digging gun emplacements in preparation for his planned attack.[216]

To the south, the opposite direction that Burnside planned to move, companies were ordered to march back and forth, and the cavalry was sent to demonstrate under enemy eyes in order to give them a false impression. Finally by mid-January, men and supplies were sufficiently assembled and ready for what the men felt would be a decisive blow against the Confederacy.[217]

On the morning of January 20, 1863, the great wagon train of pontoon boats, artillery, and supplies lined up with the Union regiments and moved northward, up the Rappahannock River. The men were enthusiastic and felt positive about this move, which seemed to be starting off very smoothly. Unknown to the Union soldiers, a massive storm had developed near the southern East Coast and started to move northward. The clouds gathered all day and grew thicker and darker as the day went on.[218]

On the evening of January 20, the rain began falling, quickly drenching the unsheltered men and horses. The torrential rain continued to fall without cessation throughout the next day. The cold, bone-chilling rain would last at least thirty hours before the storm system would pass. Burnside's army rapidly got bogged down in the mud. The temperatures hovered in the upper thirties, adding a chill to the drenched soldiers.[219] The great mule-drawn wagons carrying the pontoons churned the road into a quagmire. The wagons sank to their hubs; the artillery sank until unrecognizable except for the muzzles sticking up in the air. The exhausted horses

---

[216] www.civilwarhome.com,(Furgurson) "Burnside's Mud March," 1 (Home, www.civilwarhome.com/mudmarch.htmp.1)

[217] www.civilwarhome.com,(Furgurson) "Burnside's Mud March," 1 (Home, www.civilwarhome.com/mudmarch.htmp.1)

[218] U.K. Greg Bayne, "Burnside's Mud March," 4 (UK, americancivilwar.org.uk/news_burnsides...p.4)

[219] U.K. Greg Bayne, "Burnside's Mud March," 5 (UK, americancivilwar.org.uk/news_burnsides...p.5)

floundered, as did the men. Rudolph and the rest of the men would have had to trudge through this oozy, sticky mud, each slippery step sinking deeper into the goo, only to have their shoes sucked off when attempting to pull their feet back to the surface. The soldiers slipped and fell repeatedly, the thick mud sticking to their bodies and their equipment, adding more weight to their already heavy load.[220]

On January 21, 1863, one hundred and fifty pieces of artillery were scheduled to be in place, ready for the crossing of five pontoon bridges. Sadly, due to the severe weather conditions, there were not enough pontoons for even one single bridge.[221] Confederate pickets across the river watched the struggling Union Army with amusement. Some put up large signs on the riverbank that said, "Burnside's army's stuck in the mud." Other signs would say, "This way to Richmond."[222] The Rebels taunted and mocked Burnside's men from across the river, even sarcastically asking them if they needed their help.

The whole country was a river of mud. Gale force winds from the northeast accompanied the storm,[223] which had brought 3.2 inches of rain. The roads were rivers of deep mire, and the heavy rain had practically turned the ground into the consistency of quicksand. Whole regiments and triple teams of mules were hitched to the wagons and guns throughout the column in an almost futile attempt to pull them farther up the road. A team of twelve horses and 150 men could not pull one cannon out of the mud. Double and triple teams of horses and mules were hitched to a single

---

[220] U.K. Greg Bayne, "Burnside's Mud March," 4 (UK, americancivilwar.org.uk/news_burnsides...p.4)
[221] www.civilwarhome.com,(Furgurson) "Burnside's Mud March," 1 (Home, www.civilwarhome.com/mudmarch.htmp.1)
[222] U.K. Greg Bayne , "Burnside's Mud March," 5 (UK, americancivilwar.org.uk/news_burnsides...p.4) (UK, americancivilwar.org.uk/news_burnsides...p.5)
[223] Ibid., 5 (UK, americancivilwar.org.uk/news_burnsides...p.4) (UK, americancivilwar.org.uk/news_burnsides...p.5)

stuck pontoon wagon, with as many men as possible pushing from behind, and still it could barely be moved.[224] Dedicated troops invested great effort into moving forward even a few feet. Still the rain came down in torrents. Some regiments reportedly could only advance one and a half miles in an entire day. Roads became un-navigable and conflicting orders further confused the line of march.[225]

The deluge left the Union forces in indescribable chaos. Pontoons, wagons, and artillery were sunk deep in the mud in the center of roads the whole length of the Federal column, all the way down to the intended river crossing area. Exhausted from the effort to move their loads through the hideous medium, horses and mules lay dead in the mud where they dropped. One hundred and fifty dead animals lay lifeless in the road, many of them hardly recognizable as once living animals.[226]

The entire command was turned out in this brutal weather to repair the roads. Small trees were cut down and laid across the road side-by-side to give the many wagons and horses more buoyancy. This was no small task for the rain-soaked Union soldiers, covered in mud and shivering to the bone.

By January 22, the rain had ended but the entire Army of the Potomac was still stalled in the mud. The temperatures were hovering in the upper thirties to near forties, while the air remained damp and the sky cloudy. The objective had now changed from attacking the Confederate forces across the river to simply getting unstuck from the muck and returning to camp. Burnside tried to lift the spirits of the men by issuing liquor to the soldiers on January 22, but this only made the situation worse.[227] Many of the men became drunk, and fights

---

[224] www.civilwarhome.com,(Furgurson) "Burnside's Mud March," 1–2 (Home, www.civilwarhome.com/mudmarch.htmpp.1-2)
[225] U.K. Greg Bayne , "Burnside's Mud March," 4 (UK, americancivilwar.org.uk/news_burnsides...p.4)
[226] www.civilwarhome.com,(Furgurson) "Burnside's Mud March," 2 (Home, www.civilwarhome.com/mudmarch.htmp.2)
[227] U.K. Greg Bayne , "Burnside's Mud March," 5 (UK, americancivilwar.org.uk/news_burnsides...p.5)

broke out among the frustrated soldiers, ranging from small, individual fights to entire regiments battling one another in the sticky, gooey sludge. Still, with great effort, log roads continued to be built over the mud.

It was not until January 23, that the army began to arrive back in camp, very beaten-down from their ten mile ordeal. The campaign had been a miserable failure, and many of the men heckled Burnside as they marched through the sludge back into camp. The mire so covered them all, one regiment was indistinguishable from another. To make matters worse, many of the men, assuming they were on their way to Richmond, had foolishly burned their huts to the ground prior to leaving. By the end of the twenty-fourth, the disheveled Union forces under Burnside were once again in camp. These unfortunate few days in history would be forever known as "The Mud March."[228]

On February 10, 1863, the regiment along with its brigade, moved to Newport News Virginia. February 16, Colonel Poe resigns to accept promotion to brigadier general of the volunteers. Capt. William Humphrey was promoted to colonel, and on March 19, the regiment continued on through Baltimore, Parkersburg, and Louisville, reaching Bardstown, Kentucky on the twenty-third.[229]

In April of 1863, the 2nd Michigan was attached to 1st Brigade, 1st Division, 9th Army Corps, Army of the Ohio. Around this time, Pvt. Franklin Thompson of Flint deserted near Lebanon, Kentucky, after it was discovered that she was a woman, "and a good-looking one at that," according to Col. Poe. From April 9 through the thirtieth, the regiment was on duty at camp Dick Robinson, Kentucky.[230] A mistaken note

---

[228] www.civilwarhome.com,(Furgurson) "Burnside's Mud March," 2 (Home, www.civilwarhome.com/mudmarch.htmp.2).
[229] Civilwarintheeast.com, "2nd Michigan Infantry Regiment" (PAGE 2) (East, civilwarintheeast.com/USA/MI/2MI.php)
[230] Civilwarintheeast.com, "2nd Michigan Infantry Regiment" (PAGE 2) (East, civilwarintheeast.com/USA/MI/2MI.php)

on the bottom of one of Cpl. Lenderking's records indicates that he was to be mustered out April 10, 1863. That did not seem to happen.[231] The regiment remained in Kentucky during April, in May they moved to Columbia.

In June of 1863, they were transferred to 3rd Brigade, 1st Division, 9th Army Corps, Army of the Tennessee, to reinforce the Army of General Grant in Mississippi. From June 7 to 14, the 2nd Michigan moved in the direction of Vicksburg, Mississippi.[232] Now, Rudolph's regiment was heading to Vicksburg to join the siege at the same time. Vicksburg was a key city to the Confederate states. While in their hands, it blocked Union navigation down the Mississippi, together with control of the mouth of the Red River and of Port Hudson to the South. It also allowed communications with the states west of the river, upon which the Confederates depended on extensively for agricultural supplies. The natural defenses of the city were ideal, earning it the nickname, "The Gibraltar of the Confederacy." It was located on a high bluff overlooking the horseshoe-shaped bend in the river, making it almost impossible to approach by ship. North and east of Vicksburg was the Mississippi Delta, a practically impenetrable swamp two hundred miles north to south and up to fifty miles wide. About twelve miles up the Yazoo River were Confederate batteries and entrenchments at Heinous Bluff. On the opposite side of the river from the fortress city, the Louisiana land west of Vicksburg was also difficult, with many streams, poor country roads, and widespread winter flooding.

---

[231] The National Archives, "Rudolph Lenderking, Co. A, 2nd Michigan Infantry" (Special Muster Roll April 14,1863 (The National Archives, Record Group 94, Entry 534,Box1411)

[232] Civilwarintheeast.com, "2nd Michigan Infantry Regiment" (PAGE 2) (East, civilwarintheeast.com/USA/MI/2MI.php)

George Lenderking
27th Michigan Infantry Regiment

George's regiment was still in the process of being assembled in Michigan. He would have also heard from his family, including the injury of his younger brother Philip at Antietam. This military training would become more important as he shouldered the dangers of a soldier's life. In the recruitment of the six companies to be raised in the Lake Superior counties, only three could be enlisted. In the meantime, the recruitment of the 28th Michigan had also been going slowly. Due to the need for more troops, it was therefore determined to consolidate the two. The 27th was then ordered to break camp at Port Huron where they were currently organizing and proceed to Ypsilanti where the 28th was recruiting. The process of consolidation was completed and the united regiments became known as the 27th Michigan Infantry. This regiment was ordered into the service of the United States on April 10, 1863.[233]

Consisting of eight companies, the regiment under the command of Col. Fox proceeded to Kentucky on April 12th. The regiment consisted of 865 officers and men and was attached to the 2nd Brigade, 1st Division, 9th Army Corp, Army of the Ohio. Before leaving the state it was presented the flag by the ladies of Port Huron, which was carried throughout the remainder of the war.[234]

The first skirmish occurred with the Confederates at Jamestown, Kentucky on June 2, 1863. They were assigned to the 1st Brigade, 1st Division of the 9th Corp, Army of the Tennessee. The 27th Infantry soon received orders to march to Mississippi to reinforce General Grant's siege of Vicksburg.[235] As they advanced closer to their destination, they could hear the

---

[233] Michiganinthewar.org, 27th Regiment Michigan Volunteer Infantry (PAGE 1) (War, michiganinthewar.org/.../27thinf.htm)
[234] Ibid., (PAGE 1) (War, michiganinthewar.org/.../27thinf.htm)
[235] Civilwarintheeast.com, "27th Michigan Infantry Regiment" (PAGE 1) (East, civilwarintheeast.com/USA/MI/27MI.php)

sounds of the big guns pounding the city. Now joined to the rest of Ulysses S Grant's army, they caught their first view of the siege and the troops already entrenched. As they took their assigned position, they settled in as best they could. It also appears that George's regiment arrived there on the same day as Rudolph's and was mirror positioned only a short distance away.

They quickly learned that on May 22, 1863 several brigades had already tried assaulting the city for the second time. But after a long bitter struggle, the Confederates were still very much in control. The Union Army had suffered 3,199 casualties in the assault, and the men of the 27th could immediately see how secure the city was; the Confederates had made a strong defensive earthworks arching eastward like a shield. Their earthworks were also connected to the river, above and below the city, which itself made a natural barrier running down its backside. Realizing that the city could not be taken by assault, Grant had ordered the commencement of a siege operation; its job was to cut off all supplies going into the city and hammer them with artillery daily.[236]

---

[236] Wikipedia, "Vicksburg Campaign" (PAGE 11) (encylopedia, en.wikipedia.org/.../Vicksburg_Campaign)

Phillip Lenderking
5th Maryland Infantry Regiment

On January 2, 1863, Philip had been released from the hospital in Baltimore and returned to his regiment in the field. In the meantime, the 5th Maryland had moved to a new assignment at Harper's Ferry on September 22, just after the battle of Antietam. During October 16 and 17th, they performed a reconnaissance of the Charlestown area. In December, the regiment was assigned to the Point of Rocks, Upper Potomac, 8th Army Corps, Middle Department. While at this location, they were assigned to General Milroy's command in the Shenandoah. Their primary duty was at Point of Rocks and Maryland Heights to protect the Baltimore and Ohio Railroad.[237] It was at this location Philip was able to rejoin his regiment.

The 5th Maryland was now in winter quarters, so they had been constructing log huts that were large enough to

---

[237] Civilwarintheeast.com, "5th Maryland Infantry Regiment" (PAGE 1) (East, civikwarintheeast.com/USA/MD/5MD.php)

accommodate several men. A nearby source of trees had to first be cut and notched near both ends to fit tight at the corners, with the bottom log laying on a stone bed to prevent rot and drainage. Once the basic structure was completed, a small fireplace was formed at one end out of stone, brick, or mud, with mud squeezed in between the logs from both inside and out, and any logs in the chimney completely covered with mud. The roof was constructed from tents with sawn boards and wood planks. Finally, the huts were finished with special touches by those who would occupy them, often naming their huts after well-known hotels or restaurants back home. Once the camp was completed, it resembled a small bustling city, with streets that were very active during the day.[238]

In March of 1863, the 5th Maryland was attached to the 2nd Brigade, 1st Division, 8th Army Corps. On June 2, the regiment marched out to its new assignment at Winchester, Virginia,[239] a town that was literally the crossroads of the war and constantly changing hands. Sometime during that same day at Catoctin, Maryland, Cpl. Lenderking was promoted to sergeant while his associate Thomas Smith was demoted.[240] Upon arrival, they became part of the force of 6,900 men under Maj. Gen. Robert H. Milroy. His command consisted of three infantry brigades, under Brig. Gen. Washington L. Elliott and Cols. Andrew T. McReynolds and William G. Ely, plus two small outposts northwest of town under Col. Joseph W. Kiefer.[241] Despite the battlements bristling with heavy artillery and the lack of identified threat, the entire chain of command was uneasy with a sense of foreboding. Between June 9 and

---

[238] Service, The United States Dept. of the Interior, *The Civil War soldier, what was life as a soldier like in 1863?*, 2 (Service, Gettysburg National Military Parkp.2)
[239] Civilwarintheeast.com, 5th Maryland Infantry Regiment (PAGE 1) (East, civikwarintheeast.com/USA/MD/5MD.php)
[240] National Archives and Record Service, "Philip Lenderking" (Company Muster Roll Sept. & Oct., 1863) (National Archives and Record Service, Microcopy No. 384, roll 142, Fifth Infantry, Ke – Li)
[241] Wikipedia, "Second Battle of Winchester," 2 (Wikipedia-SBoW, 1210, ...wikipedia.org/.../Battle_of_Winchester_II p.2)

11, Milroy reinforced various locations around the perimeter of Winchester, sent all his disabled men and quartermaster stores back to Harpers Ferry, and doubled the number of men on picket duty. The rest of the men in the Federal camp were kept busy with fatigue duties, clearing away brush and trees to expand the kill zone around the forts.[242]

On June 12, a Confederate division and cavalry brigade were detected by Union troops moving north through Berryville Virginia to Martinsburg, West Virginia. A number of patrols were sent out to scour the countryside. The 12th Pennsylvania Cavalry was sent toward the location of the enemy sightings. As they trotted up the valley on the Fort Royal Road, approximately ten miles southeast of Winchester, they encountered a great Confederate force. They skirmished with the Rebel Cavalry for a short time to determine the enemy's strength, which proved to include large numbers of infantry and artillery. Afterward, with two men wounded, they reported back to their commander around 3:00 p.m..[243] By the end of the day, the Rebels were just five miles north of Front Royal, making two camps, one at Stone Bridge and the other near the Shenandoah River.[244]

The Union commander at Winchester had been plagued by Confederate raiding parties in the lower Shenandoah Valley, so one Union brigade had been posted in Berryville, to act as a base of operations for patrols of the Shenandoah River and to watch out for Confederate raiders. This brigade had orders to evacuate to Winchester upon the signal of the firing of one of the heavy artillery guns.

Around Winchester, Milroy stationed pickets and vedettes (mounted sentinel stations in advance of the pickets)

---

[242] Maier, *Leather & Steel, The 12th Pennsylvania Cavalry in the Civil War*, 81 (Maier, 2001p.81).
[243] Maier, *Leather & Steel, The 12th Pennsylvania Cavalry in the Civil War*, 83 (Maier, 2001p.83).
[244] Wikipedia, "Second Battle of Winchester," 3 (Wikipedia-SBoW, 1210, ...wikipedia.org/.../Battle_of_Winchester_II p.3)

in a tight ring around Winchester, too tight to have a good surveillance of the situations in the area close to his defenses. This was in part due to the bushwhacking of his patrols and various Confederate cavalry raids that kept occurring in his district. The vedettes farthest to the South were located at or near Parkins Mill Battery at the Opequon Creek crossing, a meager four miles south of Winchester.

Winchester was heavily fortified by forts and lunettes (earthen works that project out like a V) encircling the town, as well as along the outlying turnpike roots entering town. The strongest position was just north of town consisting of Fort Milroy, Star Fort, and West Fort, a redoubt of six guns. Within Winchester, Milroy constructed or improved ten defensive fortifications, numbered battery No. 1 through battery No. 10, making improvements on many preexisting forts and fortifications left by prior Confederate and Federal occupations. The fortifications were linked together in places with roads and trenches, and the use of these was a key to Milroy's defensive strategy. Through a combination of retreating his forces into the defensive works, and using his long-range heavy artillery, Milroy felt that he could hold out for weeks, if not months, against any force that might be thrown against him.[245]

On June 13, the weather was fine and balmy, and all was quiet at Winchester, but that soon would change. A Confederate division moving northwest on the Front Royal Pike, engaged the Union pickets, as they hid behind cedar and pine trees, bushes, field rocks, and stumps. The Union men were outnumbered ten to one but still put up a pretty good fight. But the numbers were against them. They finally were driven from behind their stone fences as a whole regiment charged the lightly manned picket line near the Parkins Mill battery, around 8:00 a.m.. Soon after, the Confederates

---

[245] Wikipedia, "Second Battle of Winchester," 3–4 (Wikipedia-SBoW, 1210, ...wikipedia.org/.../Battle_of_Winchester_II pp.3-4)

engaged in cavalry skirmishes at Hoge Run around 9:30 a.m.. Under the devastating fire of Fort Milroy's heavy guns, and the Union skirmishers along with the Federal artillery on the hill near Hollinsworth Mill, the Confederate's advance was finally halted.[246][247] The Rebels countered by bringing up a battery to engage the Union field artillery, thus driving several pieces from their front. They succeeded in establishing their lines south of town.

Meanwhile, another Confederate division had crossed west via Nineveh to Newtown and moved north on Valley Pike, arriving at the outskirts of Kernstown, where a light infantry and artillery engagement commenced around noon. The 5th Maryland containing Sergeant Lenderking was somewhere in this area when the fighting began. Eventually the Federal skirmishers in line at Prichard's Hill were also driven back, retreating to Cedar Creek Grade, where they did an about-face and briefly counterattacked. The Union position was successfully outflanked, despite the Union Cavalry attacking several times up and down the Valley Pike. Still, that position could not be held, and the Union force retreated north of Abrams Creek under the cover of the heavy guns from Brower's Hill and Fort Milroy.

Maj. Gen. Milroy still had no idea that he was facing the entire 2nd Corps of Lee's army.[248] He decided to concentrate all of his forces in the three forks defending the town. The Union high command had been afraid of this type of the scenario. General in Chief Henry W. Halleck had asked Schenck to order Milroy to fall back from Winchester to Harpers Ferry. Although Schenck had discussed evacuation with Milroy, he left no clear direction for Milroy to evacuate,

---

[246] Service, National Park (DWL &VLC), "Second Winchester (13–15 June 1863)," 2 (Service, nps.gov/hps/abpp/.../svs3-7.htmlp.2)
[247] Wikipedia, "Second Battle of Winchester," 4 (Wikipedia-SBoW, 1210, ...wikipedia.org/.../Battle_of_Winchester_II p.4)
[248] Service, National Park (DWL & VLC), "Second Winchester (13–15 June 1863)," 4 (Service, nps.gov/hps/abpp/.../svs3-7.htmlp.4)

since he had been convinced that the defensive position in Winchester was strong. Milroy, therefore, decided to disregard concerns from Washington, because he was confident that the strength of his fortifications would allow his garrison to withstand an assault or a siege.[249][250][251]

The Confederates, who had good intelligence, had foreseen that Milroy's only escape route could be successfully blocked and had preemptively moved a division toward Martinsburg, via Berryville, to cut off Milroy's expected withdraw route. That afternoon, having reached Berryville, a Confederate division and cavalry brigade attempted to capture the Union force located in the town. Just prior to the attack, a thundering roar could be heard from one of the large guns fired by Milroy's main force back at Winchester, singling the need to retreat. The Federal brigade withdrew to the Union Star Fort north of town. The Confederates only succeeded in overtaking and capturing a portion of the Federal supplied train at nearby Bunker Hill, West Virginia, taking seventy-five prisoners.[252] The telegraph lines to Winchester were then cut, eliminating Milroy's only line of communication. The Confederates reached Martinsburg by sundown, capturing the town along with five Federal artillery pieces. With the light of day departed, Milroy concentrated his forces inside the defensive triangle defined by Fort Milroy, Star Fort, and West Fort. That night, a storm arose with a heavy rain that drenched Winchester and the lower Valley all night long.[253]

---

[249] Historyofwar.org., "Second Battle of Winchester, 14 – 15 June 1863" (PAGE#?) (war.org, historyofwar.org/.../battles_winchester2...).
[250] Service, National Park (DWL & VLC), "Second Winchester (13–15 June 1863)," 2 (Service, nps.gov/hps/abpp/.../svs3-7.htmlp.2).
[251] Wikipedia, "Second Battle of Winchester," 2 (Wikipedia-SBoW, 1210, ...wikipedia.org/.../Battle_of_Winchester_II p.2).
[252] Ibid., 4 (Wikipedia-SBoW, 1210, ...wikipedia.org/.../Battle_of_Winchester_II p.4).
[253] Ibid. (Wikipedia-SBoW, 1210, ...wikipedia.org/.../Battle_of_Winchester_II p.4).

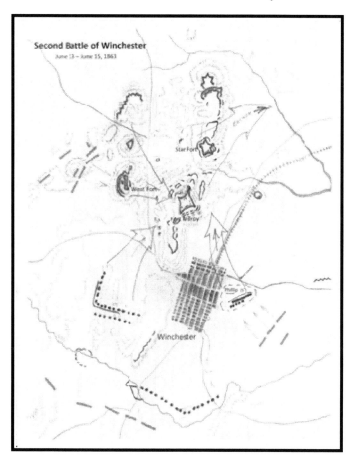

On the sunny Sunday of June 14, the 18th Connecticut and the 5th Maryland were posted to guard the east entrance to Winchester, where they would eventually contest and repulse several small probing attacks.[254]

Three detachments were sent out in different directions: toward Fort Royal, Martinsburg, and Berryville to reconnaissance the area. They found the enemy to be in great numbers on all the roads. Some Confederates had also taken possession of a large brick house surrounded by shrubbery along the Berryville road. From that position, they could fire

---

[254] Maier, *Leather & Steel, The 12th Pennsylvania Cavalry in the Civil War*, 95 (Maier, 2001p.95)

on the men behind the first line of works. In the meantime, three Confederate brigades accompanied by twenty guns, using the Apple Pie Ridge as cover, performed a flanking maneuver to Walnut Grove. As a diversionary tactic, starting around 10:00 a.m., the Confederates advanced skirmishers on the right to occupy the Federals' attention. An artillery duel was touched off with the Federal guns at Fort Milroy. The sound of Cannon did not cease until around 4 PM when the battlefield became quiet. The Confederate force had completed their flanking maneuver and had reached their intended location. Eight guns were positioned on the Brierley Farm northwest of the fort, while rwelve guns were placed in an orchard southwest of the fort. At that time the Union men and officers had no idea they were completely surrounded.[255]

The Federals, thinking that the Confederate forces may have retreated, were surprised when artillery open fired on the West Fort around 6:00 p.m., from a position expected to be void of the enemy. It began as Union soldiers lounged in the sun and rested on the cannons pondering how peaceful it finally was. Suddenly, the Confederate batteries on Bowers Hill opened up a shower of shot and shell, causing the men to tumble off the parapets and dive for cover. The mountains seemed alive with cannon fire as their round struck Union artillery pieces, blowing off their wheels and upsetting the caissons, a two wheeled wagon for transporting ammunition.[256] For forty-five minutes, twenty Confederate guns fired on the fort as a Louisiana brigade stealthily moved through the corn and wheat fields at the base of the Apple Pie Ridge.[257]

---

[255] Wikipedia, "Second Battle of Winchester," 5 (Wikipedia-SBoW, 1210, ...wikipedia.org/.../Battle_of_Winchester_II p.5)
[256] Barnhart, "The 110th Ohio volunteer infantry, the second battle of Winchester, June 13–15, 1863" (PAGE 2) (Barnhart, frontierfamilies.net/family/2ndwintr.htm)
[257] Wikipedia, "Second Battle of Winchester," 5 (Wikipedia-SBoW, 1210, ...wikipedia.org/.../Battle_of_Winchester_II p.5)

Suddenly the Confederate brigade rushed forward across the three hundred yards of open fields and swept upward into the works of the West Fort. The order was hastily given to fix bayonets as the Confederate infantry advanced out of the brush and from the ravine. The Union line only had time for one volley, which dropped many from the ranks and created large gaps in their column. The Confederates just closed their gaps and put shoulder to shoulder to return the volley, then charged with bayonets, yelling like Indians. Both gun stock and muzzle were used like clubs, jabbing and swinging in a vicious struggle to hold the line. This brief hand-to-hand struggle seemed useless as eighty Union soldiers faced many times their numbers, tens of thousands of attackers. It was a short but hellish fight as this clubbing of gun butts and thrusting a bayonets took its toll.[258]

With little choice left, it became a situation of every-man for himself. Those Federals left standing bolted through what seemed to be a gauntlet of bullets toward safety. With Confederate rounds striking all around them, wounding some and others just catching the outside of the cloth uniform, some made the desperate escape back to Fort Milroy.[259] With a mass of Confederate forces now joined in the fight, the captured artillery from the West Fort was turned around and commenced firing on Fort Milroy. The Confederate forces had successfully extended their line. During this same time, the streets of Winchester also became part of the battleground with intermittent skirmishing in the streets. Milroy's batteries at the main fort continued with the artillery duel well into the night.

At around 9:00 p.m., with only one day's rations remaining, a formal council of war was held in the Federal camp. Milroy and his officers decided to try to cut their way

---

[258] Barnhart, "The 110th Ohio volunteer infantry, the second battle of Winchester, June 13–15, 1863" (PAGE 2) (Barnhart, frontierfamilies.net/family/2ndwintr.htmp.2)
[259] Ibid. (PAGE 2) (Barnhart, frontierfamilies.net/family/2ndwintr.htmp.2)

through to Martinsburg on the old Charlestown Road. All the men, including Sergeant Lenderking, were ordered to hurriedly spike all the cannons and destroy their carriages, even cutting the spokes out of the wheels. Extra ammunition was dumped down the cisterns (large receptacles for storing water underground) of the Fort. During the several hours of intense preparation, team and artillery horses were assembled to provide transport for the teamsters, gunners, and as many infantryman as possible. When their assignment was completed, many of the men not on picket duty rested in the tents and rifle pits.[260][261][262]

As the time grew close for departure, pickets were called in where possible to do so, silently. As enemy pickets were as close as two hundred yards from the fort, there were some pickets that unfortunately were abandoned in place. The officers went around and woke the men up, instructing them to leave knapsacks and anything of weight and prepare to move out.[263]

Shortly after midnight, around 1:00 a.m., the Federal soldiers pulled their colors and quietly left their works under the cover of night. This large force of Union soldiers exited so sneakily that the nearby Confederates did not realize they had gone until morning. The column massed below by order of their numbers, on the ground between the Star Fort and Fort Munro. When all was ready, a "Forward March," was whispered, and the column proceeded forward. In silence they moved down through a bushy ravine north of the Star Fort, along the railroad line and the Valley Pike toward the Charlestown Crossing for about one

---

[260] Wikipedia, "Second Battle of Winchester," 5 (Wikipedia-SBoW, 1210, ...wikipedia.org/.../Battle_of_Winchester_II p.5)
[261] Service, National Park (CHECK AUTHOR), "Second Winchester (13–15 June 1863)," 3 (Service, nps.gov/hps/abpp/.../svs3-7.htmlp.2) (Service, nps.gov/hps/abpp/.../svs3-7.htmlp.3)
[262] Maier, *Leather & Steel, The 12th Pennsylvania Cavalry in the Civil War*, 103–104 (Maier, 2001pp.103-104)
[263] Ibid., 104 (Maier, 2001p.104)

mile where they hit the Martinsburg Road, just south of Stephenson's Depot.²⁶⁴

In the early dawn of June 15, the skirmishers before Milroy's retreating column encountered the Confederate force just four miles outside of Winchester. The Confederate commander had anticipated a possible Union withdrawal and had sent a force to this location to intercept them north of Winchester. At that point there was a railroad cut masked by a body of woods just two hundred yards from the Martinsburg Turnpike. The Confederates had deployed their regiments along the Milburn Road where it intersected with the Charlestown Road and advanced others just a little further to place two guns on either side of the Charlestown Road railroad bridge. The rest of the Confederate artillery was deployed on the heights east of Milburn Road.²⁶⁵ ²⁶⁶

The 12th Pennsylvania Cavalry Vanguard led the Federal column and was the first to collide with Confederate sharpshooters. The dark stillness of the night was shattered by shouted challenges, followed almost instantly by a burst of rifle fire, then Carbine. Against the backdrop of the dark sky and the even darker forest, the scene resembled hundreds of giant fireflies flashing in the night. As other companies of the 12th Pennsylvania Cavalry reinforced the Federal line, the Butternuts retreated and ran across the field into the inky black tree line. The sound of pounding hooves followed close behind until suddenly the lead horses nosedived forward into the ground, throwing cavalrymen into the underbrush. Telegraph wire had been strung from tree to tree that could not be seen in the darkness.²⁶⁷

---

[264] Wikipedia, "Second Battle of Winchester," 5 (Wikipedia-SBoW, 1210, ...wikipedia.org/.../Battle_of_Winchester_II p.5)

[265] Ibid. (Wikipedia-SBoW, 1210, ...wikipedia.org/.../Battle_of_Winchester_II p.5)

[266] Service, National Park (DWL & VLC), "Second Winchester (13–15 June 1863)," (PAGE#?) (Service, nps.gov/hps/abpp/.../svs3-7.html)

[267] (Maier, 2001pp.106-108) Maier, *Leather & Steel, The 12th Pennsylvania Cavalry in the Civil War*, 106-108

The Cavalry charge was halted as the danger ahead was revealed. The cavalrymen reined in their horses to a stop, sheathed their sabers, drew their carbines, and resumed the skirmish. Their right flank was suddenly slashed by a volley of rifle fire. The favor was returned with as much accuracy as possible in the dark and on the backs of skittish and rearing horses. For fifteen to twenty minutes, the enemy was revealed solely by the muzzle flashes in a violent exchange of bullets and curses. The outgunned troopers of the 12th stubbornly held their line and the Turnpike open until the 110th and 122nd Ohio entered the fray.[268]

In the meantime, Milroy faced his column to the right on the Pike and prepared to fight his way out of this murderous trap. Col. J. Warren Kiefer asked permission of General Milroy if he might charge into the woods on the Confederates. Milroy is said to have replied, "Yes, you may Col. It will keep the gap open for more of the boys to get out." Col. Kiefer pointed the way and gave the command for the men under him to charge into the woods. They moved forward doubly quick, and when in appropriate range, gave them a volley from their muskets. It must have caught the Rebels by surprise, as their response was slow, but they finally answered with artillery and musketry. The 112th Ohio contested with the Confederates, finally silencing two guns by killing their gunners, capturing two horses and a caisson. Col. Eli with two regiments advanced into the woods on the left but was forced back by superior numbers. The Confederates were being steadily reinforced, and the situation was becoming more dire every minute. The Union line retreated out of the woods and into the open field where General Milroy was waiting. Firing could now be heard from the direction of Winchester, singling the advance of Confederates to their rear. Milroy gave the last command. Pointing towards the best route of escape he said, "Every

---

[268] Ibid., 109–110 (Maier, 2001pp.109-110)

man fight your way through to Harpers Ferry. Do not go on the Pike, it is patrolled by the enemy, and you will be captured." It is said that he directed his command to split into two columns: one to proceed by way of Bath and the other by way of Smithfield toward Martinsburg.[269]

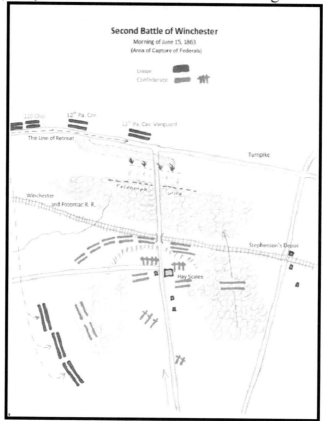

The Union Army proceeded to the attack in the hopes of finding its way out of the Confederate stranglehold steadily tightening around them. Somewhere in the confusion, the Gen.'s horse was shot out from underneath him. During the engagement on the Martinsburg Road, McReynolds withdrew his brigade and moved right off the road in an effort to reach

---

[269] Barnhart, "The 110th Ohio volunteer infantry, the second battle of Winchester, June 13–15, 1863," 2–3 (Barnhart, frontierfamilies.net/family/2ndwintr.htmpp.2-3)

Harper's Ferry. The Union men fought bravely, but with another Confederate brigade advancing up the road in line of battle engaging their rear, the odds were steadily stacking against them. This was the final blow; some of the remaining Federal officers waived the white flag. On the other hand, many of the Union men scattered as quickly as they could to the north, the northwest, and northeast hoping to escape capture. A small group of cunning men even managed to escape covertly to the southeast toward and through the Manassas Gap into Federally controlled territory. The Confederate cavalry was forced to become heavily engaged, trying to round up as many of these Federals as humanly possible.[270][271]

As the sun rose on this scene of devastation with the smell of gun smoke still hanging in the air, the carnage of the battle was revealed. Strewed over the battlefield were Union dead, some in contorted positions impossible in life while others just lay as if sleeping in their crimson-stained uniforms. Others still were mangled and torn to pieces. Equipment and hats were scattered about as were discarded rifles, blankets, haversacks, canteens, and the random shoe. Dead or dying horses lay were they fell in the night, attracting flies in ever greater numbers that swarmed to the corpses and wounded.[272]

The captured Union soldiers were in large groups as they ministered to the wounded. In these groups some men stood, sat on the ground, or squatted while waiting for instructions, which did not take long in coming. The battered Federal prisoners, shuffling and staggering, were escorted back to Winchester and herded into the same forts they had recently defended. Almost immediately the commissioned officers were called from the rest of the men and marched off toward Staunton, Virginia. A

---

[270] Service, National Park (DWL & VLC), "Second Winchester (13–15 June 1863)," 3 (Service, nps.gov/hps/abpp/.../svs3-7.htmlp.3)
[271] Wikipedia, "Second Battle of Winchester," 5 (Wikipedia-SBoW, 1210, ...wikipedia.org/.../Battle_of_Winchester_II p.5)
[272] Maier, *Leather & Steel, The 12th Pennsylvania Cavalry in the Civil War*, 117 (Maier, 2001p.117)

short time later, the noncommissioned officers and enlisted men were divided in half; one half was escorted in the same direction as their officers, while the rest of the men slept on the dirt floors of the Fort and marched out the next morning.[273]

By June 23, the Federal prisoners had reached the train station at Staunton and were being prepared for transport to Richmond. The local Confederate Militia took their possession, and unlike the Confederate soldiers, began to show the prisoners disrespect and subjected them to many indignities. They were finally piled into freight cars, where they endured a long and weary night ride. By June 25 they had reached their destination and ultimately were transferred to Belly Island Prison Camp in the James River.[274]

During this Second Battle of Winchester, the Confederate forces managed to capture twenty-eight pieces of artillery, three hundred loaded wagons, three hundred horses, a quite large amount of commissary and quartermaster's stores, along with four thousand prisoners including 373 wounded.[275] My great-great-grandfather, Sgt. Lenderking, was unfortunately one of the men captured. The Confederates had hoped to capture enough to resupply and forage, but with the capture of Winchester, they ended up with enough artillery and horses to equip a battalion of infantry and cavalry. Additionally the Confederates captured a great quantity of food, clothing, small arms, ammunition, and medical stores in Winchester.

This battle additionally saw ninety-five Union men killed, along with the Confederates' forty-seven killed, 219 wounded and three missing. Milroy along with his staff, his cavalry, and other small units, totaling about 1,200 men, did manage to escape to Harpers Ferry. In the days following the battle, 2,700 more men turned up in Bloody Run,

---

[273] Maier, *Leather & Steel, The 12th Pennsylvania Cavalry in the Civil War*, 118 (Maier, 2001p.118)
[274] Ibid., 118–119 (Maier, 2001pp.118-119)
[275] Wikipedia, "Second Battle of Winchester," 5 (Wikipedia-SBoW, 1210, ...wikipedia.org/.../Battle_of_Winchester_II p.5)

Pennsylvania.[276] But the plight of Sgt. Lenderking and the rest of the 3,999 Union prisoners would be a long, dreary trip south as a prisoner of war.[277]

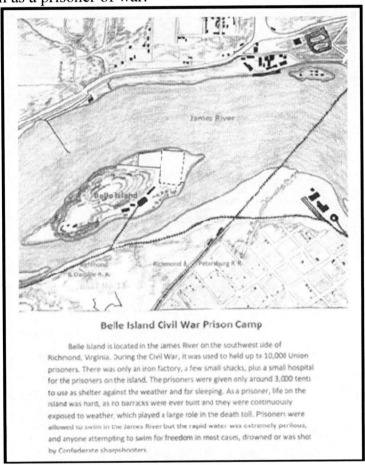

Belle Island Civil War Prison Camp

Belle Island is located in the James River on the southwest side of Richmond, Virginia. During the Civil War, it was used to hold up to 10,000 Union prisoners. There was only an iron factory, a few small shacks, plus a small hospital for the prisoners on the island. The prisoners were given only around 3,000 tents to use as shelter against the weather and for sleeping. As a prisoner, life on the island was hard, as no barracks were ever built and they were continuously exposed to weather, which played a large role in the death toll. Prisoners were allowed to swim in the James River but the rapid water was extremely perilous, and anyone attempting to swim for freedom in most cases, drowned or was shot by Confederate sharpshooters.

---

[276] Wikipedia, "Second Battle of Winchester," 6 (Wikipedia-SBoW, 1210, ...wikipedia.org/.../Battle_of_Winchester_II p.6)
[277] Digging.com, "Belle Isle Civil War Prison" (PAGE 1) (Digging.com, censusdigging.com/prison_bellisle.html)

Chapter 5
To the Battle of Fort Sanders, Knoxville

Phillip Lenderking
5th Maryland Infantry Regiment

After his captured in the Second Battle of Winchester, June 15, 1863, Sgt. Lenderking was marched south and held as a prisoner of war at Belle Island, but his confinement did not last long. By July 14, Philip had been taken to Leily Point, Virginia, where he was paroled by the Confederate Army.[278]

(Note: During the Civil War, the commanding officer at Fortress Munro had been authorized since July 12, 1862 to negotiate a general exchange of prisoners with the enemy. The stipulation of exchange was basically man for man and officer for officer, but a commanding general or admiral, for instance, was the equivalent of sixty privates or common seaman. There was a regular organized alliance to deal with the problem of civilian prisoners and the actual mechanics of parole and exchange, which further prohibited military service of released prisoners of war until exchanged. Until early 1863, the system of exchange was apparently respected by both sides, but the increasing unwillingness of the Confederacy to exchange man for man and to agree to the exchange of black troops or their white officers led to its breakdown.[279]

There were three camps established to accept paroled Confederate prisoners of war until they were exchanged for Union soldiers similarly confined in the South. When exchanges were made, the War Department required that all paroled prisoners belonging to New England and the middle states report at once to the camp in Annapolis, Maryland, as quickly as possible for their disposition.[280]

Over the course of the war, thousands of Union soldiers were held there after the exchange, until they were returned to

---

[278] National Archives and Record Service, "Philip Lenderking" (Memorandum from Prisoner of War Records) (National Archives and Record Service, Microcopy No. 384, roll 142, Fifth Infantry, Ke – Li).
[279] PA-Roots.com, "Camp Parole, Annapolis, Maryland," 3 (PA-Roots.Comp.3).
[280] Ibid., 4 (PA-Roots.Comp.4).

their regiments or sent home. Many of those who were severely wounded or diseased and did not survive are buried in their cemeteries. Camp Parole at Annapolis, Maryland was the location to which Sgt. Lenderking reported on July 15, 1863. There were eight wooden barracks erected on the campus, each meant to house 150 men, which proved to be woefully inadequate. Hospital facilities and a camp guard were inadequate and remained so despite desperate pleas to Washington by the commander. Men lived in tents, hunts they built for themselves with lumber stolen from public buildings, and a few hastily erected wooden barracks. The camp population varied from two thousand to more than fifteen thousand at any given time.)[281]

Sgt. Lenderking, as well as many other Union prisoners, were brought up the Chesapeake Bay to Annapolis by the Steamer New York in a group possibly as large as six thousand. Before entering the camp, he and the other prisoners of war were required to bathe, and their clothes and shoes were thrown into College Creek. Philip entered this overcrowded camp with a large number of others, some extremely disabled and wounded. Many of the men had been weakened by hard work or confinement in southern prisons, contracting a disease incidental to the parts from which they'd come. Some prisoners arrived in a morbid condition, as if they were carted here to be buried. The condition in which Philip found this camp was deplorable. A number of the prisoners were in such a weakened condition that they had to be carried on stretchers from the steamboat and cars.[282] Philip would have surely been glad to get out of this place once the usual military questioning and paperwork was completed and back to his regiment.

---

[281] Ibid., 2 (PA-Roots.Comp.2)
[282] PA-Roots.com, "Camp Parole, Annapolis, Maryland," 2 (PA-Roots.Comp.2)

The transport steamer New York

Prisoner Exchange

Philip's ordeal lasted about a month, ending with his return to the 5th Maryland in Baltimore. The regiment had lost so many men in the Second Battle of Winchester they were forced to return to defend Baltimore, while recruiting and refitting. Their primary duty was the defense of Baltimore, during which time they were assigned to the Middle Department, 8th Army Corps.[283] On November 4, two companies of the 5th Maryland were allowed to go home to vote. As this was Philip's hometown, I feel it safe to assume he was able to see his family during this time. His family in turn was greatly relieved to find him safely delivered to them after his grueling ordeal.

Rudolph Lenderking, 2nd Michigan Infantry Regiment

&

George Lenderking, 27th Michigan Infantry Regiment

---

[283] Civilwarintheeast.com, "2nd Michigan Infantry Regiment"(PAGE 1) (East, civilwarintheeast.com/USA/MI/2MI.php)

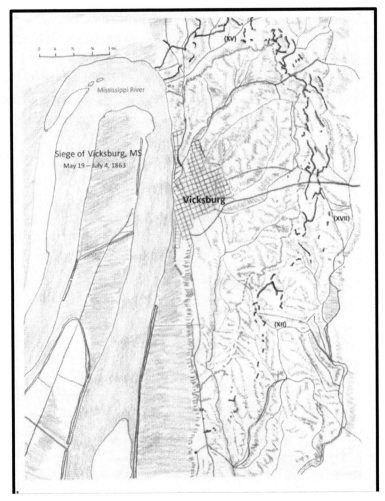

The arrival of the 2nd Michigan on June 14, 1863 brought them in view of this already massive siege of Vicksburg. The soldiers and civilians of Vicksburg had no food or supplies and were bombarded constantly by the Federal's artillery. Adm. David D. Porter's fleet also hammered Vicksburg from the river. (Note: The fleet in the river had been here for some time and first saw action on the night of the 16th of April, just prior to the first failed attack, when Grant requested Porter to take twelve vessels south past the Vicksburg batteries. In doing so, he had lost one of his ships to Confederate fire. Vicksburg was a major Confederate stronghold and contained the Confederate Army of thirty thousand men, under Lieut. Gen. John Pemberton.)[284]

The 2nd Michigan and the 27th Michigan were engaged in the siege of the city, along with the rest of the Union forces. There they stayed, entrenched with the daily thundering of cannons and, in the distance, sounds of explosions in the town. Their job was dirty and the days were long and repeated over and over like a broken record. One can easily imagine a sort of boredom that would overtake the men in such a situation. Finally, on July 3rd, hunger and the daily bombardments by Grant's artillery and Plotter's gunboats compelled Pemberton to ask for surrender terms. On July 4th, the city was finally surrendered. Its surrender to the men, along with the reported capture of Port Hudson, Louisiana, meant they had the entire Mississippi River in Union hands. They had successfully cut the Confederate forces in half.

Now that the siege was over, the men in the Federal forces could more closely see the results of their siege. The Confederates that surrendered were ragged and tired and had been reduced by disease and starvation. The residents of the city were equally so and had been forced to seek the refuge of caves and bombproof shelters in the surrounding hillsides. Their city and their homes had been devastated. But this was not a new site to the infantryman.

The number of Confederates killed and wounded in the battle of the Siege of Vicksburg numbered 2,872 men; the Union suffered 4, 910 men killed or wounded.[285] To the Confederates, the surrender on Independence Day was a bitter defeat. Union troops behaved well, mixing with Confederates and giving rations to the starving soldiers. Speculators who had been hoarding food for higher prices saw all their stores broken open and the contents thrown on

---

[284] Wikipedia, "Vicksburg Campaign," 2 (Wikipedia-V, 2011p.2)
[285] Wikipedia, "Vicksburg Campaign,"' 11–13 (Wikipedia-V, 2011pp.11-13)

the streets for the starving Rebels. The men of the two armies socialized with one another as if they had been fighting for the same cause.

On July 4, 1863, shortly after the surrender, the 2nd Michigan and 27th Michigan along with the other regiments under Burnside marched from their camp at Flower Hill under the command of Col. Humphrey. They arrived in front of Jackson on the evening of the 10th.[286][287]

Advancing on to Jackson, they prepared for the siege that would last from July 10th to July 17th. During the siege, sharpshooters watched for any targets of opportunity that they could engage. On the eleventh, the 2nd Michigan Regiment was deployed as skirmishers, charged and drove the Confederates from their rifle pits in front of town, but due to superior numbers were forced to retire. The action resulted in twelve killed, thirty-six wounded, and eight missing. On the 13th and 14th, two more men were taken prisoners and one wounded.[288]

The siege operation did have one flaw, a pontoon bridge that was guarded by the Orphan Brigade. The Orphans were in prepared trenches on the far left of the Confederate line, in front of Town Creek. Their left flank was resting on the Pearl

---

[286] Civilwarintheeast.com, "2nd Michigan Infantry Regiment"(PAGE 2) (East, civilwarintheeast.com/USA/MI/2MI.php)
[287] Civilwarintheeast.com, "27th Michigan Infantry Regiment"(PAGE 1) (East, civilwarintheeast.com/USA/MI/27MI.php)
[288] Michiganinthewar.org, "2nd Regiment Michigan Volunteer Infantry," 3 (War.org, michiganinthewar.org/infantry/2ndinf.htmp.3)

River, where the pontoon bridge was located. On July 12th, a Division of the Federal 13th Corp attacked in the center near the bridge, but the rightmost regiments of the Orphan Brigade were able to place an oblique fire into their ranks.[289] The 2nd Michigan had deployed as skirmishers on the left of the skirmish line of the 1st Brigade. The regiment moved out as directed and were initially met with only slight enemy resistance until around 6:00 a.m.. At that time a brisk fire was opened up along the whole line with the strongest posting to the right of their line in the deep water-course, and to their left in the thick woods. The fire was kept up briskly, but the enemy showed no intention of yielding their position. At 7:00 a.m. the order came down the line to charge double-quick. The regiment at once advanced with the cheer and drove the enemy skirmishers back to their reserves, strongly posted in a deep ravine. They continued their hard drive and fighting, continuing to push the Confederates out of the ravine, and back to their main supporting body, which was drawn up in line of battle on top of the south bank of the ravine. The 2nd was under terrible fire but charged up onto the main body and broke its line, driving the enemy from its fortified position.[290]

    The regiment waited for support but was surprised to find none. The regiment on its right for some reason advanced only a short distance and then fell back to its original line. Three companies to the left of the Regiment, C, H, and F did not move with the rest of the companies in the charge. For a little over forty minutes, the fighting was intense with both sides heavily engaged. The Confederates before them were quickly reinforced and holding the ground against them would become impossible. The men took whatever cover they could find, and contested the ground till the men carrying the wounded to the rear had completed their task, about three

---

[289] Brigade, "The Orphan Brigade at Jackson, Mississippi, July 1863" p. 1(Laura Cook) (Geoff Waldon, 2010) (Geoff Waldon, 2010)
[290] Humphrey, "The Jackson Campaign," 566–37 (Col. William Humphrey, 1863pp.566-37)

quarters of an hour. The regiment fell back gradually while still under fire. Once back to their lines the 2nd Michigan remained there until 3:00 a.m. the next morning when it was relieved by the 11th New Hampshire Regiment.[291]

The 27th Michigan, although not directly engaged themselves, could hear the roar of gunfire that came from the battle, as almost half of the Union troops involved were killed, wounded, or captured. George would have known Rudolph's approximate location, so he knew he was in the fight, which would have concerned him deeply. The Union men would have been cheered up somewhat despite the heavy losses by the word that the regiment shortly after the battle entered the area between the lines and captured two hundred Confederate prisoners and three Union flags. On the night of the 16th, the remaining encircled Confederate troops slipped away across the pontoon bridge over the Pearl River with the Orphans Brigade following as rearguard. The 27th Infantry lost two men who were killed and six wounded during the siege.

After the fall of Jackson, Burnside's troops, including both Rudolph's and Georgia's Regiments, destroyed several miles of railroad track of the Mississippi Central Railroad at Madison Station from July 18th to 22.[292] They continued their march to Milldale, where on July 30, Lieut. Col. Dillman resigns his command in the 2nd Michigan. Burnside's men remained there in camp until August 4th, which gave George and Rudolph an opportunity to see one another while not on duty. From August 4 to 30, the 2nd and 27th Michigan moved to Covington, where they were transferred to the 3rd Brigade, 1st Division, Ninth Army Corps, Army of the Ohio.[293]

---

[291] Ibid. (Col. William Humphrey, 1863pp.566-37)
[292] Civilwarintheeast.com, "2nd Michigan Infantry Regiment" p. 2 (East, civilwarintheeast.com/USA/MI/2MI.php)
[293] Civilwarintheeast.com, "27th Michigan Infantry Regiment" p. 1 (East, civilwarintheeast.com/USA/MI/27MI.php)

Two more men were taken prisoner by the Confederates from the 2nd Michigan and another man wounded between August 4th to the 12th as they marched to Covington, Kentucky. That also put the two brothers right across the river from Cincinnati, Ohio, where their brother Frederick was living. August 17 to 18, Burnside's Army moved on to Crab Orchard, Kentucky, via Nicholasville to begin his East Tennessee Campaign.[294]

The family knew from letters that George at this time had been ill from exposure, lack of proper food, and inadequate rest from the constant marching. Martha received a note from him from camp Nicholasville, Kentucky, dated August 31, 1863, stating that he was quite well again and that he and Rudolph were now only half a mile apart.

(Note: In the 1860s, life as a soldier was a difficult one for the thousands of young Americans who had left their home to fight for their cause. It was an experience none of them would ever forget, as military service meant many months away from home and loved ones. There were always the long hours of drilling and marching on hot dusty roads or in driving rainstorms, burdened down with a soldier's necessary items as well as personal possessions to make his life as comfortable as possible.[295] But there were also

---

[294] Michigan.org, "2nd Michigan Volunteer Infantry, "E" Company 1861–1865," 5 (Michigan.orgp.5)
[295] Service, The United States Dept. of the Interior, *The Civil War soldier, what was life as a soldier like in 1863?*, 1 (Service, Gettysburg National Military Parkp.1)

stretches of inadequate food or shelter and unhealthy conditions causing disease and for many, death. According to statistics, there were 249,458 deaths from disease in the Union Army during the Civil War and another 164,000 lost by the Confederates. That number is much higher than the 110,070 Union men or the 94,000 Confederates who died from wounds received during battles.)[296]

September 10 through the twenty-sixth, they marched to Knoxville, Tennessee, which took them over the Cumberland Mountains. September 27 through October 3, their duty was in the Knoxville area.[297]

By October 1863, Rudolph was sending his letters to his sister Martha and brother Lewis, since Philip had enlisted and was no longer home. He sent two letters that gave a feel for his army experience.[298]

> Dear Sister,
>
> At present we are resting after a march of 211 miles. . . Approximately, we shall stay here sometime because the rebels are in the mountains before us. We do not have enough troops to drive them out. The farmers are mostly for the Union and daily come to Knoxville to enlist in our Army. Some even search the country on their own and bring them to us. Also many rebels desert. . .
>
> R. Lenderking

Another letter was written to Martha dated October 19, 1863:

> Dear Sister,

---

[296] Home, Digital History (23-March, 2011) "Civil War casualties and costs of the Civil War" pp. 1-2 (Home)
[297] Civilwarintheeast.com, "2nd Michigan Infantry Regiment" p. 2 (East, civilwarintheeast.com/USA/MI/2MI.php)
[298] Wormelle, *The Lenderking Family*, 8–9 (Wormelle, 1969pp.8-9)

I did not receive your letter of September 20 until the 16th of the next month for no railroad leads to hear. The mail goes for almost 200 miles on rather rough paths and partly through mountains...

Since then, we undertook a little expedition of 86 miles, partly on the railroad and partly on foot in order to drive away a division of rebels. At Bay Springs, which is 64 miles from here, we encountered the enemy. He was driven away immediately by our cavalry that had been sent ahead as a cover... Towards four o'clock in the afternoon, our division was ordered to advance... The division suffered a loss of 10 dead in 30 wounded; our Regiment none at all...

Your loving brother,

R. Lenderking[299]

(Note: East Tennessee possessed a population largely loyal to the Union; the region was rich in grain and livestock and controlled the railroad corridor from Chattanooga to Virginia. Prior to this time, before the 2nd and 27th Michigan rejoined Burnside's command, Burnside's forces had already moved against Knoxville. He had sent a brigade under Brig. Gen. William P Sanders to strike at Knoxville with a combined force of cavalry and infantry. In mid-June, Saunders men destroyed railroads and disrupted communications around the city. One of Burnside's cavalry brigades reached Knoxville on September 2nd, virtually unopposed. When Burnside and his main force arrived in the city, there were welcomed warmly by the local population. To this point, neither of the brothers' regiments had been in the campaign Burnside was waging, but that had now changed. Burnside, now on the move again, would have the 2nd and 27th Michigan with him as he returned to Knoxville for the second time.[300]

---

[299] Wormelle, *The Lenderking Family*, 8–9 (Wormelle, 1969pp.8-9)
[300] Wikipedia, "Knoxville Campaign," 2 (Wikipedia-KCp.2)

To set the stage for what was to come, it is important to also know what the Confederate plans were at this time. Confederate President Jefferson Davis had ordered James Longstreet to advance against Burnside. Longstreet strongly objected to his orders. He felt he had insufficient numbers to go against Burnside with ten thousand men in infantry divisions under Maj. Gen. Lafayette McLaws and Brig. Gen. Micah Jenkins, and five thousand cavalrymen under Maj. Gen. Joseph Wheeler. They would be facing Burnside's twelve thousand Union infantry and 8,500 cavalrymen. He also strongly felt that the remaining forty thousand Confederates around Chattanooga, which was now under siege, would also be outnumbered by approaching reinforcements under Grant and Sherman. Longstreet argued by separating the forces he felt both ventures were doomed to failure.

Still, Longstreet had his orders and prepared his men to travel by railroad to Sweetwater Tennessee approximately halfway to Knoxville. Unfortunately the train did not arrive on time and his men were forced to start the journey off on foot. When the train finally did arrive, they were pulled by underpowered locomotives that could not negotiate all the mountain grades under load, forcing the men to dismount and walk alongside the cars in the steeper sections. The journey was further complicated by the fact that the engineers had insufficient wood for fuel, and the men had to stop and dismantle fences along the way in order to continue.[301]

In the meantime, the Lincoln administration became concerned about Burnside situation and had been urging him for weeks to leave Knoxville and head south. Upon finding out about Longstreet's advance, Burnside's orders were changed to hold the city. Burnside suggested that five thousand of his men could advance southward toward Longstreet, establish contact to slow his advance, and

---

[301] Wikipedia, "Knoxville Campaign," 3–4 (Wikipedia-KCpp.3-4)

gradually withdraw toward Knoxville. Grant recognizes this was tactically sound and accepted Burnside's proposal.)[302]

Both George and Rudolph were at this time in the Army of the Ohio under Maj. Gen. Ambrose E Burnside. He was accustomed to marching his men more than thirty miles in one day if he felt the need, and the current necessity was to advance toward Longstreet. The regiment was ordered to pack up and move out. They had already marched to Covington, then on to Crab Orchard, Kentucky, which they reached by August 30. Along the way, the 27th Michigan saw another man killed and another captured.[303] On September 10, the regiment began movement toward Knoxville, Tennessee, and saw action on October 10 at Blue Springs. The Union and Confederate cavalries had been skirmishing for a few days, when the battle commenced around 10:00 a.m. with Union Cavalry engaging the Confederates until afternoon while another regiment of mounted forces attempted to place itself in a position to cut off a Confederate retreat. Capt. Orlando M Poe, the Chief Engineer, performed a reconnaissance to identify the best location to make an infantry attack. At 3:30 p.m. Brig. Gen. Edward Ferrero's 1st Division, Ninth Corp, started its move up toward the Confederate lines. Their engagement began at 5:00 p.m. and his men broke through Confederate lines with determination, causing heavy casualties, and advancing almost to the enemy's rear before being checked.[304]

---

[302] Ibid., 4 (Wikipedia-KCp.4)
[303] Historical Data System, Inc., "George Lenderking" p. 1 (Historical Data System, regimental casualty analysis)
[304] Wikipedia, "Battle of Blue Springs" p. 1 (Wikipedia-BoBS, 2010)

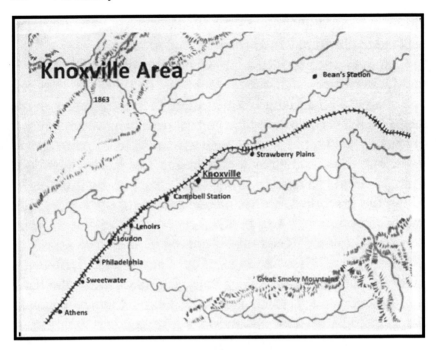

After dark, the Confederates withdrew, and the Federals took up the pursuit the next morning. Having made sure that Longstreet's advance on Knoxville had been checked by following them all the way to Huff's Ferry, Burnside decided to fall back to Lenoir's Station the following morning. The roads were in poor condition, not withstanding they still made the move in good order, with only one incident. At Loudon, the enemy took advantage of the fact the artillery was being drawn up the hill with difficulty. The attack was easily repulsed with only the loss of one caisson. That night, at the Loudon Bridge, the cavalry stayed on the east side of the Tennessee River, while the troops remained on the western side, facing the enemy. To the men, a battle appeared to be imminent. George and Rudolph, along with the men in their regiments, lay in the open field on their arms, ready for the battle they thought was coming. All the vehicles and articles that would not be used in a fight had already crossed to the other side where the cavalry was stationed. The ambulance, on the other hand, had remained with the men in the field.[305]

It was to be a long, cold, and dreary night with the rain coming down in torrents. The men were not allowed to make fires lest their position be revealed to the enemy. During the night, the enemy cavalry made a dash at the pickets, capturing two. The next morning skirmishers were thrown forward but no enemy could be found for miles. General Burnside did not advance his troops. Towards evening, the Union pickets were once more in sight of the Confederate pickets.[306]

That evening, the 2nd and 27th Michigan, as well as the rest of the Union forces under Burnside, received orders to be ready to move at 4:00 a.m. the next morning. Most men only received a short nap before they had to get up and prepare for the move. At the appointed time they received orders to fall back to Lenoir's Station. In quick order, regiment after regiment crossed the bridge without the enemy discovering their movement, abandoning Loudon by first light. The locomotive trapped on that side of the river controlled by the enemy was fired up, built up a full head of steam, and started at full speed over the abutment of the burned railroad bridge. It plunged into the bottom of the Tennessee with a huge crash. In the meantime, the pontoon bridge was quickly taken up and all the pontoons and planks were carried up the bank to be saved. As quickly as possible, they were loaded onto the train car waiting for them and taken to Knoxville to be laid across the Holston River.[307]

This was turning out to be a very cold, damp winter, yet skirmishes were fought nearly every day. On November 14, 1863, Longstreet's men erected a bridge across the Tennessee River west of Loudon, where he planned to begin his pursuit of

---

[305] Taylor, "Camp of 1st Division 9th A.C. Lenoir's Station, Tenn Novr. 1 1863" p. 1 (Taylor, November 1, 1863)
[306] Ibid. (Taylor, November 1, 1863)
[307] Ibid. (Taylor, November 1, 1863)

Burnside.[308] Around 10:00 p.m., when the federal forces were in camp at Lenore Station, the Confederates again attempted to drive in the skirmishers and again were repulsed. Early on the morning of November 15th, Burnside started to march his troops to Campbell's Station. The regiment found itself suffering from lack of rest, insufficient rations and equipment, and now another march. But it had to make a stand in defense of the supply trains or find itself in a worse situation.

Earlier, the 2nd and 27th Michigan commenced their march back in the direction of Knoxville and reached Lenoir's Station around noon. They bivouacked in the fields between the river and the station. After resting there for four hours, the 2nd Michigan moved out along the Kingston Road with the 17th Michigan, to about 250 yards in front of the Station. They formed a line to the right of the road and perpendicular to it in support of a section of battery. They remained watchful in this position until about two o'clock in the morning of the sixteenth, when they fell back to their former position in the rear of the railroad and parallel to it.[309]

---

[308] Wikipedia, "Knoxville Campaign," 4 (Wikipedia-KCp.4)
[309] Humphrey, "Chap. XXXVI" Official Reports p. 566-7 (Col. William Humphrey, 1863)

About daybreak, the 2nd Michigan acting as rearguard left the station with the 20th Michigan and moved back on the road toward Knoxville. About 9:00 a.m. they halted their march and formed a line of battle, right in front, on the right of the road facing toward Lenore station, at the rear of the Creek. One company was thrown (ordered) out as skirmishers on their right flank in support of the 17th Michigan, which had commenced skirmishing with the enemy on the other side of the creek. They remained there in line for a short time without exchanging shots with the enemy, and finally moved off by the right flank on their line of retreat, the skirmishes moving along with them on the left flank.[310]

---

[310] Byington, "Report of the Major Cornelius Byington, 2nd Michigan Infantry" p. 365-54 (Byington, 1863)

After about one mile, the 2nd Michigan was halted again and formed a line of battle in the same manner as before on the bow of an elevation, the right of the regiment in the woods and the left in the fields, and threw out one company as skirmishers in front of the regimental line. The left of the line was once again supporting one section of a battery. From this point they fell back slowly in line of battle through the woods, all the while their skirmishers exchanging shots with the enemy who followed closely behind. The enemy pressed too closely, so the line was halted and delivered a few volleys, then renewed their slow retreat. The regiment constantly repeated the halting, firing, and retreating as the Confederates continued to press them with their own brisk fire. To this point, the Regiment counted losses of about ten men killed, wounded, and missing, including one officer, Capt. Farrand, among the wounded.[311]

The 2nd Michigan continued to fall back from this line toward Campbell's Station. Longstreet's troops were paralleling Burnside's march as it appeared to be a race to Campbell's Station. The Federals realized that if Longstreet was able to cut them off, they could lose more than needed supplies, and they would be cut off from Knoxville. But despite the rain and the mud, Burnside's forces reached the vital intersection first and deployed his troops.[312] The 2nd Michigan halted in an open field and formed a line with the 20th Michigan on their left. They posted one company of skirmishers between their right flank in the woods to out into the field on their right. The latter company was relieved by skirmishers from the 23rd Michigan, as the enemy endeavored to flank them, only fifteen minutes later,[313] by throwing troops from the woods against the right flank. The Federals were hit on two sides simultaneously by

---

[311] Ibid. (Byington, 1863)
[312] Summaries, CWSAC Battle, "Campbell's Station" p. 1 (Summaries, 2006)
[313] References, Civil WareBooksOnDisk.com, "Campbell's Station, November 15, 1863" p. 1 (References)

Longstreet's troops. They were handsomely met and foiled the attempt of the enemy to get the upper hand. The fighting was brisk with a number of exchanges of volleys from both armies. It was at this time the 2nd Michigan had their heaviest losses. The enemy, having the cover of the woods, picked off the men who were highly exposed in the open field.[314]

Burnside ordered his two divisions astride the Kingston road to withdraw three quarters of a mile to a ridge in their rear. This was accomplished in good order and the Confederates ceased their attack around two p.m.. The 2nd Michigan was relieved at length by troops of the 2nd Brigade and fell back to a hollow, a short distance in rear of the line just mentioned. Toward evening, they fell back about a quarter of a mile and again formed a line on the right of the road facing the station, the 17th Michigan on their right, the 20th Michigan on their left in support of the artillery, which was posted on high ground in front of them. Around 4:00 p.m. another determined attack was launched on Burnside's left flank, but it was repelled. Another Confederate division was making an attempt to march around the Union left flank, but the short days of winter caused darkness to fall, and it was halted. The Federals suffered about three hundred casualties; 3 men were killed and eighteen others either wounded or missing

---

[314] Byington, "Report of the Major Cornelius Byington, 2nd Michigan Infantry" p. 365-54 (Byington, 1863)

from the 27th[315] and thirty men were killed, wounded, and missing from the 2nd Michigan.[316] Here they remained until dusk, when they moved out by the right flank on the Knoxville Road, arriving at Knoxville about 4:00 a.m. on the 17th. Burnside's artillery and supply trains had been able to return to Knoxville as a result Burnside continued his retrograde movement under pressure. The men under Burnside, despite the poor road conditions, lack of food, and extreme fatigue, still executed their withdrawal in an orderly fashion.[317]

Early on the morning of November 17, Burnside's battle-weary soldiers reached the outskirts of Knoxville.[318] They were met by the engineers in charge of the construction of the defensive works. They led each regiment to their assigned position of the works already constructed, but they were not complete. The men were thoroughly exhausted; many were allowed to just fall on the cold hard ground and sleep for two hours. After that short but well needed rest, the men were ordered to get up and dig with all their might in order to complete the fortifications. The men were still exhausted and had little digging equipment such as shovels and picks, but the enemy was approaching them quickly. It was hard work, but the men set to the task as their very lives depended upon it. The strengthening of the entrenchments was continued around-the-clock and male civilians were even pressed into service, as time was of the essence.[319]

With Longstreet's Army pressing closer to the city, the siege of Knoxville officially began. The 1st Division of Cavalry was commanded by recently promoted Brig. Gen. W. P. Saunders, who had successfully led the cavalry that was

---

[315] Michiganinthewar.org, "27th Regiment Michigan Volunteer Infantry" p. 2 (War, michiganinthewar.org/.../27thinf.htm)
[316] Michiganinthewar.org., "2nd Regiment Michigan Volunteer Infantry" p. 4 (War.org, michiganinthewar.org/infantry/2ndinf.htm)
[317] Byington, "Report of the Major Cornelius Byington, 2nd Michigan Infantry" 365-54 (Byington, 1863)
[318] Reference, Civil War, "Knoxville Siege," 1 (Reference, 2010p.1)
[319] Nosworthy, *Roll Call to Destiny*, 200 (Nosworthy, 2008p.200)

screening Burnside's withdrawal. On the day of the 17th, Burnside stationed Sanders' cavalry a mile west of the city on the Kingston road to hold Longstreet's approaching army in check. This gave Burnside more time to fortify his position.[320] [321] By the afternoon of the eighteenth, Burnside was nearing completion of his works and sent orders for the cavalry to withdraw into the city. The order had no sooner reached Brig. Gen. Sanders when he became mortally wounded and fell. The remainder of his command, however, was safely withdrawn within the defenses.[322]

Knoxville lies between two streams that flow in a southerly direction and both empty into the Holston River at the southern most limit of the city. On the west side of the town, a line of works were built starting a quarter-mile below Knoxville's city limits. The works extended out in a northwesterly direction and then angled more northerly across the Kingston road to a point six hundred yards beyond.[323] It was here that Burnside constructed fortress earthworks built upon a hill, using uncompleted Confederate earthen works already laid. The fort was built in an irregular quadrilateral form that is now known as Fort Sanders.[324] (Note: the fort was originally named Fort Loudon. But the officers under Burnside recommended the bastion be renamed in honor of slain cavalry officer William Sanders who had been mortally wounded a few days earlier.)[325] Snipers were a constant threat so on November 19, another man was wounded in the 2nd Michigan.[326]

---

[320] System, Historical Data The Union Army, vol. 6, "Knoxville, Tennessee (Siege of) November 17–December 4, 1863" pp. 1-2 (System, Battle History)
[321] Ibid. The Union Army, vol. 6, (System, Battle History) (System, Battle History)
[322] Reference, Civil War eBooksOnDisk.com 2011, "Knoxville Siege," (Reference, 2010p.1) 2 (Reference, 2010p.2)
[323] Ibid. (Reference, 2010p.2)
[324] System, Historical Data The Union Army, vol. 6,, "Knoxville, Tennessee (Siege of) November 17–December 4, 1863" pp. 1-2 (System, Battle History)
[325] Nosworthy, *Roll Call to Destiny*, 201-202 (Nosworthy, 2008pp.201-202)
[326] History Data System, Inc., "2nd MI Infantry (3-years)" The Union Army, vol. 6, pp. 1-2 (History Data System, P.O. Box 35, Duxbury, MA 02331)

It did not take long for the Confederates to move in and occupy the territory that was recently vacated by Sanders' cavalry. The Confederates however, were not well equipped for siege operation and were running short on supplies. Longstreet had planned an attack as early as November 20 but changed his mind, feeling it made more sense to wait for the reinforcements under Brig. Gen. Bushrod Johnson, who was bringing an additional 3,500 men in the cavalry brigade of Gruimble Jones. All the while, the Federals worked hard and long every day to add strength to their breastworks.

(Note: the union forces at Knoxville at that point had little food, and their uniforms were very worn. The situation was severe enough that supplies had to reach them in a makeshift manner. Local loyalists gathered supplies and food upstream and were allowed to float down the river. The Union forces in turn stretched the barrier of sorts across the river to catch the bundles. It was carried out in sufficient quantities to be considered very successful.)[327]

Confederate sharpshooters were sent forward to set up residence in a house, from which they set up a nuisance fire on the Federal line. The 17th Michigan was ordered to make a sortie to the house and burn it down. The Confederates were soon driven from the structure and it was set ablaze.[328][329]

Friday the twenty-first, it rained most of the day, and Saturday the twenty-second, the Federal forces continued to strengthen the defenses around the city. On the twenty-third, the 2nd Michigan marched out to the Confederate earthen works in the front of the fort and with fierce fighting, took possession of them. However, due to lack of support, they had

---

[327] Historyofthewar.org, "Battle of Knoxville, 29 November 1863," 4 (War.orgp.4)
[328] Reference, Civil War (AUTHOR?), "Knoxville Siege," (Reference, 2010p.1) 2 (Reference, 2010p.2)
[329] System, Historical Data The Union Army, vol. 6,, "Knoxville, Tennessee (Siege of) November 17–December 4, 1863" pp. 1-2 (System, Battle History)

to withdraw back to the safety of their own fortifications.[330] A temporary truce was called to retrieve their wounded, during which time a number of Rebels rushed out of the rifle pits to strip the dead. Later that night, the pickets at another location were driven in by the Confederates. The next morning, the Federals pushed forward and after a difficult struggle in which they lost 22 men,[331] they reestablished their lines.

On the twenty-fourth, Longstreet sent a portion of his forces to the south side of the Holston River. The next day, they attacked Shackelford's cavalry's position atop the hill on the south side of the river. The Confederate attacker's desperate attempt only succeeded in causing themselves heavier losses as they were repulsed.[332]

---

[330] Reference, Civil War eBooksOnDisk.com, 2011, "Knoxville Siege," (Reference, 2010p.1) 2 (Reference, 2010p.2)
[331] System, Historical Data The Union Army, vol. 6,, "Knoxville, Tennessee (Siege of) November 17–December 4, 1863" pp. 1-2 (System, Battle History)
[332] (Reference, 2010p.3) Reference, Civil War The Union Army, vol. 6,, "Knoxville Siege," (Reference, 2010p.1) 3

Also on November 24, the 2nd Michigan had orders to assault the enemy picket lines in front of their position. Except for those serving as pickets, the regiment marched out and reached the line of their own pickets, and then were ordered to charge double quick and move to the left oblique. They swiftly reached and cleared the enemy's entrenched pickets where they halted and took cover. The regiment held the enemy entrenchments for over half an hour while subject to heavy musketry fire from their left and front, as well as from Rebel sharpshooters on their right flank. It was here that Major Cornelius Byington, Adjutant Noble, and Lieutenants Gilpin and Frank Zoeliner were instantly killed or mortally wounded.[333] The 2nd then fell back to the reserves of the pickets at the railroad and came to a standstill. The men had commenced falling from the time they left their picket line until the time they returned to their lines one hour later. Throughout this day, eighty men were killed, sixty-nine wounded, twelve taken prisoner, and one man was missing.[334]

The next day, the Federal garrison did little more than watch and wait. The following day, the twenty-seventh, Longstreet's skirmishers were busy probing the defenses on both sides of the river. During that time, another man was killed from the 2nd Michigan by a sniper. Then on the twenty-eighth, three more men were captured by the Rebels. As evening approached, Confederate artillery fire opened up on Fort Sanders from a hill overlooking the stronghold. It soon became apparent that this was where Longstreet was planning an attack, so Burnside ordered reinforcements to the fort.[335]

Under the cover of darkness, a strong wave of skirmishers began advancing forward. By midnight they were

---

[333] Michiganinthewar.org., "2nd Regiment Michigan Volunteer Infantry," 4 (War.org, michiganinthewar.org/infantry/2ndinf.htmp.4)
[334] History Data System, Inc., "2nd MI Infantry (3-years)" p. 4 (History Data System, P.O. Box 35, Duxbury, MA 02331)
[335] Reference, Civil War (AUTHOR?), "Knoxville Siege," 3 (Reference, 2010p.3)

in range of the fort. (Note: Longstreet claimed later that as his men moved forward they were able to capture many of the outlying union rifle pits along with sixty to seventy prisoners.) The skirmishers ceased activity now for several hours and waited in the nasty, cold-drizzling night. These severe conditions were as hard on the bodies of the men as on their dispositions.[336]

The officers and men felt that the assault was imminent. In preparation, the men were awoken early the next morning. They immediately went to their assigned duty stations and loaded all spare rifle muskets. The rifles were then stacked in convenient locations along the fortifications. The artillery was readied and most were double shotted, canister with about twenty-six iron balls per can so at close range it acts like a shotgun. The canister was loaded in the twelve-pound howitzers but one artillery piece, in the bastion to the right of the fort, was triple shotted, and to be withheld until the attackers were in the ditch. Artillerymen stood ready at each piece with the lanyard in his hand, ready to fire. Several rows of twenty-pounder parrot shells with five-second fuses were placed in strategic locations along the north and west walls. They had an evil reputation, so the men near their locations were very uneasy.[337] Some Union soldiers were ordered to poor buckets of water down the already frozen and slippery slope on the outside of the fort.[338] When all the preparations were completed, the men were ordered to stay low behind the parapet and the cotton bales that were placed on its top. It felt like a long, cold wait as in their stillness, their bodies became chilled to the bone and their fingers almost frozen.[339]

(Note: Cotton bales that were periodically placed along the top of the walls weighed approximately five hundred pounds each. They vary slightly in size, sixty to seventy

---

[336] Nosworthy, *Roll Call to Destiny*, 215–216 (Nosworthy, 2008pp.215-216)
[337] Ibid., 219-220 (Nosworthy, 2008pp.219-220)
[338] Ibid., 221 (Nosworthy, 2008p.221)
[339] Ibid., 219 (Nosworthy, 2008p.219)

inches long, thirty-two to thirty-five inches wide, and twelve to twenty-two inches thick. It is likely that several bales were stacked on top of each other in these positions and would have made good cover for any man hiding behind them.)

In the early morning, while it was still dark, small Union detachments were sent out from the fort. Some stayed close by to act as sentries while others assumed temporary defensive positions in rifle pits. Around 6:30 a.m.,[340] as the day was beginning to break, Longstreet open fired from five artillery locations seven hundred to 1,500 yards from the fort. The hazy flashes of enemy guns appeared in the still, dark ground below the horizon. The rounds could be heard as they whistled through the sky into sudden impacts at the fort; but many of the shells exploded in the air, too high to do any real damage. Still, as they grew closer and then exploded, the shrill shell shrieks would play on the morale of the men.[341]

The Union sentries and skirmishers knew it was time to withdraw into the fortifications, which they did with haste. A portion of the picket on Fort Sander's east side was made up of companies of the 2nd Michigan, who occupied short rifle pits adjoining the left rampart of the fort. Being on the side closer to Knoxville, the opposite side of the fort where the attack was occurring, Companies A, H, G, and F moved inside and were placed in positions for defending a portion of the principal works. The other six companies K, B, I, E, C and D, were stationed in the rifle pits extending from the right rampart of the fort, with the 20th Michigan between them and the Fort as well. They would continue to hold a portion of these rifle pits throughout the attack and until the Rebel forces were finally driven back.[342] [343]

---

[340] System, Historical Data The Union Army, vol. 6, "Knoxville, Tennessee (Siege of) November 17–December 4, 1863" p. 2 (System, Battle History)
[341] Nosworthy, *Roll Call to Destiny*, 216–217 (Nosworthy, 2008pp.216-217)
[342] Michiganinthewar.org., "2nd Regiment Michigan Volunteer Infantry," 4 (War.org, michiganinthewar.org/infantry/2ndinf.htmp.4)

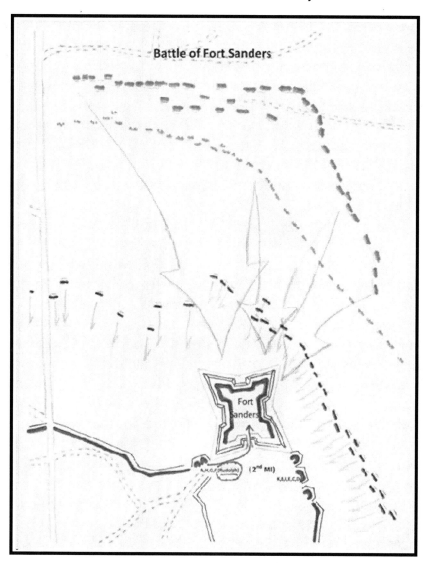

Positioned in rifle pits down near the river, the 29th Massachusetts that was in the second brigade along with the 27th Michigan did not fall back fast enough and was ordered to do so immediately. Company B of the 79th New York volunteers had gotten into their rifle pits in front of the fort

---

[343] Michigan,org, "2nd Michigan Volunteer Infantry, "E" Company 1861–1865" p. 2 (Michigan.orgp.7)

just prior to the beginning of the shelling and decided to wait to withdraw until the shelling ceased. One shell fell short behind their position, dislodging and splintering a stump, sending wood and dirt into the air. The artillery shells still shrieking overhead became random as they worked behind the fort's defensive works. When the twenty-minute[344] bombardment ceased, it was early dawn, and the men from the 79th New York ran back to the Fort double quick. The last men to return took up the planks across the ditch and carried them into the fort.[345]

The cannon fire and shrill shrieks of the artillery shells were quickly replaced with heavy musketry fire along the whole of Longstreet's line. The drizzle like rain had stopped, but the air was still thick and heavy with moisture. A ground fog had developed in the low-lying areas of the attackers but did not reach the Union defensive positions in the fort. This thick heavy air, muffled the sound of the powerful musketry fire, turning the hundreds of cracks of gunfire into continual pips strung out along a long line. The Confederate skirmishers had carefully aimed at the gun emplacements and Union men they could see behind the parapets. Their volley soon created hundreds of eerie zips and dull thuds, which erupted along the top of the fort after only a brief delay. This deadly hail sent every man diving for cover.[346] It appeared as if even the cannons could not be used to return fire. But this was a mere deception on the Union's part as many men were just staying low, keeping out of sight to give the enemy false confidence. Also, despite the excellent marksmanship of the Confederates, only one Union soldier was struck and killed before taking cover, probably due in part to poor visibility.

---

[344] Reference, Civil War (AUTHOR?), "Knoxville Siege," 3 (Reference, 2010p.3)
[345] Nosworthy, *Roll Call to Destiny*, 217 (Nosworthy, 2008p.217)
[346] Ibid., 217–218 (Nosworthy, 2008pp.217-218)

The main attacking Confederate body began to form up behind the skirmishers. The column of regiments was ordered to advance on the fort which they did in proper fashion. Initially, the fog covered their advance that was slow but zealous. The men seemed to be enthusiastic and with high hopes of success in their mission. The columns of men, with their heads down moved quietly forward. The heavy tread of the men could be heard from the fort as they moved ever closer. As the attackers began to exit the fog, they reached the entanglements of telegraph wire that was stretched from tree stump, to tree stump, to tree stump, low to the ground.[347] Many men, not seeing the tripwire, started toppling to the ground into a pile. Caught by surprise, the men in the rear, not aware of what was taking place at the front of their column, continued to push forward, aggravating the traffic jam and increasing the amount of men in a heap on the ground. This drastically slowed their advance and caused much confusion. Still wanting to push forward, the column split and spread out in order to clear the entanglements, fallen logs with sharpened branches, and men still trying to get out of the trip piles. With the enemy in view, Union artillery placed in barbettes, peeking through the parapet, open fired, delivering several rounds of canister into the attackers. Now clear of any obstacles, except for the many tree stumps scattered about the terrain, the Confederate advance toward the fort picked up to that of a run.[348]

---

[347] Summaries, CWSAC Battle, "Fort Saunders" p. 1 (Summaries, Reference #: TN025, Preservation Priority: IV2 (Class B))
[348] Nosworthy, *Roll Call to Destiny*, 218–219 (Nosworthy, 2008pp.218-219)

Fort Sanders after the battle

Upon reaching the fort's outer ditch, the attackers were surprisingly and abruptly halted. They expected the ditch to be only about four feet deep, when in fact it was twelve feet wide and eight to ten feet deep with vertical sides. Above that, the fort's exterior slope was almost vertical.[349] The final surprise was another tripwire placed close to the top edge of the ditch. Crossing the ditch was nearly impossible, especially during withering defensive fire from musketry and canister

---

[349] Wikipedia, "Knoxville Campaign," 5 (Wikipedia-KCp.5)

now raining down on them. Confederate officers did not intentionally lead their men into the deep trench, because without scaling ladders, very few would be able to enter the fort. But as before, the column from behind still pushed forward in large numbers, forcing many to trip and fall into the deep channel. Once the men started falling into the ditch, the force of the men pushing forward turned it into a cascade of tumbling men and arms. Pandemonium quickly ensued among the attacking forces.[350]

The Federals were able to direct artillery and musketry fire directly into the attackers from both sides in crossfire. This was the moment they had waited for, as piles of Confederate attackers struggled in the bottom of the ditch, all tangled up with one another. The order was given, and the triple-shotted artillery piece fired into the swirling mass. It was an instant swath of death and destruction—the carnage was terrible. Despite the horror, the Confederate attackers only momentarily hesitated; then the confusion started to dissipate. Man after man now deliberately jumped into the trench to look for a way forward. Before them was an eight-or-so-foot earthen walling, just below a twelve foot, 45° upward-sloped parapet.[351]

Inside the Fort, a number of Union officers were encouraging their men to deliberately target the Confederate officers below. The Union men took aim and fired from the embrasures beside the artillery pieces and from cotton bales on top of the parapet, then ducked back behind to reload in safety. The Confederate attackers not in the ditch took what cover they could behind tree stumps to shield those trying to scale the walls. They would fire, reload, and fire again as fast as they could. The attacking sharpshooters would note the position of a Union soldier, take aim, and wait for him to come out for another shot. The moment he would show himself, the musket

---

[350] Nosworthy, *Roll Call to Destiny*, 220–221 (Nosworthy, 2008pp.220-221)
[351] Ibid., 221 (Nosworthy, 2008p.221)

would explode a deadly round. A number of Union soldiers fell in this manner all along the battle line.[352]

The shape of the Union fort allowed the artillery emplacements to enfilade the ditch with devastating results. The smart Confederate soldier would hesitate until after the artillery had shot its load, then jump into the ditch and attempt to climb out the other side before another round could be loaded and fired. In the ditch, they were like sitting ducks in a shooting gallery, desperately climbing on one another's shoulders and trying to dig their fingers into the hardened earth to get to the base of the parapet. The murderous fire raining down on them was stopping many from advancing any further. There was one reported dead spot beneath one of the bastions for the Confederate attackers, who would momentarily huddle down before bravely moving on to scale the outside walls.[353]

Several Confederate attackers brought two or three boards that were used across the ditch. Still, in the vicious

---

[352] Nosworthy, *Roll Call to Destiny*, 221–222 (Nosworthy, 2008pp.221-222)
[353] Ibid., 222 (Nosworthy, 2008p.222)

crossfire from muskets and cannons, balance was hard to maintain and a number trying to cross never made it to the other side. Those attackers that did make it across would still be confronted by the steep frozen earthen works. The berm usually found just above a trench where it met the parapet at a 45° angle of an earthen fort had been cut away in preparation for the attack. This made it extremely hard to get a toehold in the frozen earth, and the water poured down the sides of the fort earlier made it icy slick as well.[354]

Initially, those attackers seeking entrance into the fort would find the embrasure for the defending artillery easier to reach as it was cut midway up the parapet. If the cannon had recently been fired, it could be a temporary corridor into the fort. As the initial Confederate officers and trickles of men first reached such a position, they were quickly outnumbered and captured. As the numbers of attackers reaching those positions increased, the situation became more critical. At one embrasure where a twelve-pounder howitzer appeared to have run out of ammunition, Confederate attackers stormed in and demanded their surrender, but one of the artillerymen calmly pulled the lanyard and eliminated the threat. The artillery crew had held back the last round for such an occasion. The howitzer was then rolled into the embrasure and used as a plug as the artillerymen armed themselves with muskets.[355]

Against all odds, the attackers were starting to reach the top of the parapet in larger numbers. One Union soldier grabbed an ax and violently dispatched three Confederate intruders. That soldier was exposed to a murderous fire from below, so several of his comrades quickly pulled him back behind cover. One Confederate soldier bearing his regiment's flag was reaching the top of the parapet and planted the flag in the hard ground to pull himself up. On seeing this flag, the Union soldiers displayed a noticeable increase in alarm, similar to the state of a large bee's

---

[354] Historyofwar.org, "Battle of Knoxville, 29 November 1863" p. 4 (War.org)
[355] Nosworthy, *Roll Call to Destiny*, 224 (Nosworthy, 2008p.224)

nest invaded by an enemy. That Confederate soldier who had reached the top of the parapet with his flag planted was immediately—and simultaneously—shot by a number of Union defenders. His lifeless body, now riddled with bullets, rolled down onto other attackers still trying to scale the outside of the parapet.[356]

At the height of the battle, two Union officers worked in unison with the twenty-pounder parrot shells that had been stacked earlier along the northern and western walls and put them to good use. As quickly as possible, one would pick up the shell, the other light it, and it would be rolled down to the attackers in the ditch. Their work was swiftly followed by violent explosions in quick succession in the crowded trench, causing great carnage.[357]

As many as one hundred men managed to scale the parapet during the peak of the battle, many of whom were knocked back or killed. One of those men was reportedly an officer, who saw the opposite side of the fort with little to no defenses. He desperately tried to convince those behind him to work their way to the other side and attack there. But amidst the confusion of battle, the sound of cannons, the musketry fire of hundreds of men, and the shouts of encouragement and desperation, it was totally in vain. Those on the parapet who were not killed quickly found themselves surrounded with no avenue of retreat. Surrender was their only option. The slaughter was horrifying.[358]

Another wave of Confederates advanced towards the fort in two lines but their advance was cut short. Men started to leave the fight and stagger back to their lines with no more fight left in them. Union reinforcements began arriving and advanced at a run into the area of the hardest fighting. Companies A, C, D, and K from the 29th Massachusetts and

---

[356] Nosworthy, *Roll Call to Destiny*, 223 (Nosworthy, 2008p.223)
[357] Ibid., 224 (Nosworthy, 2008p.224)
[358] Ibid., 223 (Nosworthy, 2008p.223)

Company C from the 20th Michigan engaged the enemy at once. There was still much confusion but the retiring numbers continued to grow until the attack finally broke off entirely. With no more strength or will left for this fight, the bulk of the Confederate forces withdrew, and the battle was over.

One company of the 2nd Michigan and one from the 29th were hastily sent out to demand the surrender of any Confederate men still standing. They did so eagerly and without delay, and scores surrendered, having no spirit left to fight. They were promptly formed up and taken back through the embrasures into the security of the fort. The Union soldiers offered help to those men who needed it, despite the fact that moments ago they were mortal enemies.[359]

The attack lasted twenty minutes and resulted in extremely lopsided casualties. Burnside estimated the enemy lost one thousand men killed and wounded, but Longstreet reported only 129 killed, 458 wounded and 226 missing.[360] The Union only lost thirteen men. The 2nd Michigan recorded having five men wounded, one man taken prisoner, and another man missing. The 27th Michigan during the siege suffered the loss of three men killed, two men wounded, sixteen captured and one missing. The total Union losses for the siege cost a total of ninety-two men killed, 394 wounded, and 207 captured or missing.[361]

According to a record I found in Phillips papers, it was on this day of November 29, 1863, that Corporal Rudolph Lenderking was wounded in front of Fort Sanders.[362] The only time anyone from the 2nd Michigan was outside of the fort and under fire was at the very end of the battle. The retreating Confederates were still sporadically firing to cover

---

[359] Nosworthy, *Roll Call to Destiny*, 226–227 (Nosworthy, 2008pp.226-227)
[360] Reference, Civil War (AUTHOR?), "Knoxville Siege ," 3 (Reference, 2010p.3)
[361] Ibid. (Reference, 2010p.3)
[362] Records, National Archives – Pension, "Philip Lenderking" Request for back pay owed family (Records)

their retreat when men from the 2nd Michigan and others rushed out to take prisoners.

Corporal Lenderking was wounded in the right thigh with a mini ball that badly shattered his femur bone. (Note: As this was mentioned in the family transcripts later, Rudolph must have been conscious enough after the battle to speak to George and relate to him where he was shot.) He was cared for as best they could, but with such a wound, little could be done for this extremely painful injury. He was ultimately removed from the scene of battle and taken to the hospital in Knoxville;[363] I'm sure a most agonizing trip. Being in close proximity, his brother George from the 27th Michigan would have surely found time to visit him upon learning of his condition. After seeing many wounded on the battlefield, his heart surly dropped at seeing the condition of his brother. A Dr. Cogswell from the 29th Massachusetts viewed his wound containing the almost powdered bone and decided that the only course of action was to amputate the upper third of his thigh. The anesthetic was poor if not nonexistent, making the operation a painfully grueling and bloody work. Corporal Rudolph Lenderking obviously became extremely feverish and sickly as his wound became infected, leading to his death on December 2, 1863. His passing would've struck the family very hard as his brother George notified them shortly after. According to records, he was laid to rest in the Knoxville Cemetery.[364]

---

[363] Service, The National Archives and Record, "Rudolph Lenderking" Company Muster Roll, Nov. & Dec., 1863 (Service)
[364] Ibid. p. 1(Service)

Chapter 6
To the Battle of the Wilderness

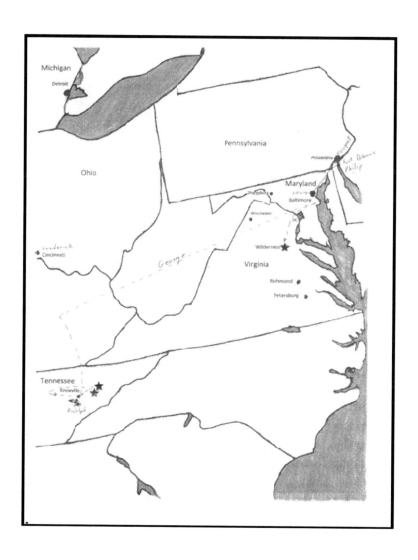

Phillip Lenderking
5th Maryland Infantry Regiment

In January of 1864, the 5th Maryland was assigned to the District of Delaware, Middle Department and transferred to Fort Delaware.[365] The regiment continued to build its strength as men continued to flow in, either as new recruits or other parolees. During that night of March 9, 1864, another detachment of the 5th Maryland volunteers came in. On March 16, 1864, "Old Schley" of the 5th Maryland arrived with some sixty more of his men.

While at Fort Delaware, the men of the 5th Maryland performed their guard duties as well as drilling and preparing to once again enter the war. Sgt. Lenderking, being a member of the band, would likewise be entertaining the men and doing other jobs as required. In March of 1864, the Fort Delaware Cornet Band was giving performances in Delaware City, Wilmington, Chester, and Philadelphia. The band also

---

[365] Civilwarintheeast.com, "5th Maryland Infantry Regiment" p. 1 (East, civikwarintheeast.com/USA/MD/5MD.php)

performed a benefit concert for the Ladies Aid Society of Salem New Jersey during that same month. A picture of the band in the book, *Images of America, Fort Delaware*, has a picture of the band on page thirty-one. A musician who bears a striking resemblance to Sgt. Philip Lenderking is located eighth from either end.[366] After all, soldiers love to sing, and there were many tunes popular with the men. Regimental and brigade bands often played during the evening hours; some of the more popular tunes were the "Battle Cry of Freedom," "Battle Hymn of the Republic" and "Tenting on the Old Campground," as well as softer songs like "Aura Lea."

In the morning reveille was sounded at 5:00 a.m. to begin the day, followed by an assembly for morning roll call and breakfast call. Drums were usually used to announce daily activities and were part of an infantryman's daily routine. Sick call was sounded soon after breakfast, followed by assemblies for guard duty, drill, or to begin to march. The sound of drums at fort and military encampments were also commonplace for parades, and to call men to attention, but they could also be used to signal maneuvers or serve as signals for men to load and fire their weapons.[367]

At times, especially while in camp, the soldiers would also have free time, which many spent playing card games, reading, pitching horseshoes or team sports such as baseball, which was rapidly gaining favor among the Northern troops. Soldiers also played a formal football, which at that time resembled more of a huge brawl than the sport you see today. Men also participated in foot races, horse races, boxing matches, music, and other activities to pass the time. Once a regiment marched out in an active campaign, many of these things would be left behind as their activities would be mostly

---

[366] Mackie and Lee, *Images of America, Fort Delaware,* 31 (MacKie, 2010p.31)
[367] Service, The United States Dept. of the Interior, *The Civil War soldier, what was life as a soldier like in 1863?*, 2 (Service, Gettysburg National Military Parkp.2)

restricted to writing, cleaning uniforms and equipment. Many would just pass free time with sleeping.[368]

Religion was a very important part of the soldiers' daily routine. Many of the men attended church services on a regular basis, and some even carried small Bibles or Testaments in their personal items. Regimental and brigade chaplains were quite plentiful and acted as assistance in field hospitals, comforting the sick and wounded and writing letters home for those who could not write. Chaplains also held field services for their respective regiments, and most accompanied the soldiers as they marched into the battlefield.[369] So it is not surprising to find Sgt. Lenderking running some errands for a chaplain while in Fort Delaware. It appears the chaplain needed some things removed from a train, which Sgt. Lenderking was glad to do. He climbed up onto the train car at the station of the B&O Railroad and was hurrying to perform his task when he slipped and lost his footing. He soon found himself falling over the edge of the car and hit the ground with a thud. To his misfortune, he landed on his thumb and dislocated it at the proximal joint, which was not only painful at the time, but would also cause him continued pain for the remainder of his life.[370]

George Lenderking
27th Michigan Infantry Regiment

Longstreet had abandoned the siege of Knoxville on December 4 upon the approach of Gen. Sherman with an additional 25,000 men to break the siege. Longstreet

---

[368] Service, *The United States Dept. of the Interior*, "The Civil War soldier, what was life as a soldier like in 1863?," 3–4 (Service, Gettysburg National Military Parkpp.3-4)

[369] Ibid. (Service, Gettysburg National Military Parkp.5)

[370] Records, National Archives–Pension, "Philip Lenderking" Dr. Report, F.Y. MacDonald, March 22, 1880 (Records)

withdrew his men toward Rogersville, Tennessee, some sixty-five miles northwest of Knoxville where he planned to prepare to go into winter quarters. During the siege, the 27th Michigan took an active part in its defense and had lost a total of fifty-four men, either killed or wounded.[371]

The 27th with others set out in pursuit of Longstreet on December 6. By December 13, some of the Federal's cavalry had reached Bean's Station on the Holston River. Longstreet decided to go back and attack the station in hopes of defeating part of the Union Army and stopping their pursuit. Gen. Shackelford who commanded the Union cavalry sent word back to general Parke and suggested that the infantry be marched up in his support. The following morning the infantry set out on its march to Bean's Station.

By 2:00 a.m. on December 14, one of the three Confederate columns began skirmishing with the Union pickets about three miles north of the station. The Union pickets held the lines as best they could but soon it developed into a general engagement. The Confederate assault was too overwhelming. The Union cavalry was slowly forced back. The Union infantry now deployed for the assault and fought on vigorously throughout most of the day. Confederate flanking attacks and other assaults occurred at various times and locations but the Federals continued to hold until Southern reinforcements arrived. By nightfall, the Federals retreated through Beans Gap and on to Blain's Crossroads where they again dug in. Longstreet set out to attack the Union forces again the next morning, but as he approached them he found them well entrenched and withdrew.[372] The fighting had been fierce, resulting in seven hundred Union and nine hundred Confederates killed or wounded.[373] The 27th Michigan has lost

---

[371] Michiganinthewar.com, "27th Regiment Michigan Volunteer Infantry" p. 2 (War, michiganinthewar.org/.../27thinf.htm)

[372] Wikipedia, "Knoxville Campaign," 5–6 (Wikipedia-KCpp.5-6)

[373] Historyofwar.org, "Battle of Bean Station, 14 December 1863" p. 1 (War.Org, historyofwar.org/.../battles_beans_station)

another man wounded, six men captured, and one man missing over this course of time.[374]

The 27th Michigan continued operations in East Tennessee till March of 1864. In the cold winter months, the regiment saw less action, but there was still the occasional skirmish. But even worse than the fighting in these cold winter days, the 27th suffered hardships and severities along the campaign as they were poorly supplied with rations, tents, blankets, and clothing. Many of their shoes were worn out by the constant marching, either in deep mud or over the frozen ground.

(Note: At this time shirts and undergarments were universally of cotton material and also sent to the soldiers from home. Union soldiers' blouse and trousers were wool and died dark blue until 1862 when the trouser color was altered to a lighter shade of blue. The floppy crown forage-cap was made of wool broadcloth with a leather visor and was usually adorned with brass letters of the regiment and company to which the soldier belonged. But long campaigns and heavy fighting would leave the soldiers' clothing torn,

---

[374] Historical Data System, Inc., "George Lenderking" p.2 (Historical Data System, regimental casualty analysis)

with occasional holes from bullets that barely missed, making it necessary for the garment to be mended or replace.)[375]

At this time, George learned of the capture of his brother Philip at the Second Battle of Winchester and his timely release. However, being in such close proximity to the battle in which Rudolph was mortally wounded weighed heavily on his mind as he continued his regimental duties. In January 12, 1864, he expressed his sadness to the family upon learning of the death of Rudolph at the camp near Knoxville, Tennessee. On January 31, 1864, he also said this:

> I feel very lonely and fed up with this life of a soldier. Though near Knoxville, we still have half rations and these are very small. About two weeks ago, the 9th Army Corps had hardly any rags on our bodies and for eight days we had only two spoonfuls of flour a day. If we had not been able to buy a little something to eat, we would've died of starvation. Now things are a little better.
>
> George Lenderking[376]

By January 22, they had reached Armstrong's Ferry. From January 24 through March 2, they advanced to Morristown, then to Mossy Creek, Tennessee. Finally, the regiment was reinforced with two additional companies I and K, along with some new recruits from the state, in all a total of 362 men.[377]

March 17 through April 5, they moved on to Baxter, Tenn., Knoxville, Tenn., then to Nicholasville, Ky. and thence to Annapolis, Md. Two companies of sharpshooters were added to their roles and they were assigned to the 1st Brigade, 3rd Division, 9th Army Corps, Army of the

---

[375] Service, The United States Dept. of the Interior, *The Civil War soldier, what was life as a soldier like in 1863?*, 3 (Service, Gettysburg National Military Parkp.3)
[376] Wormelle, *The Lenderking Family*, 9–10 (Wormelle, 1969pp.9-10)
[377] Michiganinthewar.org., "27th Regiment Michigan Volunteer Infantry" p. 2 (War, michiganinthewar.org/.../27thinf.htm)

Potomac.[378] It was also at this time that 2 Corporal George (Lenderking) Landerking was promoted in rank to full corporal.[379]

Grant's campaign objective was to find Lee's army and destroy it. On May 4th, 1864, just after midnight, the Army of the Potomac began crossing the Rapidan River at three separate points. The plan was to converge on the Wilderness Tavern, near the edge of the Wilderness of Spotsylvania, and then move on to more open ground. Lieut. Gen. Ulysses S Grant did not desire to engage Lee's army in this area. The early settlers here had cut down the native forest, leaving only a secondary growth of dense shrubs. You literally could not see a soldier fifty yards ahead of you.[380] This rough terrain, which was virtually unsettled, was nearly impenetrable for military maneuvers. The 5th Corps under, Maj. Gen. Warren, and the 6th Corps, under Maj. Gen. John Sedgwick crossed the Rapidan at Germanna Ford, and proceeded on to the Wilderness Tavern. While waiting for the wagon train following them, they set up camp under recommendation of Maj. Gen. Mead. The wagon train, despite Grant's insisting that the army travel light with minimal artillery and supplies, had a logistical tail almost seventy miles long. It was estimated that Mead's supply trains included an estimated 4,300 wagons, 835 ambulances, and a herd of cattle. The 9th Corps under Burnside, originally held in reserve to guard the Orange and Alexander Railroad, was positioned behind the very lengthy supply trains.[381]

The 2nd Corps, under Maj. Gen. Winfield S. Hancock, would cross to the east of Ely's Ford and advanced to the Spotsylvania Court House by way of Chancellorsville,

---

[378] Ibid. p. 2 (War, michiganinthewar.org/.../27thinf.htm)
[379] The National Archives, "George Lenderking, Co. A, Michigan infantry" Company Muster Roll Mar. & April, 1864 (Archives, 1867)
[380] Historical Data System, Inc., "Wilderness Virginia, May 5–17th, 1864" p.1 (Historical Data System, PO Box 35, Duxbury,MA 02331)
[381] Wikipedia, "Battle of the Wilderness," 3 (Wikipedia-BotW, 2009,p.3)

which was reached by the afternoon of May 5, and Todd's Tavern. Grant had stressed that speed was of the essence because the army was vulnerable as it moved through this thin stretch.

An erroneous report was received by Meade stating that the Confederate cavalry under Jeb Stuart was operating in his army's rear. He immediately ordered the bulk of his cavalry to move east to deal with the perceived threat, thus leaving his army blind.[382]

(Note: In the meantime, Gen. Robert E. Lee, leading the Confederate Army of Northern Virginia, had reconnaissance of the movement of Grant's army. He estimated Grant's strength was 118,000 men with superior artillery to his 65,000 men. Lee reasoned the fighting in the tangled woods would eliminate Grant's artillery advantage, and cause confusion among his infantry who had less familiarity with the area.)[383]

Early on the morning of May 5, Warren's 5th Corps was advancing toward the Plank Road when a Confederate force appeared to their west. Grant was quickly notified and quickly instructed, "If any opportunity presents itself of pitching into a part of Lee's army, do so without giving time for disposition." Assuming this to be a small Confederate force, Meade halted his army and directed Warren to attack. As Warren approached the Confederate earthen works on the clearing known as Saunders Field, he held back the attack, feeling he had insufficient troops. He requested a delay from Meade, until reinforcements could arrive, but Meade in his frustration ordered him to attack.[384]

---

[382] Wikipedia, "Battle of the Wilderness," 5 (Wikipedia-BotW, 2009,p.5)
[383] Ibid., 4 (Wikipedia-BotW, 2009,p.4)
[384] Historical Data System, Inc., "Wilderness Virginia, May 5–17th, 1864" pp. 1-2 (Historical Data System, PO Box 35, Duxbury,MA 02331)

Once the Union men advanced and the attack began, it was just past the noon hour. It took but a short time before one brigade had to take cover in a gully to avoid the inflating fire from the Confederate lines. Johnson's left held against repeated assaults, but Griffin, along with a brigade from Wadsworth division, broke through the Rebel center south of the Turnpike. That success would be short-lived as the Federals were soon forced to fall back from lack of support. Wright's division of Sedgwick's 6th Corps was unable to advance to the Confederate skirmishers located in this dense undergrowth. The battle lines were pushed back and forth as both sides fought desperately for their ground. The battle continued to grow, engaging more and more troops from both sides. Burnside's 9th Corps was sent for and ordered across the river to join the army now engaged in battle.[385]

Another Confederate column advanced steadily up the Orange Plank Road in an attempt to flank the Union's far left. Fortunately, it was detected by the Federals early enough to prevent another surprise. Getty's Federal division was

---

[385] Wikipedia, "Battle of the Wilderness," 5–6 (Wikipedia-BotW, 2009, pp.5-6)

ordered to move further south to hold the intersection of Brock and Orange Plank Roads. A. P. Hill's 3rd Corps continued its advance up the Orange Plank Road and attacked. The Federals were slowly being pushed back until Hancock's 2nd Corps arrived to reinforce Getty's left flank. Fierce fighting continued until nightfall with neither side gaining an advantage.[386]

On the morning of May 6, around 5:00 a.m., Grants Federals seized the initiative. The 5th and 6th Corps resumed their assault against the Confederate positions along the Turnpike to the Federal right. Simultaneously, 2nd Corps and Getty's division would attack the Confederate line on the Federal's left flank. Initially, the Federal advance steadily made its way through A. P. Hill's line across the Orange Plank Road. The Confederate lines were pushed back to Tapp's farm, where they were reinforced by Longstreet's troops.[387]

In the meantime, Burnside's 9th Corps was expected to move into the gap in the center. But the regiment had only recently been able to cross the Rapidan River's pontoon bridge at Germanna Ford the evening before. Two companies of the regiment were on the picket line during the night,[388] and the balance of the regiment held in reserve.[389] Early that morning, at first light, the 27th withdrew from its position and marched several miles to the left, where it formed its lines to prepare its advance upon the enemy. The battle was already heavily engaged as the 9th Corps advanced down the plank road. It was already around 7:00 a.m., and the sound of heavy artillery and fighting to their right, just two miles south of their position roared like thunder.

---

[386] Ibid., 6–7 (Wikipedia-BotW, 2009, pp.6-7)
[387] Historical Data System, Inc., "Wilderness Virginia, May 5–17th, 1864" p. 3 (Historical Data System, PO Box 35, Duxbury,MA 02331)
[388] Vosper, *Official Reports, Wilderness* p. 959-67 (Vosper, 1864)
[389] Cannon, *The Wilderness Campaign, May 1864*, 183 (Cannon, 1993p.183)

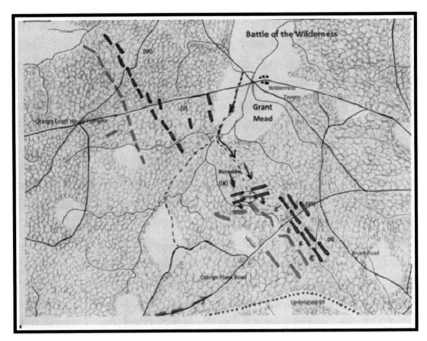

The column finally turned to the right onto an old road that wound through the thick woods toward the center of the fighting. Its movement forward was at a snail's pace as the soldiers proceeded with extreme caution. Visibility was limited, making it extremely difficult for officers to exercise effective control. Movement through this thick underbrush caused men to thrash noisily and blindly forward, making them perfect targets for the concealed Confederates ahead. Attacking or retreating formations could not be maintained in this near jungle-like terrain. The maps the officers used proved to be thoroughly unreliable.[390] By 10:50 a.m. they had only traveled a mile and a half, with the battle still a mile away. Grant was becoming anxious and sent word to Burnside of the necessity to move with speed and attack immediately. Hancock had been heavily engaged and

---

[390] Wikipedia, "Battle of the Wilderness," 4 (Wikipedia-BotW, 2009, p.4)

expecting Burnside for the past three hours, and had been maneuvering his troops according to that expectation.[391]

Longstreet struck the Federal's left flank by way of an unfinished railroad track to the South of the Union lines. Upon commencement of the attack, he was able to dislodge one Federal position after another. The Confederates advanced nearly to Brock Road by early afternoon when Longstreet was wounded by friendly fire, and the attack began to fall apart.[392]

Finally around 2:00 p.m., Burnside's troops were ready to attack south on the left flank of the Confederates 1st Corps, north of the Plank Road. Many of the men were set up in supporting roles and on guard duty, with only three brigades committed to the attack. They advanced forward in skillful fashion and touched the left flank of Field's

---

[391] Cannon, *The Wilderness Campaign, May 1864*, 182–183 (Cannon, 1993pp.182-183)
[392] Wikipedia, "Battle of the Wilderness," 8–9 (Wikipedia-BotW, 2009, pp.8-9)

Confederate division. Both sides were fully engaged with the heavy firing of musketry. Confederate bullets whistled by the men like hail, cutting leaves and branches that subsequently fell to the ground. Constantly firing, reloading, and re-firing their muskets, they pressed forward with constant persistence. The 45th Pennsylvania had gotten close enough to the enemy defenses to plant their colors despite the heavy resistance, but finally they had to withdraw. There was much confusion, smoke, and burning leaves, along with the thick smell of spent black powder. With nothing further to be gained, the Federal troops were drawn back and entrenched.[393]

Lee was not able to launch a second assault until about 4:00 p.m., but by that time, reinforcements had arrived to shore up Union defenses. Thirteen brigades were sent in on the Confederate right against the Federal lines on Brock Road. The bloodshed was renewed with the tempest of musketry. Both sides leveled their muskets and blasted away at each other for the better part of half and hour. One soldier referred to this time as one continuous roll of thunder that was long, deep and heavy, and fearful to listen too. The fighting was so fierce that part of the Union breastworks caught fire. The resulting blaze and its thick choking smoke forced some

---

[393] Cannon, *The Wilderness Campaign, May 1864*, 183 (Cannon, 1993p.183)

troops to fall back. The Confederates quickly moved in to fill the void. Burnside took the offensive around 5:30 p.m. in order to come to Hancock's aid. The tempest of musketry and bloodshed still failed to accomplish much but the wounding of Confederate Brig. Gen. E. A. Perry. Both sides had exhausted all their options, so after much brutal fighting, the conflict finally sputtered out in the southern half of the battlegrounds.[394][395]

In the northern portion of the lines of both enemies, the battle was renewed with intensity. Around 7:30 p.m., bitter fighting erupted as the Confederate forces attempted to outflank the Union to the far right. Again the Union lines were shifted and much improved fighting took place. Now with all opportunities exhausted and the daylight fading, the day's combat and bloodshed finally waned, winding down to an end.[396][397]

At the end of the day's battle of May 6, 1864, Cpl. Landerking was presumed to be a prisoner of war. Subsequent follow-ups showed no signs of him anywhere. He did not appear in the lists of Confederate prisoners, nor did the family that he was very close to all of his life ever hear from him again. As time went on, even the army began to feel he must have been killed at the Battle of the Wilderness; but without more evidence, he could only be listed under "no proof of death."[398] In the end, all that could be said was that as the light faded from day into night, or as the cannon and musket smoke faded from the battlefield, so also did Cpl. Landerking fade from the field of battle.

---

[394] Historical Data System, "Wilderness Virginia, May 5–17th, 1864" (Historical Data System, PO Box 35, Duxbury, MA 02331)
[395] Wikipedia, "Battle of the Wilderness," 9 (Wikipedia-BotW, 2009, p.9)
[396] Historical Data System, Inc., Wilderness Virginia, May 5 – 17th, 1864 (Historical Data System, PO Box 35, Duxbury, MA 02331)
[397] Wikipedia, "Battle of the Wilderness," 9 (Wikipedia-BotW, 2009, p.9)
[398] The National Archives, *George Lenderking, Co. A, Michigan infantry* Adjutant General's Office, November 19, 1867 (Archives, 1867)

Missing In Action!

The Battle of the Wilderness lasted from May 5 to May 7. The estimated casualties and losses were listed on the Confederate side at around 11,125. Out of that number, 1,495 men were killed, 7,928 wounded, and 1,702 men captured or missing. The Union losses were 17,666, out of which 2,246 were listed as killed, 12,037 wounded, and 3,383 men captured or missing. The 27th Michigan lost in this battle an estimated 187 men killed, wounded, and missing.[399]

---

[399] Historical Data System, Inc., "George Lenderking" The Union Army, Vol. 6 (Historical Data System, regimental casualty analysis)

Chapter 7
To Bermuda Hundred

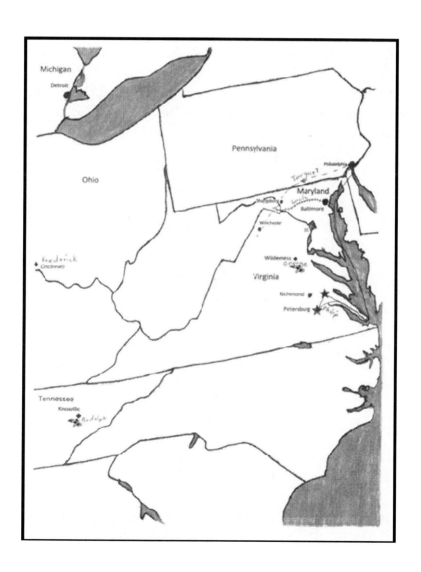

Lewis (Lenderking) Landerking
Company E, 12th Maryland Infantry

Lewis Lenderking was the youngest brother of Philip, Rudolph, George, and Frederick. He had recently moved from Germany to the United States and was living in Baltimore, Maryland. He had gray eyes, light hair, a light complexion, and stood five feet, five inches high. His primary work with that of a farmer.

Upon reaching the age of 18, he considered joining the military as his brothers had done. He also would have been very aware of the dangers of being a soldier from all the letters sent home by his brothers in the field. Still, on July 20, 1864, he enlisted in company A, 12th Maryland infantry as a private for 100 days.[400]

---

[400] National Archives Microfilm, "Lewis Lenderking, Company A 12th Maryland Infantry, (100 days unit)" Company Muster-in and Descriptive Roll, July 20, 1864 (Publication, National Archives and Record Service, Washington DC)

The 12th Infantry was organized in Baltimore, Maryland, during the months of June and July as a short one hundred day emergency / security measure. Lieut. Col. John L. Bishop was in charge of the regiment during its brief term of service. Upon recruiting a sufficient number, they became a official regiment on July 30, 1864, consisting of a battalion of five companies: A, B, C, D, and E. The regiment was attached to the 1st Separate Brigade, 8th Army Corps to September 1864. They were then transferred to the Reserve Division of the Department of West Virginia at Harpers Ferry.[401]

Tougart Snyder
Company H, 12th Pennsylvania Cavalry

In 1864, my great-great-grandfather on my mother's side, Tougart Snyder, was a 42-year-old carpenter who relocated here from Germany. At the time of the Civil War he was living in Chambersburg, Pennsylvania. He had a dark complexion, blue eyes, gray hair and stood about five foot ten inches high. On September 14, 1864, he enlisted in Company H of the 12th Pennsylvania Cavalry. Taugart was a substitute for a thirty-one-year-old man named James C. Shipley from Liberty Township, Pennsylvania. What some people may not understand or realize is that during the Civil War, people could arrange for someone else to go into the military service in their place. So in some way my great-great-grandfather had some form of contact with Mr. Shipley prior to that time that led to his substituting for him.[402]

My great-great-grandfather, now Private Snyder, began his training. The cavalry was initially used for scouting purposes and to guard supply trains. They were armed with breech loading

---

[401] Civilwarintheeast.com, "12th Maryland infantry Regiment" Maryland – Massachusetts Regimental Histories p1237) (East, civilwarintheeast.com/USA/.../12MD.php)
[402] The National Archives, "Tougart (Schneider) Snyder" Muster and Descriptive Roll for a Detachment of Substitutes forward, Sept. 14, 1864 (Archives, National Archives and Record Service, Washington DC)

carbines, sabers, and pistols. Cavalry divisions would act as fast moving skirmishers and in many battles did their fighting either mounted or on foot.[403] So the cavalrymen had to learn about all the military equipment needed by the infantry soldier to fight and stay alive on the field, along with extra duties pertaining to their horses. Horses needed to be fed and watered daily, and required great care to maintain their health and strength. Cavalrymen also needed to know how to care for the equipment such as saddles and bridals. They would often train in cavalry maneuvers and tactics without horses before they ever got to ride. When fighting from atop a horse, cavalrymen would only get one shot from their breech-loading carbines, which could not be reloaded easily while riding. Therefore the cavalrymen would switch to their pistols and finally their sabers, which they drilled with both on foot and horseback.[404]

When Private Snyder reached the 12th Pennsylvania Cavalry it was a Reserve Division, attached to the Department of West Virginia.[405] It was now late fall and the weather was growing steadily colder. He found the regiment originally formed around the Philadelphia area to be poorly equipped in many ways and not very respected by some of the officers.

---

[403] Service, The United States Dept. of the Interior, *The Civil War soldier, what was life as a soldier like in 1863?,* 6 (Service, Gettysburg National Military Parkp.6)
[404] Ibid. p.2 (Service, Gettysburg National Military Parkp.2)
[405] Civilwarintheeast.com, "12th Pennsylvania Cavalry Regiment" p. 2 (East.Com, civilwarintheeast.com/../PA12cav.php)

(Comment: I would like to mention at this time that as I started to research the 12th, I was surprised to find how poorly supplied the 12th had been throughout most of the war. I have read reports that the regiment periodically lacked in carbines, pistols, sabers, saddles and even horses. Many of the weapons they possessed were old and used. As a result, a number of the men would have lacked one piece of equipment or another at the time they had to go into the field. Yet consistently, the commanding officers always seemed to expect them to perform as well in the field as a completely equipped cavalry unit.)

As winter was setting in, hostilities with the Confederate guerrillas were slowing down. It was just as hard for the enemy to live and maneuver in the cold-weather as it was for the 12th Pennsylvania. The guerrilla threat was still very present in the area, so Private Snyder like the rest had to be very careful when on picket duty or out on patrol.

Phillip Lenderking
5th Maryland Infantry Regiment

Initially, Philip and the family would have been notified by the army of their belief that George was captured in the Battle of the Wilderness. As Philip had been released only a month after his capture, their hopes would initially have been high, expecting George to return soon. But as time went on with no word or confirmation of his capture from the Confederate ranks, it became more and more likely that George had been killed. Receiving no more letters from him along with the uncertain possibility of his death would have weighed heavily on the whole family for some time.

On June 4, 1864, Philip and the 5th Maryland were once again packing up and getting ready to move out. They had just received orders to join the army in the field; they were assigned to the 3rd Brigade, 2nd Division, 18th Army Corps, Army of the James.[406]

---

[406] Civilwarintheeast.com, "5th Maryland Infantry Regiment" p. 1 (East, civikwarintheeast.com/USA/MD/5MD.php)

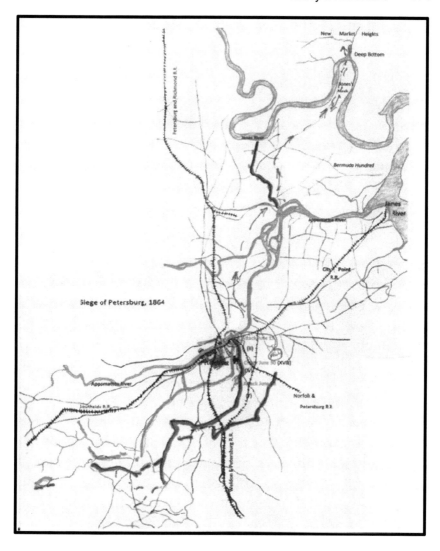

The 5th Maryland had arrived at what some people now call the Siege of Petersburg, Virginia, just in time to participate in the initial attempts to capture the city. Petersburg was protected by multiple lines of fortifications, the outermost of which was known as the Dimmock Line, a line of earthen works approximately ten miles long, located east of the city. Around 2,500 Confederates were stretched thinly along this defensive line. On June 8, the Union force of approximately 4,500 men prepared themselves for an attack against the outer works.

Brig. Gen. Edward W. Hinks 3rd division of the 18th Corps was assigned to attack the Dimmock Line east of the city. Brig. Gen. August V. Kautz's cavalry division of 1,300 cavalrymen was to sweep around Petersburg and strike it from the southeast. The troops moved out on the night of June 8 but made poor progress. It was not until around 3:40 a.m. on June 9 that the Union division crossed the Appomattox River. Finally around 7:00 a.m. both Gilmore and Hanks encountered the enemy but stopped at their fronts to await the cavalry. Kautz's cavalry division did not arrive until noon, having been delayed en route by numerous enemy pickets.

The assault was finally launched on the Dimmock Line where it crossed the Jerusalem Plank Road. A Confederate battery was located in that same area, manned by 150 militiamen. Kautz first launched a probing attack of the 11th Pennsylvania cavalry against the Home Guard, which consisted primarily of teenagers, elderly men, and some wounded soldiers from city hospitals. The Federal cavalry action paused as the Home Guard, after heavy losses, retreated to the city. Kautz, in the meantime, could not hear any activity on Gilmore's front, and presuming he was left on his own, he withdrew. This brief battle resulted in eighty casualties on the Confederate line and another forty Union cavalrymen.

On June 14, Lieut. Gen. Ulysses S. Grant directed Butler to augment the 18th Corps, commanded by Brig. Gen. William F. "Baldy" Smith, to the strength of sixteen thousand men, including Kautz's cavalry division, and to use the same route employed in the unsuccessful attack of June 9 for another assault. Baldy Smith and his men, which included the 5th Maryland, crossed the Appomattox River shortly after dawn on June 15. Kautz's cavalry was leading the advance and encountered an unexpectedly strong works at Baylor's farm northeast of Petersburg. Hinks's men launched two attacks on the Confederate stronghold and finally captured the Cannon, but the overall advance was then delayed until early afternoon.[407]

Maj. Gen. Smith delayed in attacking the Confederate earthen works until around 7 p.m.. Before him in the Confederate works were 2,200 troops defending the Dimmock line. The Confederates had insufficient infantrymen so even in this concentrated area, they were spaced and unacceptable ten feet apart. Smith deployed a strong skirmish line that swept over the earthen works on a three and a half mile front, causing the Confederates to retreat to a weaker defensive line on Harrison's Creek. Smith decided to wait until dawn the next morning to resume his attack, not realizing that the undefended city was immediately to his front. It was around this same time that Maj. Gen. Winfield S. Hancock, the 2nd Corps commander who outranked him, arrived and conferred with Smith. There was some uncertainty concerning his orders and the description of forces before him, so Hancock uncharacteristically deferred to Smith's. judgment and also decided to wait.

---

[407] Wikipedia, "Siege of Petersburg," 5–6 (Wikipedia-SoP, 2011pp.5-6)

General Beauregard, the defending Confederate commander, seized the opportunity to call for reinforcements. He called for his remaining 3,200 men that were bottling up Butler's army up at Bermuda Hundred to disengage and join the defenses at Petersburg. By the morning of the 16th, Beauregard had deployed about fourteen thousand men in his defensive line up against the fifty thousand Federals now facing him.[408]

Grant arrived with Burnside's 9th Corps and immediately ordered a reconnaissance of the enemy's defensive line to look for weak points. Hancock, who was a temporary commander of the Army of the Potomac, directed Smith's 18th Corps on the right, his Second Corps in the center, and Burnside's 9th Corps on the left. At 5:30 p.m., the order was given to advance, and all three corps began moving forward at a slow pace. The Confederates fought fiercely and erected new breastworks to the rear as breakthroughs occurred in their lines. General Meade arrived and assumed command of the 2nd Corps, and ordered the second attack. Toward the center, the 1st Division of the 2nd Corps under Brig. Gen. Francis E. Barlow pushed forward and overran the breastworks before them, but a counterattack drove them back, resulting in the capture of a large number of his men. The survivors quickly dug in close to the enemy works and held their positions. Another long night was spent by the Federal forces hunkered down, waiting for further orders.[409]

Early in the morning of June 17, two brigades of Burnside's 9th Corps stealthily approached the Confederate line and launched a surprise attack at first light. The advance was initially successful in the capturing of nearly a mile of Confederate fortifications and about six hundred prisoners. Continuing to move forward, the Federals were suddenly surprised to find another line of enemy entrenchments, as a

---

[408] Wikipedia, "Siege of Petersburg," 6–7 (Wikipedia-SoP, 2011pp.6-7)
[409] Wikipedia, "Siege of Petersburg." 7 (Wikipedia-SoP, 2011p.7)

blistering fire erupted that finally broke their advance. Two more assaults were launched by the 9th Corps, the first around 2:00 p.m., and the second in the evening, but both failed.

In the meantime, the Confederate engineers were constructing a new defensive position a mile west of the Dimmock Line, which they occupied by nightfall. With the arrival of two more Confederate divisions around 3:00 a.m., the Confederates now had twenty thousand men to defend the city. The Federal 5th Corps also arrived to reinforce Grant's army, which now numbered 67,000 men.

The 1st Union attack began at dawn of the eighteenth on the Federal right by the 2nd and 18th Corps. The 2nd Corps, still in the middle, were surprised to make such rapid progress against the Confederate line, not realizing that it had been moved back the night before. When they finally encountered the new Confederate line, the attack immediately ground to a halt and casualties quickly began to mount. There was a heavy engagement with blistering volleys being exchanged back and forth that lasted for hours with much bloodshed.

At noon, Wilcox's division of the 9th Corps led a new attack and suffered significant losses in the marsh and open fields they had to traverse. Warren's 5th Corps was also halted by a murderous hail of shots and shells unleashed by the Confederate line before them. At 6:30 p.m., Meade ordered a final assault but again was met by murderous fire. The 1st Maine Heavy Artillery Regiment, one of the leading regiments, lost 632 of its nine hundred men, considered the heaviest single battery loss of any regiment during the entire war. The failure of this attack was only emphasized by surrenders and losses of men. The past four days of fighting left the Federals with insignificant gains so Meade ordered his army to dig in and the siege began. Union casualties for this action were 11,386, of which 1,688 were killed, 8,513 wounded and 1,185 men missing or captured. The Confederates lost around 4,000 men: 200 killed, 2,900 wounded and 900 missing or captured. The

5th Maryland saw one man killed, five wounded 304 men captured, and another man missing.[410]

The area east of Petersburg had turned into a large camping area that would resemble a huge bustling city of white canvas, which sometimes would be obscured by smoke from hundreds of campfires. There would be the constant movement of men and equipment up and down the roads in all directions. The individual soldier's home in camp was a piece of canvas issued for use during an active campaign. Two men could button their individual pieces together to make a small "dog tent", as soldiers would call them. The tents could be easily pitched by tying each to a rifle stuck in the ground, or by stringing it to a bayonet or up to fence rails if available. Two soldiers were supposed to be able to crawl into it but the common joke was that only a dog could manage to crawl under this tent and stay dry in the rain.[411]

Sgt. Lenderking as well as the rest of the 5th Maryland were then dug into the trenches outside of Petersburg. For some, it would be long and boring despite the constant attempt of snipers to pick someone off in their front lines. Most were out in the open and subject to whatever the weather threw at them. In the rain, they would be soaked and muddy, while the hot humid weather would make their wool uniforms unbearable. On other days the sun would come out and bake them, their little piece of canvas the only shade available. Sgt. Lenderking and the rest of the band did all they could to cheer up and encourage the men with songs, while performing whatever duties were assigned them.

---

[410] Wikipedia, "Siege of Petersburg," 7–8 (Wikipedia-SoP, 2011pp.7-8).
[411] Service, The United States Dept. of the Interior, *The Civil War soldier, what was life as a soldier like in 1863?*, 1 (Service, Gettysburg National Military Parkp.1)

Often the conversation would be about the war and the events taking place around them. It would be especially discouraging to hear news of Federal actions that didn't seem to bring the end of the war any closer, such as the event that took place between June 21 and 23. Two Union corps were attempting to disrupt the Confederate Railroad but were caught by surprise from the rear. The troops of the 2nd Corps were able to rally around the earthen works they had constructed the night before and stabilize their lines just prior to darkness, which ended the fighting. The next day they advanced in the hopes of regaining lost ground but the Confederates had already pulled back and abandoned the earthen works they had captured. A heavy skirmish line was ordered out by Gen. Meade from the 6th Corps in an attempt to reach the welding railroad. The track had only begun to be dismantled when a large Confederate infantry force attached, taking numerous prisoners. Such operations were very costly to morale, as well as to their numbers, as Union casualties were 2,962, significantly greater than the Confederates loss of 572 men. The only point gained by all that loss of life was a short portion of track being destroyed.[412]

Another big event that the men in the trenches would discuss was the Wilson-Kautz raid that took place between June 22 and July 1. Early in the morning of June 22, 3,300 men and twelve guns organized into two batteries, which departed the Mount Sinai Church. They began to destroy railroad track and cars of the Weldon Railroad at Reams Station, seven miles south of Petersburg. Kautz's men moved to the west to Ford's Station and began destroying track, locomotives, and cars on the South Side Railroad.[413]

On the twenty-third, a Confederate force struck the rear of Wilson's column and started their pursuit. Wilson followed Kautz along the South Side Railroad, destroying about thirty miles of track as they went. Wilson and Kautz continued tearing up track south to the Staunton River Bridge at Roanoke Station where they encountered approximately one thousand men of the Home Guard. After heavy fighting they were forced to turn back to the east with Confederate forces attempting to catch up with them.

On the afternoon of June 28, Wilson and Kautz were surprised when they reached Stony Creek Station and found Confederate infantry blocking their path. A battle ensued as the men tried to break through but had to fall back when the left flank of the Union forces were threatened to be enveloped. The Federals changed direction and took a back road in the direction of Reams Station, but were again attacked late in the day. The Union cavalry managed to slip out of the trap under the cover of darkness and rode north to the Halifax Road for the supposed security of Reams Station.

---

[412] Wikipedia, "Siege of Petersburg," 8–9 (Wikipedia-SoP, 2011pp.8-9)
[413] Ibid., 9–10 (Wikipedia-SoP, 2011pp.9-10)

On June 29, Kautz approached Reams Station from the west, expecting to find friendly forces, but instead found a division of Confederate infantry blockading the approaches to the Halifax Road and the railroad. The Rebels had constructed strong earthen works from which they could defend their position easily. Still, Kautz's cavalry attacked but were unsuccessful, only to receive a counterattack against the flank of the Pennsylvanians. On the Stage Road to the north of the station, the Confederate brigades finally managed to outflank the Federal left and force them to turn. Wilson sent a message north requesting help from Meade at City Point.[414]

Under severe pressure from the Confederate forces, they felt as if they were caught in a trap and had no promise of immediate aid. Wilson and Kautz's Raiders burned their wagons and destroyed their artillery pieces, fleeing to the North before the reinforcements arrived. There were hundreds of Union men taken prisoner and what was to become known as, "a wild skedaddle." Sadly, at least three hundred escaped slaves who had joined the Union cavalrymen during the raid were abandoned during the retreat. The Raiders were finally to reenter federal lines around 2:00 p.m. on July 1 after destroying sixty miles of track, which took the Confederates several weeks to repair. The cost for the raid was high with 1,445 Union casualties, approximately a quarter of their force. Wilson counted 33 men killed, 108 wounded, and 674 captured or missing; Kautz accounted for 48 men killed, 153 wounded, and 429 captured or missing. Everyone seemed to have an opinion as to whether or not the raid was a success or a dismal failure.[415]

In late July, Grant ordered Hancock's Second Corps and two divisions of Sheridan's Cavalry Corps to cross the river to Deep Bottom by pontoon bridge and advance

---

[414] Wikipedia, "Siege of Petersburg," p. 11 (Wikipedia-SoP, 2011p.11)
[415] Wikipedia, "Siege of Petersburg," 10–11 (Wikipedia-SoP, 2011pp.10-11)

against the Confederate capital. Sheridan's first objective was to ride around the city to the north and west and cut the Virginia Central Railroad, which was supplying Richmond from the Shenandoah Valley. As the Union men prepared themselves for the move, the Confederates also got wind of the impending activity, which implies a significant structure of spies within the Union camp. Over 16,500 Confederate soldiers moved east on New Market Road and took up positions on the eastern face of New Market Height.

Hancock and Sheridan crossed the pontoon bridge, starting at 3:00 a.m. on July 27. The second Corps took up position on the east bank of Bailey's Creek, from New Market Road to near Fussell's Mill. Sheridan's cavalry captured the high ground on the right, overlooking the millpond, but they were quickly counterattacked and driven back. The Confederate works on the West bank of Bailey's Creek was formidable, so Hancock chose not to attack it, but instead spent the rest of the day performing reconnaissance.[416]

---

[416] Ibid.,11–12 (Wikipedia-SoP, 2011pp.11-12)

Hancock's men had become stymied at Bailey's Creek as more Confederate reinforcements were brought up from Petersburg. On the morning of July 28, Grant reinforced Hancock's position with a brigade from the 19th Corps. Sheridan's cavalrymen were just beginning an attack on the Confederate left wing when three brigades attacked Sheridan's right flank, thus disrupting the cavalry's advance. The attackers were surprised when they were unexpectedly hit by heavy fire from the new Union repeating carbines. Sheridan's cavalry reserves quickly pursued and captured nearly two hundred prisoners, the final action of the day. Having drawn sufficient Confederate soldiers out of Petersburg, the Union advance was terminated that same afternoon. Union casualties for what would be called the First Battle of Deep Bottom was sixty-two men killed, 340 men wounded and eighty-six missing or captured; the Confederate cavalry's losses were eighty men killed, 391 wounded, and 208 men missing or captured.

Early on the morning of July 30, the dark trenches were alive with activity. Brig. Gen. James H Ledlie's 1st Division was lined up in preparation for the assault, but he failed to brief the men on what was expected of them when their advance was to commence. The Brig. Gen. proceeded well behind the lines and got drunk, providing no leadership at all. Other divisions also lined up in line of battle behind Ledlie's 1st division and made ready for an advance. The 5th Maryland division was positioned further back as reserves, should the assault be successful. No one was quite sure what was to happen as they were mostly unaware of the secret tunnel that had been dug. The shaft or mine was around 511 feet long ending in a T-shape that extended out seventy-five feet in both directions. That section had also been filled with eight thousand pounds of gunpowder some twenty feet underneath the Confederate works.[417]

---

[417] Wikipedia, "Siege of Petersburg," 12 (Wikipedia-SoP, 2011p.12)

At 4:44 a.m., the charges exploded violently with a deafening roar. A huge amount of earth was thrown up into the air mixed with somewhere between 250 and 350 instantly killed Confederate soldiers and guns. The sky then proceeded to rain down that bloody debris over a large area. The crater that was created was 170 feet long, sixty to eighty feet wide and thirty feet deep. Ledlie's 1st Division was untrained and completely unprepared for the explosion and hesitated for about ten minutes before leaving their pre-advance entrenchments. When they finally did, instead of moving along the edge of the crater into the Confederate works, they moved down into the crater itself. Since this was not the plan movement, there were no ladders provided for the men to use in exiting the crater at the other end. The Confederates quickly rallied and gathered as many troops together as they could for a counterattack. Within an hour's time, the Confederates formed up around the crater and fired rifles and artillery down into its depths, making the Union forces the target of a "turkey shoot." The assault was failing miserably, but Burnside still sent more men down into the crater. Under considerable flanking fire, the next few hours was the scene of much bloodshed and slaughter. The remaining trapped men of the 9th Corps attempted to escape the crater in the onslaught,[418] climbing on one another's shoulders and digging foot holds.

---

[418] Wikipedia, "Siege of Petersburg," p. 13 (Wikipedia-SoP, 2011p.13)

Some Union troops eventually did find their way around the right side of the crater, advanced into the earthen works and assaulted the Confederate line. The Confederates were finally driven back for several hours in a vicious hand-to-hand combat. Finally, more rallied Confederates charged out of the sunken gully area about two hundred yards from the right side of the Union advance. The Federals were finally forced back from the Confederate earthen works toward their own lines to the east. Union casualties numbered 504 men killed, 1,881 wounded, and another 1,413 missing or captured. Confederate losses were approximately two hundred men killed, nine hundred wounded and four hundred men missing or captured.[419]

I'm sure that the men in the trenches around Petersburg, as well as Sgt. Lenderking, were relieved to hear the Brig. Gen. James H. Ledlie was dismissed for his poor conduct during the battle. It was bad enough he had not explained to the men leading the advance what was expected of them, but to be reportedly drunk well behind the lines, providing no

---

[419] Wikipedia, "Siege of Petersburg," 12–13 (Wikipedia-SoP, 2011pp.12-13)

leadership at all, was disgraceful. The men also had little respect for Burnside, who was also relieved of his command, as many of the casualties that were incurred that day were from the division he foolishly sent down into the pit with no means of escape.

Philip and the 5th Maryland continued their duties in the trenches with much repetitive action. A soldier's life did not always mean fighting. There were other fatigue duties that would be assigned such as gathering wood for the cook's fire or water details. Metal had to be polished and clean, especially muskets and pistols. Fields had to be cleared for parades and drills, plus many long hours were spent pacing up and down a well-trodden line while on guard duty. While in the trenches, they spent many lengthy stretches of just waiting and watching. Weather conditions made no difference, for these duties needed to be completed rain or shine, day or night, always watching for the enemy that might be lurking somewhere nearby. A furlough was hard to come by as every man was needed in the field, so few men ever had the chance to get away, let alone visit home.[420]

Still, the days dragged on. Another battle took place at Deep Bottom between August 14 and the 20th with little Federal success. The number of Union casualties was approximately 2,900 men, some due to heatstroke, while the Confederate casualties were somewhat less at 1,500 men. Occasionally, there would be some Union successes such as the operation against the Weldon Railroad near Globe Tavern. The Federals were always pleased to be able to tear up tracks belonging to the Confederate railroad and thus disrupt supply routes, such as the action taken August 18 to 21. Still, when you count the wounded and killed, it all came at a high cost. The Federal losses for that action were 251 men killed, 1,148 wounded, and 2,897 men missing or captured. The

---

[420] Service, The United States Dept. of the Interior, *The Civil War soldier, what was life as a soldier like in 1863?,* 1 (Service, Gettysburg National Military Parkp.1)

Confederates on the other hand lost 211 men killed, 990 wounded, and 419 missing or captured. The Confederates also lost a key section of the Weldon railroad and were forced to carry supplies by wagon thirty miles from the railroad at Stony Creek.[421]

Another bloody attack at Reams Station on August 25 did nothing for the morale of the men in the trenches. The 2nd Corps lost another 117 men killed, 439 wounded, and 2,048 missing or captured, out of which the Union cavalry loss 145 men. The Confederates on the other hand lost 814 men, including the cavalry's sixteen men killed, seventy-five wounded and three missing. The loss of all these men had resulted in the further disrupting of the Confederate supply lines.[422]

Possibly the most embarrassing incident to the Federals at Petersburg took place at 12:00 a.m. on September 16. The Confederates launched an attack just five miles East of Grant's headquarters and captured 2,486 beef cattle. Only 120 enlisted men and thirty civilians attended them while carrying no arms. The Confederates proceeded to drive their prize south toward Cook's Bridge while 2,100 Union cavalrymen pursued close behind. The Rebels simply retraced their steps back to Petersburg, where they turned the cattle over to the Confederate commissary department. The Confederates feasted upon the Federal cattle for days in front of the Union lines, taunting them regularly. For the men in the Union trenches eating hardtack, this would truly have been a tough reality to swallow.[423]

Many men in the 5th Maryland, including Sgt. Lenderking, were rapidly reaching the end of the army's three-year term. Many of them were pondering whether or not to reenlist, while others were finally looking forward to the

---

[421] Wikipedia, "Siege of Petersburg," 14–15 (Wikipedia-SoP, 2011pp.14-15)

[422] Ibid., 16–17 (Wikipedia-SoP, 2011pp.16-17)

[423] Wikipedia, "Siege of Petersburg," 17 (Wikipedia-SoP, 2011p.17)

chance of returning home to their families. Undoubtedly, receiving orders to march out to battle at this time would cause much anxiety in the men, particularly those looking forward to leaving for home.

(Note: the battle of Chaffin's Farm, New Market Heights, took place between September 29 and 30, 1864. It is listed that the 5th Maryland participated in this battle, yet the Union order of battle I found does not list them specifically. It does, however, list the 2nd Brigade of the 1st Division of the 18th Army Corps of which they were apart,[424] so I will include it here.)

---

[424] Civilwarintheeast.com, "5th Maryland Infantry Regiment" p. 1 (East, civikwarintheeast.com/USA/MD/5MD.php)

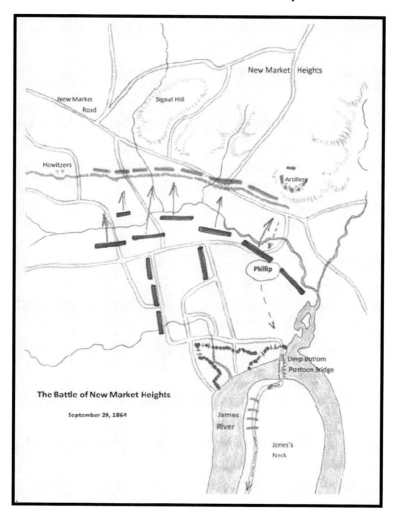

The Battle of New Market Heights
September 29, 1864

During the night of September 28–29, the 10th Corps and 18th Corps crossed the James River on a newly constructed pontoon bridge to Aiken's Landing. Their objective was to assault the Confederate defenses, Fort Harrison, north of the river on New Market Heights. The attack began at dawn as the Union 10th Corps, containing a brigade of Union colored troops, pushed hard against the Heights. There was much heroic fighting that took place that day, which would cause some to receive the medal of honor, Christian Fleetwood to name one. The Confederate forces quickly rallied and stopped the Union advance on Fort Harrison to push them back. The Union line was bolstered and they again stormed the Heights. The Confederate left flank was routed, thus turning the tide of battle. Confederate troops were forced to pull back to Fort Greg, Gilmore, and Johnson. The 10th Corps turned to the northwest along the New Market Road and moved against the secondary line of Rebel works. One Union division assaulted the small salient known as Fort Gilmore while the brigade of U.S. Colored Troops were led against Fort Greg just south of Fort Gilmore. Again these attacks were marked by heroism among the colored troops but despite their actions, the Union line was finally repulsed.[425]

Roughly during this same time, the 18th Corps under Maj. Gen. Edward Ord, led the assault against Fort Harrison to the West of New Market Heights. The 1st Division, which also should include the 5th Maryland, rushed across an open field and took cover in a slight depression just in front of the fort. After a few moments rest, the charge resumed and they successfully took the earthen works. The Confederate defenders broke to the rear, seeking refuge behind their second line of defenses. With all three brigade commanders either wounded or killed, the Union attackers had become disorganized. Ord personally attempted to rally the troops in order to continue their successful attack, but he too fell critically wounded, thus putting an end to the fighting.[426]

On September 30, the Confederate's uncoordinated counterattack was unsuccessful. The Confederates were forced to cut off the captured forts and shift more troops north toward Richmond, further weakening their lines at Petersburg. It is unlikely however that Philip would have been there on the day of the counterattack. He had to report back to Bermuda Hundred across the river and a little south of

---

[425] Wikipedia, "Battle of Chaffin's Farm / New Market" p. 2 (Wikipedia-BoCF, 2011)
[426] Ibid., 2–3 (Wikipedia-BoCF, 2011pp.2-3)

the location of the last battle, because on September 30 of 1864, Sgt. Philip Lenderking was mustered out. Since his pay had not been settled since January 1, it was time to get the Union books in order. His entire draw so far for the year was twelve dollars and seventy-eight cents which would be subtracted from that which he was to be paid. He was also due the soldier's allowance for the time he was in captivity, which amounted to thirty days at thirty cents a day, reaching a total of nine dollars. Three dollars were also subtracted for equipment lost. In the end, he was due one hundred dollars and discharged October 7, 1864 at Bermuda Hundred, Virginia by expiration of his terms of service.[427]

It is not surprising that Philip did not reenlist like some of the other men. His oldest brother Frederick was back home in Ohio with his hand permanently crippled from his wound in the Battle of Springfield, Missouri. His brother Rudolf had been killed in the battle of Fort Sanders in Knoxville, and his other brother George, they believed, was likely killed at the Battle of the Wilderness. His younger brother Lewis was then still serving in the hundred day regiment, which caused him some concern. Finally, he himself had been wounded in the head at Antietam, for which he would suffer back pains, headaches, and other medical problems for the rest of his life. It was time for him to go home.

After the Civil War, Philip Lenderking went to Lexington, Virginia to work until 1868, after which he migrated back to Baltimore where he had previously worked as a tinsmith in the Mount Clara Baltimore and Ohio Railroad repair shops. His reason for returning was to marry Mary Sophia Stieg, daughter of the Honorable Mr. Stieg of York, Pennsylvania. He wrote to Mr. Stieg on January 3, 1868, the following letter:[428]

---

[427] National Archives and Record Service, "Philip Lenderking" Company Muster-out Roll, April 30, 1864 (National Archives and Record Service, Microcopy No. 384, roll 142, Fifth Infantry, Ke – Li)
[428] Wormelle, *The Lenderking Family*, 10–11 (Wormelle, 1969pp.10-11)

I take up the pen to impart to you a matter which is very close to me. When I visited you and your family at Christmas, I did not have a mind to marry your daughter Sophia so soon, but times and people are changeable, and thus it has been with me. After a discussion I arrived at the decision to marry your daughter as soon as possible, namely on the 23rd of this month, for it has to happen sometimes. I should have liked to impart the matter to you in person, as such things can be discussed better by talking then by writing. But it went with me and Sophia as it goes with all young people; we had so much to discuss but forgot the main thing, namely that we should tell you everything and beg your advice, assent and blessing.

So I beg you now to grant me the above-mentioned and to pardon my forgetfulness in negligence. Upon what I shall consider myself one of the happiest people who live in this world.

With the hope that these lines find you in good health and that you will grant my request, I remain,

Your most devoted,

Philip H Lenderking

Best regards to everyone.

On January 23, 1868, Philip Heinrich Lenderking married Sophia Stieg. Their wedding photo that was taken a few months later is shown below:

Family Picture

Chapter 8
To the End of the War

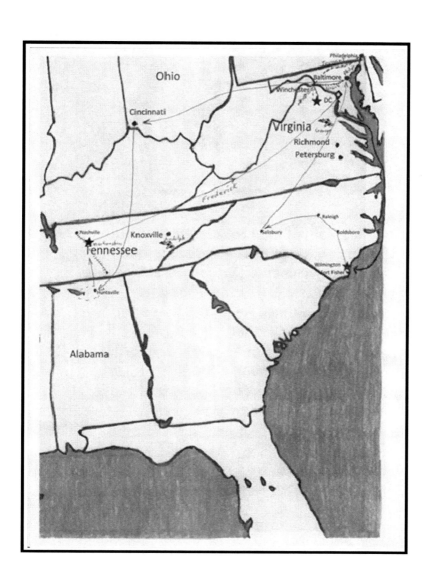

Lewis (Lenderking) Landerking
12th Maryland Infantry

The primary duty of the 12th Maryland Infantry was to guard the Baltimore and Ohio Railroad between Baltimore, Maryland, and Kearneysville for their hundred-day term until November, 1864. It was no small task protecting these long rigid lines of railroad track that were of great strategic importance. On July 7, 1864, a Confederate raiding party hit the railroad just twelve miles north of Washington, D.C. and again on October 14, John Mosby's Raiders derailed the Western express just eleven miles west of Harpers Ferry. It is estimated that by the end of the war over 18,000 men would have been occupied guarding this valuable lifeline.[429] A number of the men of the 12th Maryland Infantry reenlisted for one year and were assigned to the 1st Eastern Shore Maryland Infantry after completing their time of service. The

---

[429] Aronson, "Strategic Supply of Civil War Armies," 3 (Aronson, ...cox.net/.../STRATEGIC_SUPPLY_OF_CIV...p.3)

rest, including Private Lewis Lenderking, mustered out as a unit November 14, 1864. During this time they only lost two men by disease.[430] The Lenderking family was glad to see their youngest member safe at home at last.

Frederick Lenderking, (Second Enlistment)
Co. H, 181st Ohio Infantry Volunteers

Everyone in the family was aware that Lewis joined the infantry shortly after he had turned eighteen, but it appears no one in the family was aware of Frederick's plans. Despite the fact that his left hand possessed very little function as a result of his injury in the battle of Springfield Missouri, Frederick reenlisted, in the Ohio infantry.

His reenlistment appears in the 174th Regiment of Ohio Volunteer Infantry but his service was in the 181st. After careful examination of the documentation, it appears that at the time Frederick reenlisted, the 174th Regiment Infantry had already left the state of Ohio for Nashville, Tennessee on September 23, arriving on September 26.[431] Frederick's reenlistment was on September 28, after they had already departed. The 181st Ohio Infantry, on the other hand, mustered in for one year of service at camp Dennison, October 15, 1864, with 1,007 men under Col. John O'Dowd. It could be that the paperwork used was readily available because of the 174th regiment's recent enlistments; this could have been used for Frederick's enlistment in the 174th but also so that he could be held for the 181st that was just beginning its recruitment.

---

[430] Civilwarintheeast.com, "12th Maryland infantry Regiment" p. 1 (East, civilwarintheeast.com/USA/.../12MD.php)
[431] Stevens, "174th Ohio infantry" p. 1 (Stevens, http://www.ohiocivilwar.com/cw174.html)

[Declaration of Recruit form for Friedrich Lenderking, Cincinnati, Ohio]

You can see in the paperwork above that this is Frederick; it lists that this is his second enlistment and that the last place he served was in Fremont Bodyguard, along with his discharge date.

The paperwork also reveals that his occupation at the time was that of a boatman. He had previously been a saddler, but the injury of his hand prevented him from doing the kind of fine, detailed work needed in that trade. Along Cincinnati, Ohio, is the Ohio River where much commerce takes place, so he obviously changed his occupation and worked there up to this time. Frederick was now twenty-nine years old, with blue eyes, auburn hair, dark complexion and stood five feet, eight inches high. He received a one hundred dollar enlistment bounty, which I'm sure he could have used at the time. With the injury to his left hand, he could not be expected to stand on the line and load and fire a musket, so he was put in a support role, driving supply wagons as a teamster.[432]

(Note: in order to understand what Frederick's job really entailed you must understand a little bit about how the troops received supplies in the field. One of the primary ways supplies were delivered was by the waterways of the country. But that left many areas still some distance from any navigable waterway, so the railroad held a very high and strategic importance. This is why many battles were fought to

---

[432] The National Archives, "Frederick Lenderking, The 181st Ohio Infantry" Company Muster Roll, May 8, 1865 (Archives, National Archives and Record Service, Washington DC)

control these locations, as they were vital supply routes for both armies. Even with the many miles of track that existed at the time, you still had locations that were far from even the train tracks that crisscrossed the country, so supply depots were established at strategic locations called advanced depots. From there, military supply wagons carried the rations, ammunition, and other needed goods to temporary depots closer to the troops in the field. From those points, the various items were divided up and sent to the corps, division, and brigade levels. At the brigade, a regimental officer heading a special detail received the food and delivered it to the regimental commissary, who in turn distributed it to the separate companies for issue to each soldier.

Consideration had to be taken as to what supplies were most vital. Weapons and ammunition, for example, were expended in the constant skirmishing and battles, Whereas clothing and shelter for the most part could be ignored to a point under the right conditions because they lasted longer. Rations on the other hand, had to be provided constantly and in large amounts if the army was to maintain discipline, morale, and the energy it needed to fight.[433]

A wagon pulled by six horses could carry a maximum of two thousand pounds. If it had to clear hilly or rough terrain, the amount of weight would have to be reduced accordingly. It was estimated that each man required four pounds of transport capacity per day, so the basic assumption was that one wagon could supply five hundred men daily, if it could make a round-trip per day. So naturally, if you're two days away from the supplied depot, it would take twice as many wagons to supply the men in the field. So if you're looking at an army of one hundred thousand men that are approximately ten days of travel away from the supplied depot, you would require four

---

[433] Aronson, "Strategic Supply of Civil War Armies," 1 (Aronson, ...cox.net/.../STRATEGIC_SUPPLY_OF_CIV...p.1)

thousand wagons running constantly to supply that portion of the army. This is all further complicated by the fact that the animals pulling the wagons needed forty pounds of fodder per day, and the men running the wagons needed supplies of their own as well.[434] Wagons would be located on the wagon train by order of priority, ammunition, troops, artillery, and at the rear, quartermaster supplies.

Many of the wagons that were used at that time were a standard ten feet long. They could be pulled from either end and were covered by a canvas top containing the name of the corps, the unit and possibly the contents. A grease bucket for the wheels and a water bucket were hung under the back and near the rear axle. Also on a rear was the feed box used to feed the team of horses or mules that would stand on polls for feeding. Mostly mule teams were used to pull wagons as they were more available and had better endurance, despite the fact they were not as steady under fire. Although some horses were used, they were more readily found as artillery teams and ambulances where speed and stability was more important.[435])

The 181st Ohio Infantry left the state October 24 and reported to Huntsville, Alabama by October 29, attached to the District of Northern Alabama, where their primary duty was at Huntsville and Decatur where one man was wounded. In early November they moved north into Tennessee to Murfreesboro, in defense of the Nashville and Chattanooga railroad.[436]

---

[434] Aronson, "Strategic Supply of Civil War Armies," 5 (Aronson, ...cox.net/.../STRATEGIC_SUPPLY_OF_CIV...p.5)
[435] Cruise, "Mule-Drawn Wagon Trains, the Cleveland Civil War Roundtable, 2001, 2008" pp. 1-2 (Cruise, clevelandandcivilwarroundtable.com/.../wag...)
[436] Stevens, "181st Ohio Infantry" p. 1 (Stevens, http://www.ohiocivilwar.com/cw181.html)

On December 4, a Confederate force attached Blockhouse No. 7 that was protecting the railroad crossing at Overall Creek. Finding it too well defended and not able to make any headway, the Confederates split their force the next day and moved towards Murfreesboro. One Rebel column attached Blockhouse No. 4 while the other attacked the fortress on the nearby hill, capturing both. More Rebels came in and joined the attack force and continued the advance towards Murfreesboro in two separate columns. The Union forces retreated back into the Fortress Rosencrantz fortifications with the Confederates making camp just outside the town. The next day the Confederates attacked with little success and the battle degraded into a staring contest between both armies. On the morning of the seventh, two Union brigades moved out and again engaged the Confederates, resulting in part of the Confederate force breaking and running and the other part making a more orderly retreat. In the attack, the Confederates had managed to destroy some railroad track, several blockhouses, and some homes, and temporarily disrupt Union operations in the area. The Union Army felt it was nothing more than a minor irritation.[437] [438] The 181st Ohio Infantry saw one man killed and another sixteen wounded in this action.[439]

On December 7, the last day of the siege of Murfreesboro, the 181st Ohio advanced to Wilkinson's Pike just outside of Murfreesboro. They eventually moved back into the town but again advanced back to that same position December 13–14. Frederick continued his supply runs for the regiment at Murfreesboro until December 24 when the 181st Ohio moved to Columbia, Tennessee, and then on toward Washington, D.C. the same day.[440]

In January of 1865, they were switched to the 3rd Brigade, 2nd Division, 23rd Army Corps, Army of the Ohio, Department of North Carolina. On January 15 they boarded ships and headed south. On February 9 they arrived at their destination, Fort Fisher, North Carolina, where they joined Sherman.[441] The scene they viewed upon their arrival must have been something to behold, as the battle for Fort Fisher had just concluded and there were some fifty warships in the area.

---

[437] CWSAC, "Battle Summaries, "Murfreesboro, Reference #:TN037, Preservation Priority:II.4 (Class D), Stone River NB" p. 1 (CWSAC Battle Summaries, nps.gov/hps/abpp/battles/tn037.htm)
[438] Wikipedia, "Third Battle of Murfreesboro" p. 2 (Wikipedia, ...wikipedia.org/.../Third_Battle_of_Murfreesboro) (Wikipedia, ...wikipedia.org/.../Third_Battle_of_Murfreesboro)
[439] Historical Data Systems, Inc., "181st Ohio infantry" p. 1 (Historical Data Systems, PO Box 35, Duxbury,MA 02331)
[440] Stevens, "181st Ohio Infantry" p. 1 (Stevens, http://www.ohiocivilwar.com/cw181.html)
[441] Stevens, "181st Ohio Infantry" p. 1. (Stevens, http://www.ohiocivilwar.com/cw181.html) (Stevens, http://www.ohiocivilwar.com/cw181.html)

Operations against Hoke began on February 11 and would last through the fourteenth.[442] These operations commenced with an attack against the Sugar Loaf Line where they drove back the Confederate defenders. The Union troops were then carried to the west bank of the Cape Fear River to prepare for the attack on Fort Anderson. The Union gunboats in the river deployed a fake monitor, causing the Confederates to detonate their water mines. They then proceeded to move in and bombard the fort, destroying all twelve of their guns. The Union troops then moved into the Fort through swampy ground and captured it quite easily as the Confederates were already in retreat. By February 19, the Union troops had caught up with the retreating Confederates, after being ferried back across the river. The Federals again had to wade through swampy water to attack the Confederate line. The Confederates were then routed from their positions and 375 were taken prisoner along with two pieces of artillery. This placed the gunboats within range of Wilmington, which the Confederates quickly abandoned. On February 22 the Union forces marched in and took possession of the town. The town of Wilmington was of strategic importance as its capture closed the last major port of the Confederate States. The town up to this time had been a major part of the blockade runners, running tobacco, cotton, and other goods to Britain, the Bahamas, and Bermuda.[443][444]

The 181st Ohio continued to advance northward towards Goldsboro on March 6 through the twenty-first.[445] From the timeline, it appears they arrived in the area as the battle of Bentonville was coming to an end. General Sherman had

---

[442] Ibid., p. 1 (Stevens, http://www.ohiocivilwar.com/cw181.html)
[443] Timeline X, "The Battle of Wilmington, February 11, 1865–February 22, 1865" p. 1 (Timeline, www.xtimeline.com/evt/view.aspx?id=2...)
[444] Wikipedia, "Battle of Wilmington, 2011" pp. 1-2 (Wikipedia, en.wikipedia.org/../Battle_of_Wilmington)
[445] Stevens, "181st Ohio Infantry" p. 1 (Stevens, http://www.ohiocivilwar.com/cw181.html)

been chasing the Confederates up through the Carolinas, constantly whittling their numbers down and keeping them on the move. Then on April 9, Lee surrendered at the Appomattox courthouse, causing the Confederates' General Johnston to meet with General Sherman between the lines. After three separate days of discussion, April 17, 18, and 26, 1865, Johnston surrendered his Confederate Army of 89,270 soldiers. After the surrender, Sherman issued ten days' rations to the hungry Confederate soldiers, as well as horses and mules for them to use on their farms. Some food rations were also given to the local population in the area.[446]

---

[446] Wikipedia, "Joseph E. Johnston, 2011" p. 9 (Wikipedia, en.wikipedia.org/wiki/Joseph_E_Johnston)

During this same time, the 181st Ohio advanced on Raleigh from April 10 to the 14 and occupied the town. By April 26 they had moved on to the Benton house where they heard of the surrender of Johnston. As conditions in the area were normalized, they had duty first at Raleigh, then Greensboro and Salisbury till July. The records show that on June 17, 1865, Frederick was relieved of his duty as a teamster in the supplied train and was ordered to report to his company for duty.[447] The remaining 850 men under Col. John E. Hudson mustered out July 29, 1865, and returned to camp Denison in Ohio by way of Baltimore, Maryland.[448]

Unfortunately, no one seems to know what happened to Frederick after the war. All records of him just seemed to vanish at that point. Whether he traveled west as many did after the Civil War or died for an unknown reason prior to the next census is still a mystery.

Tougart Snyder
12th Pennsylvania Cavalry

In northern Virginia, colder weather had slowed down the frequency of attacks from those loyal to the Confederacy, but the attacks did continue. There was a skirmish on November 12 as Hilltown and Mount Zion Church and another took place on November 24 at Newtown, where one man went missing. Then another attack took place November 29 at Charlestown while the 12th was on detachment.[449] That attack of two hundred Confederates left one man killed, one

---

[447] The National Archives, "Frederick Lenderking, The 181st Ohio Infantry" S.O. No. 103, June 17, 1865 (Archives, National Archives and Record Service, Washington DC)
[448] Stevens, "181st Ohio Infantry" p. 1 (Stevens, http://www.ohiocivilwar.com/cw181.html)
[449] Civilwarintheeast.com, "12th Maryland infantry Regiment" p. 3 (East, civilwarintheeast.com/USA/.../12MD.php)

wounded[450] and nineteen horses stolen. The Rebels only lost one man killed and three wounded.

On December 15, 1864, Col. Poe was discharged and Capt. Marcus A. Reno (whose name will be better remembered in history for the battle of the Little Bighorn than it will be for the Civil War) of the first regular cavalry was commissioned to succeed him. The 12th Pennsylvania cavalry was assigned to the 3rd Infantry Division in the west. Capt. Reno, sensing a lack of discipline, immediately began issuing orders making life much stricter for the regiment. His orders were very detailed, including such find points as to how to go about picking up trash around the camp.[451]

Pvt. Snyder, as well as the rest of the regiment, would have found drilling in the shivering-cold months and practicing with their weaponry very difficult. As mentioned before, the 12th was lacking in equipment. Many of the men still didn't have essential carbines, and the ones that did were very used and imperfect ones. It is therefore not hard to believe that in one reported instance, at a practice firing, ten out of fifty failed to go off. Lack of cleaning the weapons did account for some of the misfires, but far too many were just plain defective. There was an attempt by some of the men to improve the situation. but their efforts had little effect.[452]

On December 21 of the previous year, there was a report that Col. Mosby had been mortally wounded; he had been shot in his abdomen two inches below the navel and was left for dead. As a result, there was an unusual lull in the area's guerrilla activity, but this would be short-lived as he recovered in two months time.[453] On January 17 one of their

---

[450] Historical Data System, Inc., "Regimental Casualty Analysis, 12 PA Cavalry" p. 1 (Historical Data System, PO Box 35, Duxbury, MA 02331)
[451] Maier, *Leather & Steel, The 12th Pennsylvania Cavalry in the Civil War*, 279–289 (Maier, 2001pp.279-280)
[452] Ibid., 280 (Maier,2001p.280)
[453] Wikipedia, "John S Mosby," 5 (Wikipedia, en.wikipedia.org/wiki/John_S_Mosbyp.5)

spies was captured in camp, and on the nineteenth, the guerrillas derailed a freight train near Duffield's Station. At the end of the month, the regiment secretly moved out to smash and destroy all ferry boats up and down the Shenandoah River. Their orders were to destroy all ferry boats from Harpers Ferry all the way up to Barry's Ferry. Command didn't want anyone to realize what they were doing, so the Rebels could not hide or save a few boats for the use of Confederate guerrillas.[454]

On the cold, dark night of January 30, shortly after 11:00 p.m., the whole regiment was awakened abruptly by the sound of a shot from a picket inside their camp. Startled, everyone grabbed their carbines and pistols and ran out of their huts, many only half dressed in their long-johns. In the light of the scattered camp fires, several of Mosby's men were seen mounting their horses at the stable area, gathering horses. A few others were scattered about the camp holding several prisoners. Realizing that their camp had been invaded, pandemonium set in. The men of the 12th started shouting and everyone raised their arms to fire on the Raiders, who were grossly outnumbered. By this time the Raiders were riding as hard as they could down the main road of the camp. They rode low in the saddle toward the gate with eight horses in tow, firing into the huts with their pistols as they galloped. Within the camp the 12th's responded with flashes of fire and cracks of shots erupting with smoke. Bullets followed, whizzing by the Raiders on all sides and from all directions as they exited the gate and made their escape. Moments later, on a Charlestown street, Union troops posted there, took their turn at them. Despite the many rounds shot at the escaping confederates, it seemed none were hit. It was soon discovered, however, that a number of men were missing, probably captured.[455]

---

[454] Maier, *Leather & Steel, The 12th Pennsylvania Cavalry in the Civil War*, 281 (Maier, 2001p.281)
[455] Maier, *Leather & Steel, The 12th Pennsylvania Cavalry in the Civil War*, 282–283 (Maier, 2001pp.282-283)

(Note: It was not until after the war that Confederate documents showed that on that night, a group of thirty of Mosby's men were out to do damage to the B&O Railroad. Finding it too heavily guarded, half of their man returned to their camp while the other half decided to look for targets of opportunity. In the dark, they managed to capture two men on patrol and forced them at gunpoint to disclose the night's countersigns. Although wary of a trap, they wanted to find out if the countersign worked. The Raiders soon found two more men on picket duty and tried giving them the countersign. Having received the proper countersign, the two men relaxed their guard and quickly were taken prisoner. It was reported that one of those men was very talkative with the revolver aimed at him. But it seems he was not giving all the correct information as he provided a false name of an officer. A short time later, a four-man patrol was spotted. The Raiders gave the countersign and used the false name of the officer they had received. Despite the fact that the name was incorrect, the patrol still fell for it. They also relaxed their guard and were promptly captured as well. All these prisoners were sent back under guard as the remaining Raiders moved on. Next they used the name on the picket at the entrance of the camp and promptly captured him. Now in the camp, a man of the 12th exited one of the tents for firewood, so they quickly grabbed him before he could cause alarm. Their plan, it seems, was to steal as many horses as they could. Unfortunately when they approached another picket and demanded his surrender, the Raider got a bullet shot at him instead. With the alarm now raised, they had no recourse but to flee the area as fast as they could with whatever they had managed to steal thus far.)[456]

Col. Reno was not very happy about the total chaos that had taken place during the recent raid. The following morning, it is recorded that he called the whole regiment out to dress them down. He proceeded to question their manhood, their courage, their patriotism, and then proceeded to issue orders and instructions as to how to properly respond should something like this ever happen again. It seems that he was interested in having the officers come out, assess the situation and issue the appropriate commands to the men who in turn would closely carry those orders out.[457]

I am sure the men in closest proximity to the Raiders, realized the urgency of the situation. The question was, if they quietly stood there waiting for an officer to come and assess the situation, would they even have time for a response? And those in the back part of the camp, far from where the raiders were located, must have felt the words Col. Reno spoke were unfair to them. I am sure Pvt. Snyder and the rest of the Regiment were very bewildered by this whole affair.

Three days later another train was reported derailed by about thirty Raiders. The O.R. Report of February 4, 1865, states Col. Reno had two contingents of men, one led by 1st

---

[456] Maier, *Leather & Steel, The 12th Pennsylvania Cavalry in the Civil War*, 281–282 (Maier, 2001pp.281-282)
[457] Maier, *Leather & Steel, The 12th Pennsylvania Cavalry in the Civil War*, 283–284 (Maier, 2001pp.283-284)

Lieutenant Guild the other by 2nd Lieutenant Chase, go after the thirty Raiders. In the darkness, 2nd Lieutenant Chase's detachment fired upon the other detachment, wounding one man. Meanwhile, Mosby's Raiders escaped. It quickly got around camp what had happened and about Col. Reno ordering the arrest of 2nd Lieutenant Chase over the incident.[458] The regiment didn't have long to find out the fate of 2nd Lieutenant Chase. Ten days later, without a court-martial, he was discharged from service.

Besides the talk about officers' actions on and off the field, as the men sat around the campfire during their free time, they would also talk of their experiences while out on patrol. Some would talk of their trips on the side called, "barn-yards". Trips like these where taken by slipping off quietly to forage for different supplies that they felt were needed. They would also have stories of people who were killed, such as the man and his friend who, stumbled upon a Confederate in a barn. As the man attempted to make his escape from them, the musket fire brought other Butternuts (another name for Confederate soldiers because of the color of their uniform), to the scene. The one who escaped lived to tell of how his friend was shot multiple times and killed while trying to climb over the garden fence and escape. Stories like this would inflame the men against Mosby's Rangers (another name for Mosby's Raiders) feeling such a killing unnecessary as he had no real chance to escape or defend himself.[459] Reports of casualties for the 12th Pennsylvania Cavalry from the first half of February reports 2 men were killed and 1 man wounded.[460]

By mid-February, the cold was giving way for warmer weather. Cold rains were starting to come down periodically as

---

[458] Reno, "Affair at Harpers Ferry February 3, 1865 (Detached)" CHAPT. LVIII, P. 455-95 (Col. M a Reno, O. R. Report, National Archives, Washington DC)
[459] Maier, *Leather & Steel, The 12th Pennsylvania Cavalry in the Civil War*, 285–286 (Maier, 2001pp.285-286)
[460] Historical Data System, Inc., "Regimental Casualty Analysis, 12 PA Cavalry" p. 1 (Historical Data System, PO Box 35, Duxbury, MA 02331)

the ground was beginning to thaw. The thick sticky mud was everywhere you went. For Pvt. Snyder and the rest of the regiment, drilling in the mud would now become a regular routine, if they were not trapped in their tents. Keeping themselves and their equipment clean must have been a daunting task. By February 20, Mosby's Rangers were spotted in Loudoun Valley along with three companies of the 6th Virginia Cavalry, one company from the 12th Virginia Cavalry and more coming in. Generally there was an estimated 1,200 to 1,400 men gathering for future hostilities.[461]

It was around this time that the 3rd Massachusetts Cavalry, which was doing the same duty as the 12th, was recalled to Harpers Ferry from Duffield's Station where they had been all winter. The men of the 12th were now left to cover all the territory from Charlestown to Halltown. They were especially supposed to watch the Shenandoah River area around Berryville. Even so, things were calm for a while. The Confederate threat was still existent but not very active. The 12th started increasing their patrols as the weather became more favorable. It was important to keep watch on the lower Valley and areas near Mosby's men in order to keep them contained.[462] During this time, skirmishes were on the increase with the Rebels.

As if the Confederate presence was not enough, on March 4, 1865, Col. Reno, remembering the raid of January 30, chose this time to put on a drill to see how the men would react to a similar situation. Several men, remembering the scolding they had received earlier, reportedly went and hid behind trees and peeked around to see what was happening. Several guards were not found at their post. But worst of all, the duty officers were totally absent from camp. They were taking what is called a "French furlough," which resulted in

---

[461] Ibid., 289 (Maier, 2001p.289)
[462] Maier, *Leather & Steel, The 12th Pennsylvania Cavalry in the Civil War*, 289–290 (Maier, 2001pp.289-290).

the arrest of three men. Col. Reno was not very happy or impressed by the results of the drill.[463]

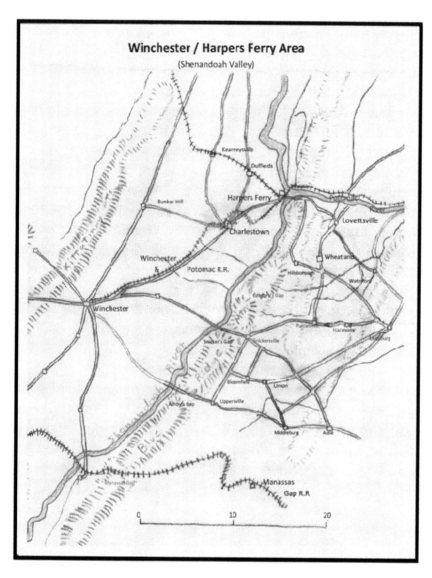

On March 8, new information started to arrive about Mosby's build up. Later that same day, it was reported Mosby and about three hundred men were spotted crossing the

---

[463] Ibid., 284 (Maier, 2001p.284)

Shenandoah River at Snicker's Ferry. It was reported they were headed toward the village of White Post, then through one of the gaps in the Blue Ridge Mountains. This caused some concern as Mosby's Rangers and the rest of these men were now on the same side of the mountains as the 12th. Patrols were therefore increased in the area in between them to keep Mosby's men from doing more damage.[464]

A few days later, Col. Reno returned unexpectedly from his furlough in Harrisburg. The regiment was quickly given the order to prepare to move out and for each man to take eight days rations with him. They moved out early the next morning, around 6:00 a.m., and by 9:30 a.m. they were crossing the river at Harpers Ferry. They joined several other cavalry units and proceeded south through Lovettsville, Virginia. As they advanced they set fires to haystacks and other forage found in the possession of people that they felt were disloyal to the Union. The 12th had a minor skirmish along the way with a small group of butternuts and captured six. At the end of the day they rendezvoused with an infantry regiment and encamped at Hillsborough. The night's rest was laced with the intermittent shots fired at pickets.[465]

The next morning, the infantry regiment headed south while the cavalry went through Wheatland, Waterford, and Leesburg, continuing to destroy anything they felt the Confederate raiders could use. The 12th then turned west and started its trek toward Purcellville to meet up with the infantry, which it did about midday. A roving skirmish line was set up to protect the column as it continued to move toward Purcellville with little resistance.[466]

The column had passed through Harmony, "Hamilton Village," with the 12th Pennsylvania scouting in the lead as the column searched for barns to check and forage to

---

[464] Ibid., 291 (Maier, 2001p.291)
[465] Reno," O R report" CHAPT. LVIII, p. 535-95 (Col. M A Reno, March 29, 1865,)
[466] Ibid. CHAPT. LVIII, p. 535-95 (Col. M A Reno, March 29, 1865,)

destroy. Up until this time, the day had been uneventful. The repetitious marching and stopping to torch the haystacks and search barns had become routine. As the 12th reached an area about a mile and a half east of Purcellville, about six to twelve of Mosby's Rangers were spotted in the center of the road. The Rebels dashed off with the 12th right behind them. Suddenly the thick underbrush to the left side abruptly erupted with the firing of revolvers and chilling Rebel cries. It appeared as if all of Mosby's Rangers were charging out toward them. They hit the flank and the front of the 12th Pennsylvania as hard as they could, crashing like a great gray wave into the Union blue column. Like the swirling of water in the rapids, the two opposing cavalries mixed together in mortal combat. For several minutes the pistols cracked and flashed with smoke, which mixed with dust kicked up by the horse's hooves. The sounds of grunting and whinnying horses and sabers clanging entered the mix. But Mosby's men had the upper hand, and in time the 12th Pennsylvania broke and fell back toward Harmony," Hamilton Village."[467][468]

The running battle continued as Mosby's men stayed close behind the 12th, firing into their retreating ranks. Back near Harmony, the 12th turned and tried to rally and clashed desperately against the Raiders. The clash was desperate and violent, but the day was not lost. Some of the Union infantry had taken cover behind the hedgerow not far off and used a well-directed volley into the confederates. They burst out of the thicket and charged the embattled cavalries. Now losing the upper hand, the Raiders quickly retired from the battle. With the current fight seemingly at an end, the regiment made camp for the night on a farm located nearby.[469] During the

---

[467] Reno, "O R report" CHAPT. LVIII, p. 535-95 (Col. M A Reno, March 29, 1865,)
[468] Maier, *Leather & Steel, The 12th Pennsylvania Cavalry in the Civil War*, 293–294 (Maier, 2001pp.293-294)
[469] Reno, "O R report" CHAPT. LVIII, p. 535-95 (Col. M A Reno, March 29, 1865,)

battle, one officer and five men were killed with an additional two officers and seventeen men wounded.[470]

That cold, rain-soaked night of March 22 wasn't very restful. Intermittent gunfire between Ranger snipers and Union pickets could be heard throughout the night. In the morning hours the Union troops burned the barn and wagon shed that was full of corn, not wanting the Raiders to get any of it. Col. Reno ordered his column southward toward the village of Bloomfield as they continued their mission to destroy food and forage that would aid the enemy. Late in the day, as they were nearing Bloomfield, a number of Mosby's scouts again skirmished sharply with the 12th Pennsylvania.[471]

The next day, March 23, the Union forces moved slowly near Moose Creek[472] on their five to six mile trip to Upperville. Between the burning, searching, and skirmishing with the Rebels, the Union forces kept extremely busy. March 24 was much the same with the Federal column now turning east toward Middleburg, still shadowed by the Rangers. The only real show the Rangers put on that day was a failed attempt to attack the wagon train near the Goose Creek Bridge, but with artillery and infantry there ready for them,

---

[470] Gayley, "12th Pennsylvania Cavalry Pennsylvania Volunteers" p.8 (Gayley, pa-roots.com/.../12thcavorg.htmlp.8)

[471] Reno, "O R report" CHAPT. LVIII, p. 535-95 (Col. M A Reno, March 29, 1865,)

[472] Civilwarintheeast.com, "12th Maryland infantry Regiment" p. 3 (East, civilwarintheeast.com/USA/.../12MD.php)

they quickly changed their minds. By the end of the day, the 8th Illinois Cavalry and a section of artillery met up with Reno's column. The following day, the entire Union column turned back northward toward Harpers Ferry. They passed through the village of Union and Purcellville with little to no resistance from the Confederate Raiders. Upon returning to their base camp, the 12th resumed their normal routine, which lasted for several days.[473][474]

March 28, the 12th Pennsylvania found themselves taking inventories and disposing of accumulated extraneous properties. They had orders to prepare for relocation. On April 1st they were up at 5:00 a.m., and by 8:00 a.m. had begun a very slow, hard, and dusty trip. It was so slow in fact that they barely made it to the outskirts of Berryville, where they camped for the night. The next day at 7:00 a.m. they resumed their march. They soon discovered this was really a huge reconnaissance in forced expedition up the valley. By the end of the day they were still only about two miles south of Winchester.

On April 3, the column continued to slowly work their way up the Valley Turnpike. But today the news of the capture of Richmond Virginia raced up and down the column like a wildfire. That night there was talk of peace and home, but there was also the dread that with the end of the war insight, one might end up being the last to die. On the next morning, the 12th Pennsylvania hurried their breakfast, for they had the advanced part of the column. At Ebensburg, they charged some Rebels and drove them through the town into the mountains. When the 12th made camp that night near Mt. Jackson, they didn't know at that time, the regiment's last fight was over.[475][476]

---

[473] Maier, *Leather & Steel, The 12th Pennsylvania Cavalry in the Civil War*, 301–302 (Maier, 2001pp.301-302)

[474] Reno, "O R report" CHAPT. LVIII, p. 535-95 (Col. M A Reno, March 29, 1865,)

[475] Maier, *Leather & Steel, The 12th Pennsylvania Cavalry in the Civil War*, 303 (Maier, 2001p.303)

With the reconnaissance concluded, the 12th Pennsylvania journeyed back down the valley to Winchester, where they set up another base camp. It was on the trek back down to Winchester, April 7, when everyone learned of the Confederate defeat at Sailors Creek and the capture of one-third of Lee's army. In honor of the victory, in one accord, all the men in the 12th gave three cheers, "Huzzah! Huzzah! Huzzah!"[477] in April, their duty assignment was at Winchester and in the Shenandoah Valley attached to the Cavalry of the Army of the Shenandoah.[478] Around midnight of April 9, the 12th Pennsylvania, now in a new base camp, received word of the surrender of Lee's army at Appomattox Courthouse. A two hundred gun salute took place and a three-day celebration commenced. Great cheering and rejoicing could be heard throughout the camp. The war was over! There was a grand parade in the town nearby and two companies of Rebels came in and surrendered. But the 12th had to get back to work, because even though the war was won, they still had a job to do. Their job was now that of peacekeeper until such time that a local government could be reestablished.[479] The regiment was also to help in the processing and paroling of the thousands of butternuts who were surrendering every day.[480]

On April 16, a delegation of Mosby's Rangers approached the pickets just outside Winchester. They came in under a white flag, which was fashioned out of a white handkerchief. Among them was the second in command of Lieutenant Colonel William Chapman and William Mosby,

---

[476] Gayley, "12th Pennsylvania Cavalry Pennsylvania Volunteers," 8–9 (Gayley, pa-roots.com/.../12thcavorg.htmlpp.8-9).

[477] Maier, *Leather & Steel, The 12th Pennsylvania Cavalry in the Civil War*, 304 (Maier, 2001p.304).

[478] Civilwarintheeast.com, "12th Maryland infantry Regiment" p. 3 (East, civilwarintheeast.com/USA/.../12MD.php).

[479] Maier, *Leather & Steel, The 12th Pennsylvania Cavalry in the Civil War*, 305 (Maier, 2001p.305).

[480] Gayley, "12th Pennsylvania Cavalry Pennsylvania Volunteers," 9 (Gayley, pa-roots.com/.../12thcavorg.htmlp.9).

the younger brother of their leader. They came bearing a letter from Mosby to the Union leader here at camp. They were promptly escorted to Col. Reno's tent where they talked for a spell and finally were escorted to Maj. Gen. Hancock's headquarters to deliver their message. The main message basically stated that Mosby was not prepared to surrender but would participate in a cease-fire until such time as he could learn more concerning the fate of the Confederacy. The Union officers confirmed the Confederacy had ceased to exist. An order was also given that Mosby report to them in a few days.[481] It appears that Col. Mosby did not report in as requested because shortly thereafter, Maj. Gen. Hancock placed a $5,000 bounty on his head, but he eluded capture until the end of June, when Ulysses S. Grant intervened directly in the case and paroled Mosby.[482]

How strange these days must have felt to Private Snyder and the rest of the regiment. As time went on, it must have seemed odd to pass Confederate soldiers in arms in this peaceful setting. In the town, more and more people continued to come in and congregate. Both blue and gray were passing each other without hostilities. For the men of the 12th, in between their patrols and picket duty, which amounted more to a police duty, there were also duties such as drills, cleaning equipment, and inspections. But in their spare time that was steadily on the increase, there was plenty of lager to drink as well. The men were looking forward to going home.

On June 2˙ enlistments of a number of the one-year men had finally come to an end. They were mustering out and allowed to go home. Those left behind became even more

---

[481] Maier, *Leather & Steel, The 12th Pennsylvania Cavalry in the Civil War*, 305–306 (Maier, 2001p.305) (Maier, 2001pp.305-306).
[482] Wikipedia, "John S Mosby," 5 (Wikipedia, en.wikipedia.org/wiki/John_S_Mosby)

restless and longed to head home themselves; time just seemed to drag.[483]

On July 10, the orders finally arrived to send the regiment home. The morning of July 12, at 2:00 a.m., everyone leaped out of their racks and hurriedly packed for their trip. At 4:00 a.m. they started their march to Woodstock. The next day they departed Woodstock at 3:00 a.m. and arrived at Stephenson's Train Depot at 2:00 p.m. in the afternoon. They soon found out their train would not arrive for several more days. After so much waiting, the day before the train came turned into a serious celebration. When the train finally arrived in Philadelphia, the 12th marched to their barracks at Camp Cadwallader. There, they joined six other PA regiments and were relieved of their arms.[484] On July 20, in accordance with General Order #83, my great-great-grandfather Taugart Snyder mustered out of the 12th Pennsylvania Cavalry along with the rest of the remaining men.[485] [486] They were all finally sent home to their families and loved ones as the Civil War 12th Pennsylvania cavalry ceased to exist.

---

[483] Maier, *Leather & Steel, The 12th Pennsylvania Cavalry in the Civil War*, 310 (Maier, 2001p.310)
[484] Ibid., 312–313 (Maier, 2001pp.312-313)
[485] Gayley, "12th Pennsylvania Cavalry Pennsylvania Volunteers" p. 9 (Gayley, pa-roots.com/.../12thcavorg.html)
[486] Civilwarintheeast.com, " 12th Maryland infantry Regiment" p. 3 (East, civilwarintheeast.com/USA/.../12MD.php)

To the Honorable the Judges of the District Court for the City and County of Philadelphia.

The Petition of *Taugart Snyder* A *Private* Soldier in the *Vol* Army of the United States, Respectfully Sheweth:

That he enlisted in Company *H. Capt. George W. Henries*, *12th* Regiment, *Penn. Cavalry* Army of the United States, on the *14th* day of *Sept.* A.D. 18*64* and was honorably discharged from the service on the *First* day of *June* 18*65*; and that he has resided in the United States for a period of one year and upwards, and that it is bona fide his intention to become a citizen of the United States, and of renouncing forever all allegiance and fidelity to any foreign Prince, Potentate, State or Sovereignty whatever, and particularly to the *King of Saxony*

He therefore prays that, on his making the proof and taking the oath prescribed by law, he may be admitted a Citizen of the United States of America,

and he will ever pray, &c.

Traugott Schneider

Earnest Hermann a Citizen of the United States of America, being duly sworn according to law, saith, that he knows and is well acquainted with *Taugart Snyder* the Petitioner; that to his knowledge he has resided in the United States one year, and during the said period he has behaved as a man of good moral character, attached to the principles of the Constitution of the United States, and well disposed to the good order and happiness of the same and that he is the identical person who enlisted in Company *H. 12th Penn Cavy* Regiment, as set forth in the discharge hereto annexed.

Sworn in open Court
30th Sept. 1872

Alex: P Keyser for Prothonotary.

1321 North 4th

I, *Taugart Snyder* do swear that the contents of my petition are true; that I will support the Constitution of the United States, and I now renounce and relinquish any title or order of nobility to which I am now or hereafter may be entitled; and I do absolutely and entirely renounce and abjure all allegiance and fidelity to any foreign Prince, Potentate, State or Sovereignty whatever, and particularly to the *King of Saxony* of whom I was born a subject.

Sworn in open Court,
30th day of *Sept.* A.D. 187*2*

Traugott Schneider

221 Cumberland

As the document shown above may be hard to read, I shall repeat it here in larger print.

United States of America

Be it Remembered, That at the District Court for the city and County of Philadelphia, held at Philadelphia in the Commonwealth of Pennsylvania, in the United States of America, on the _Thirteenth_ day of _September_ in the year of our Lord 18_72_ _Taugart Snyder_ appeared and exhibited a petition to said Court, praying to be admitted to become a CITIZEN OF THE UNITED STATES; and it appearing to said court that the said _Taugart Snyder_ was a regularly ENLISTED SOLDIER of the United States, that he enlisted on the _14th_ day of _September_ A.D. 186_4_, was honorably discharged from said service on the _First_ day of _June_ A.D. 186_5_

And Whereas, By an act of Congress approved the 17th day of July, 1862, it is provided as follows: "That any alien, of the age of twenty-one years and upwards, who has enlisted, or shall enlist in the armies of the United States, either the regular or the volunteer forces, and have been or shall be here after honorably discharged, may be admitted to become a citizen of the United States, upon this petition without any previous declaration of his intent to become a citizen of the United States, and that he shall not be required to prove more than one year's residence within the United States previous to his application to become such citizen; and that the Court admitting such alien shall, in addition to such proof of residence and good moral character as is now provided by law, be satisfied, by competent proof, of such person having been honorably discharged from the services of the United States as aforesaid." And due and satisfactory proof having been submitted to the said Court that the said

petitioner was a regularly enlisted soldier of the United States, and was honorably discharged from the service, and that he is a man of good moral character, attached to the principles of the CONSTITUTION OF THE UNIDED STATES, and well disposed to the good order and happiness of the same; and having declared on his solemn *Oath* before the said Court, that he would support the CONSTITUTION OF THE UNIDED STATES, and that he did absolutely and entirely renounce and abjure or all allegiance and fidelity to every foreign prince, potentate, state and sovereignty whatsoever, and particularly to the *King of Saxony* of who he was before a subject; and having in all respects complied with the laws in regard to Naturalization, in his case made and provided: Thereupon the Court admitted the said *Taugart Snyder* to become a citizen of the United States, and ordered all proceedings aforesaid to be recorded by the Prothonotary of said court, which was done accordingly.

Chapter 9

In Their Hearts, They Were Americans!

After the end of the Civil War and the fighting was over, those brave souls that fought to preserve the Union who came from other parts of the world to start a new life became citizens. When you think about it, of the 2.2 million Union soldiers who fought in the Civil War, 54.6 percent were foreigners, of whom 25-33 percent were foreign-born. (Sources do very on this subject)

1,000,000 (45.4 percent of all Union soldiers) were native-born Americans of British ancestry. 516,000 of whom about

175,000- 216,000 were born in Germany.

210,000 (9.5 percent) were African-American. Half were free men who lived in the North, and half were ex-slaves or escaped slaves from the South. They served in more than 160 "colored" regiments.

150,000-200,000 were Irish.

90,000 were Dutch.

50,000 were born in England

50,000 were Canadian.

40,000 were French or French Canadian. About half were born in United States of America the other half in Québec.

20,000 Scandinavian (Norwegian, Swedish, Finnish, and Danish)

7,000 Italian

7,000 Jewish

6,000 Mexican

5,000 Polish

3,600-4,000 were Native American

Several Hundred were of other various nationalities. [487] [488] [489] [490] [491]

Of the approximately four thousand Hungarian immigrants who were in the United States at the time of the Civil War, eight hundred served in the Union Army, or 20 percent. This degree of participation exceeds that of any other ethnic group in America. Out of that eight hundred who served, 130 were officers. Among those officers were five Brigadier Generals, fifteen Colonels, fourteen Majors, fifteen Captains, and several subalterns and surgeons.[492] The majority of these Hungarians serving under the Union flag, did so for several distinct reasons. During the Hungarian war of independence in 1848, these men fought for the liberation of Hungary. One of their greatest achievements was the freeing of the serfs in Hungary. Still they left their homeland

---

[487] McPherson, "Immigrants in the Union and Confederate Army during the Civil War" p. 1 (McPherson, What They Fought For, 1861 – 1865 (Louisiana State University press, 1994))
[488] Waskie, "Foreign Soldiers in the American Civil War" pp. 1-4 (Waskie, wesclark.com/jw/foreign_soldiers.html)
[489] Stoddard and Murphy, "Ethnic Makeup of the Civil War" p. 1 (Brook C. Stoddard & Daniel P. Murphy, netplaces.com/...ethnic-makeup-of-the...)
[490] Yank and Reb, "History 269 The Civil War and Reconstruction" p. 1 (Billy Yank and Johnny Reb, virginiawestern.edu/.../Soldiers.html)
[491] Wikipedia, "Union Army," 6 (Wikipedia-UA, 2011p.6)
[492] Clevelandmemory.org, "Hungarians and Their Communities in Cleveland, chapter 2," 89–91 (memories.org, Cleveland memories.org/.../pg089.htm pp.89-91)

because they could no longer live under the oppressive and tyrannical rule of the Austrians. Rather than surrender their advanced social and political ideas, they chose to live in exile. Now living here in United States, a country whose constitution assured freedom and democracy, how could they fight for the retention of slavery?

My ancestors like all these other families had the courage to leave their homes, travel halfway around the world, and come here to a new country. To them this was the land of opportunity where every man is equal. Here, they believed in the idea that a man can breathe and even grow rich; that every man was as good as the man standing next to them.

People do not change their citizenship from one country to another unless they feel their freedoms are repressed and they can do better somewhere else. All those I have spoken with who have come to this country today have done so because the country they left was repressive in nature and did not recognize their God given rights.

Until the United States was formed as a republic under its Constitution, the countries of the world were ruled by kings, queens, and dictators of all sorts. As early as 1770, the Earl of Chatham made a statement in the House of Lords in the United Kingdom, "Unlimited power is apt to corrupt the minds of those who possess it."[493] In 1887 Lord Acton expressed his opinion to Bishop Creighton in a letter: "power tends to corrupt, and absolute power corrupts absolutely. Great men are almost always bad men."[494] So our ancestors, as they came here to this country to begin a new life, fully understood the concept, "Power corrupts; absolute power corrupts absolutely." What better place to come then to this new republic with limited government, controlled by the people that it governs; a country that is of the people, for the people, and by the people.

---

[493] The Phrase Finder, "Power corrupts; absolute power corrupts absolutely" p. 1 (Finder, phrases.org.uk/.../Absolute-power-corru...)
[494] Ibid. p. 1 (Finder, phrases.org.uk/.../Absolute-power-corru...)

My great-great-grandfathers Tougart Snyder and Philip, his four brothers Frederick, Rudolph, George, and Louis, and all the others who came to this country in those hard times, came in the light of day, ready to pay whatever price was required. The price for each man was not always equal. George and Rudolph gave the ultimate price of their lives; Frederick and Philip suffered wounds and partial disabilities; Tougart served less than a year while escaping harm and Lewis only served one hundred days. But the price one pays is not what is important. What is significant is what is in one's heart. They came, each one, ready to pay in full measure the price for liberty. For they knew that to bargain over the price could leave one's heart-broken in the end if one doesn't achieve the targeted goal. As my ancestors have shown, liberty can be elusive and difficult to achieve.

Nor did these people come to this country expecting a free ride or handout. They had a strong sense of who they were as individuals, founded in faith and knowledge of what God expected of them. They readily understood concepts like that found in First Timothy 5:8, "But if any provide not for his own, and especially for those of his own house, he hath denied the faith, and is worse than an infidel."[495]

They also came ready to embrace completely their new life here in United States. My ancestors were never known to fly the German flag, neither at their home or at their place of business; they were Americans and flew the American flag accordingly. Again, if you look at their oath of allegiance to the United States and the Constitution, one should quickly realize that each word needs to be understood and strongly felt. Matthew 6:24 states, " No man can serve two masters: for either he will hate the one, and love the other; or else he will hold to the one, and despise the other."[496] In the same

---

[495] Holy Bible, King James Reference p. 1617 (Holy Bible, Zondervan, Grand Rapids, MI 49530 USA)
[496] Ibid. p. 1302 (Holy Bible, Zondervan, Grand Rapids, MI 49530 USA)

manner, in your heart, you cannot be citizens in two countries.

I recently had the grand opportunity to be in Gettysburg on Remembrance Day weekend, and I witnessed a number of people being given the oath of U.S. citizenship and allegiance to the U.S. Constitution. I think it says it best, so I included it here.

I hereby declare; on oath,

- that I absolutely and entirely renounce and abjure all allegiance and fidelity to any foreign prince, potentate, state or sovereignty of whom of which I have heretofore been a subject or citizen;
- that I will support and defend the Constitution and laws of the United States of America against all enemies, foreign and domestic;
- that I will bear true faith and allegiance to the same;
- that I will bear arms on behalf of the United States when required by law;
- that I will perform noncombatant service in the Armed Forces of the United States when required by law;
- that I will perform work of national importance under civilian direction when required by law;
- and that I will take obligation freely without any mental reservation or purpose of evasion; so help me God.
- In acknowledgement therefore I have here unto affixed my signature.[497][498]

---

[497] Longley (About.com), "The Oath of U.S. Citizenship and Allegiance to the U.S. Constitution" p. 1(Robert Longley, usgovinfo.about.com/.../oathofcitizen.htm) (DON'T SEE THIS IN BIBLIOGRAPHY)

I started doing this research with a strong sense of being a Bramble. But now looking back at the family's ancestry, I am also a Leveridge, a Wood, a Udich, a Bachofer, a Buehler, a Whitman, a Snyder, a Stieg and a Lenderking, and these are just the ones I found going back to the Civil War. I further realize that for each generation I look back, the family names in my roots nearly doubles. And from each brother and sister of a grandfather, a grandmother, and so on, a different shoot rises up. The concept of the family tree only works tracing the lines of an individual person. As a family, it represents more by a multi-stemmed "bush," which keeps spreading out more and more over time. And considering this, the irony of my last name being Bramble is not lost on me.

In my mind I now picture family as a broader concept. I also picture those now entering this country much differently as well. For as you go back in time our roots may touch at some distant place; and if not so, our branches may touch at some future time. In the end, we all want the same thing; we desire to be able to live freely and be happy. But as long as there are men on this planet that desire to control everything we do, that liberty is in jeopardy. We must all work together and strive for liberty as our ancestors did, and to maintain it diligently lest it be permanently lost.

The American's Creed

by William Tyler Page

I believe in the United States of America as a government of the people, by the people, for the people; whose just powers are derived from the consent of the governed; a democracy in a republic; a sovereign Nation of many sovereign States; a perfect union, one and inseparable; established upon these principles of freedom, equality,

---

[498] Wikipedia, "Oath of Allegiance (United States)" pp. 1-2 (Wikipedia, 2010 ...wikipedia.org/.../Oath_of_Allegiance_(...)

justice, and humanity for which American patriots sacrificed their lives and fortunes.

I therefore believe it is my duty to my country to love it, to support its Constitution, to obey its laws, to respect its flag, and to defend it against all enemies.[499][500]

Written in 1917, accepted by the United States House of Representatives on April 3, 1918

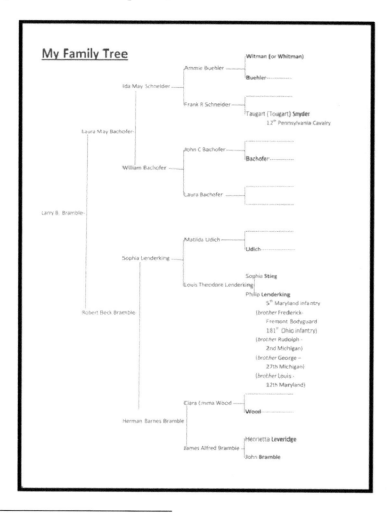

---

[499] www.ushistory.org, "The American's Creed" p. 1 (Page, www.ushistory.org/documents/creed.htm)
[500] Wikipedia, "The American's Creed" p. 1 (Page, en.wikipedia.org/wiki/American's_Creed)

Library of Congress Credits

The Lexington of 1861   Page 8

Digital ID: (digital file from b&w film copy neg.) cph 3a08162
http://hdl.loc.gov/loc.pnp/cph.3a08162

Reproduction Number: LC-USZC4-1736 (color film copy transparency) LC-USZ62-4817 (b&w film copy neg.) LC-USZC2-2750 (color film copy slide) LC-USZCN4-351 (color film copy neg.)

Repository: Library of Congress Prints and Photographs Division, Washington, D.C. 20540 USA http://hdl.loc.gov/loc.pnp/pp.print

Encampment of Army of the Potomac at Cumberland Landing on Pamunkey River; 5 Union soldiers seated on Hill in the foreground   Page 10

Digital ID: (digital file from b&w film copy neg.) cph 3b14106
http://hdl.loc.gov/loc.pnp/cph.3b14106 Reproduction Number: LC-USZ62-66616 (b&w film copy neg.)

Repository: Library of Congress Prints and Photographs Division, Washington, D.C. 20540 USA http://hdl.loc.gov/loc.pnp/pp.print

Siege of Yorktown, Va. Views of Federal Battery, No. 4   Page 34

Digital ID: (b&w film copy neg.) cph 3b15635
http://hdl.loc.gov/loc.pnp/cph.3b15635

Reproduction Number: LC-USZ62-68172 (b&w film copy neg.)

Repository: Library of Congress Prints and Photographs Division, Washington, D.C. 20540 USA http://hdl.loc.gov/loc.pnp/pp.print

Fair Oaks, Virginia. Prof. Thaddeus S. Lowe replenishing balloon INTREPED from balloon CONSTITUTION   Page 34

Digital ID: (digital file from original neg. of right half) cwpb 01562 http://hdl.loc.gov/loc.pnp/cwpb.01562

Reproduction Number: LC-DIG-cwpb-01563 (digital file from original neg. of left half)

DC-DIG-cwpb-01562 (digital file from original neg. of right half)

Repository: Library of Congress Prints and Photographs Division, Washington, D.C. 20540 USA http://hdl.loc.gov/loc.pnp/pp.print

[Petersburg, Va. Company F,114th Pennsylvania infantry (Zouaves) with fixed bayonets] Page 58

Digital ID (digital film from original neg.) cwpb 03880 http://hdl.loc.gov/loc.pnp/cwpb.03880 Reproduction Number: LC-DIG-cwpb-03880 (digital file from original neg.)

LC-B8171-7143 (b&w film neg.)

Repository: Library of Congress Prints and Photographs Division, Washington, D.C. 20540 USA http://hdl.loc.gov/loc.pnp/pp.print

[Beaufort, S.C. 50th Pennsylvania infantry and parade formation Page 64

Digital ID: (digital file from original neg.) cwpb 00741 http://hdl.loc.gov/loc.pnp/cwpb.00741 Reproduction Number: LC-DIG-cwpb-00741 (digital file from original neg.)

LC-B8171-0156 (b&w film copy neg.)

Repository: Library of Congress Prints and Photographs Division, Washington, D.C. 20540 USA http://hdl.loc.gov/loc.pnp/pp.print

The "Sunken Road" at Antietam Page 80

Digital ID: (digital file from original item) ppmsca 07751 http://hdl.log.gov/loc.pnp/ppmsca.07751

Reproduction Number: LC-DIG-ppmsca-07751 (digital file from original item)

LC-USZ62-114376 (b&w film copy neg.)

LC-B8171-553 (b&w film copy neg.)

Repository: Library of Congress Prints and Photographs Division, Washington, D.C. 20540 USA http://hdl.loc.gov/loc.pnp/pp.print

Antietam, Maryland. Bodies in front of the DUNKER CHURCH Page 81

Digital ID: (digital file from original neg.) cwph 01099
http://hdl.loc.gov/loc.pnp/cwpb.01099

Reproduction Number: LC-DIG –cwpb-01099 (digital file from original neg.)

Repository: Library of Congress Prints and Photographs Division, Washington, D.C. 20540 USA http://hdl.loc.gov/loc.pnp/pp.print

Antietam, Maryland. Ditch with bodies of soldiers on right wing used as a rifle pit by Confederates Page 81

Digital ID: (digital file from original neg.) cwpb 01102
http://hdl.loc.gov/loc.pnp/cwpb.01102 Reproduction Number: LC-DIG-cwpb-01102 (digital file from original neg.)

Repository: Library of Congress Prints and Photographs Division, Washington, D.C. 20540 USA http://hdl.loc.gov/loc.pnp/pp.print

[Civil War camp scene Bird's-eye view of troops in formation and tents in backgrd.] Page 95

Digital ID: (digital file from b&w film copy neg.) cph 3b29527
http://hdl.loc.gov/loc.pnp/cph.3b29527

Reproduction Number: LC-USZ62-82883 (b&w film copy neg.)

Repository: Library of Congress Prints and Photographs Division, Washington, D.C. 20540 USA http://hdl.loc.gov/loc.pnp/pp.print

Aiken's Landing Virginia, Steamer New York waiting for exchange of prisoners Page 114

ID: (digital file from original neg. of right half) cwpb 02050
http://bdl.loc.gov/loc.pnp/cwpd.02050 Reproduction Number: LC-DIG-cwpb-02050 (digital file from original neg. of right half)

LC-DIG-cwpb-02052 (digital file from original neg. of variant, left half) LC-DIG-cwpb-02051 (digital file from original neg. of variant, right half) LC-B8171-2619 (b&w film neg.)

Repository: Library of Congress Prints and Photographs Division, Washington, D.C. 20540 USA http://hdl.loc.gov/loc.pnp/pp.print

Embarkation of exchanged Union prisoners at Aiken's Landing, February 21, 1865   Page 114

Digital ID: (b&w film copy neg.) cph 3c32751
http://hdl.loc.gov/loc.pnp/cph.3c32751

Reproduction Number: LC-USZ62-132751 (b&w film copy neg.)

Repository Library of Congress Prints and Photographs Division, Washington, D.C. 20540 USA http://hdl.loc.gov/loc.pnp/pp.print

[Fort Sanders, Knoxville, Tennessee]   Page 142

Digital ID: (digital file from original neg. of right half) cwpb 03507 http://hdl.log.gov/loc.pnp/cwpb.03507

Reproduction Number: LC-DIG-cwpb-03506 (digital file from original neg. of left half)

LC-DIG-cwpb-03507 (digital file from original neg. of right half)

Repository: Library of Congress Prints and Photographs Division, Washington, D.C. 20540 USA http://hdl.loc.gov/loc.pnp/pp.print

Drilling troops here Washington D.C.   Page 150

Digital ID: (digital file from original item) ppmsc 03310
http://hdl.log.gov/loc.pnp/ppmsc.03310

Reproduction Number: LC-DIG-ppmsc-03310 (digital file from original item)

LC-USZC4-7963 (color film copy transparency) LC-B8184-B526 (b&w film copy neg.)

Repository: Library of Congress Prints and Photographs Division, Washington, D.C. 20540 USA
http://hdl.loc.gov/loc.pnp/pp.print

Larry B. Bramble 237

Petersburg, Virginia. Soldiers quarters   Page 177

Digital ID: (digital file from original neg.) cwpb 01305
http://hdl.log.gov/loc.pnp/cwpb.01305

Reproduction Number: LC-DIG-cwpb-01305 (digital file from original neg.)

Repository: Library of Congress Prints and Photographs Division, Washington, D.C. 20540 USA http://hdl.loc.gov/loc.pnp/pp.print

Ammunition Train 3d Division, Cavalry Corps   Page 197

Digital ID: (digital file from b&w film copy neg.) cph 3b45393
http://hdl.loc.gov/loc.pnp/cph.3b45393 Reproduction Number: LC-USZ62-99347 (b&w file copy neg.)

Repository: Library of Congress Prints and Photographs Division, Washington, D.C. 20540 USA http://hdl.loc.gov/loc.pnp/pp.print

Richmond, Virginia Wagon Train of Military Telegraph Corps   Page 200

Digital ID: (digital file from original neg.) cwpb 03735
http://hdl.loc.gov/loc.pnp/cwpb.03735 Reproduction Number: LC-DIG-cwpb-03735 (digital file from original neg.)

LC–B8171–7183 (b&w film nag.)

Repository: Library of Congress Prints and Photographs Division, Washington, D.C. 20540 USA http://hdl.loc.gov/loc.pnp/pp.print

Petersburg, Virginia The first Federal wagon train entering the town   Page 203

Digital ID: (digital file from original neg. of left half) cwpb 01286
http://hdl.loc.gov/loc.pnp/cwpb.01286 Reproduction Number: LC-DIG-cwpb-01286 (digital file from original neg. of left half)

LC-DIG-cwpb-01287 (digital file from original nag of right half)

LC-B8171–0951(b&w film copy neg.)

Repository: Library of Congress Prints and Photographs Division, Washington, D.C. 20540 USA http://hdl.loc.gov/loc.pnp/pp.print

Camp of the 18th Pennsylvania Cavalry, February 1864   Page 207

Digital ID: (digital file from b&w film copy neg.) cph 3b47403
http://hdl.loc.gov/loc.pnp/cph.3b47403

Reproduction Number LC-USZ62-92389 (b&w film copy neg.)

Repository: Library of Congress Prints and Photographs Division, Washington, D.C. 20540 space USA
http://hdl.loc.gov/loc.pnp/pp.print

Clip Art and Map Credits

Bombardment of Fort Sumter	http://www.wpclipart.com	page 6
The Division of States during the War	http://www.wpclipart.com	page 9
Chapter 2 Movements Map	My adaptation	page 11
2nd Michigan near Bull Run	www.PictureHistory.com MES12653	page 12
Musket clipart	www.jewish-history.com/clipartgallery/illus.html	page 13
Bull Run area map	My adaptation	page 16
Springfield area battle map	My adaptation	page 24
Cavalry picture	www.ghead.awardspace.com/clipart/	page 29
Clipart of wounded	www.jewish-history.com/clipartgallery/illus.html	page 30
Chapter 3 movements map	My adaptation	page 31
Peninsula Campaign map	My adaptation	page 32

Battle clipart	http://www.wpclipart.com	page 33
Battle of Fair Oaks maps	My adaptation	page 39
Battle clipart	http://www.wpclipart.com	page 40
Seven Days battle map, First three days	My adaptation	page 40
Seven days battle continues map	My adaptation	page 41
Seven days battle, sixth day	My adaptation	page 42
Battle clipart	http://www.wpclipart.com	page 43
Seven days battle, Malvern Hill	My adaptation	page 46
Battle clipart	http://www.wpclipart.com	page 47
Battle clipart	http://www.wpclipart.com	page 49
Second Bull Run battle map	My adaptation	page 51
Battle clipart	http://www.wpclipart.com	page 54
Battle clipart	http://www.wpclipart.com	page 57
Antietam pre-battle map	My adaptation	page 69
Antietam battle map	My adaptation	page 74
Antietam battle clipart	http://www.wpclipart.com	page 75
Chapter 4 movements map	My adaptation	page 83
Battle clipart	http://www.wpclipart.com	page 94
Second battle of Winchester map	My adaptation	page 101
Second battle of Winchester battle map	My adaptation	page 107
Belle island prison camp area	My adaptation	page 110

Chapter 5 movements map	My adaptation	page 111
Musket clipart	www.jewish-history.com/clipartgallery/illus.html	page 115
Vicksburg siege map	My adaptation	page 116
Battle of Jackson	http://www.wpclipart.com	page 118
Pontoon bridge At Cincinnati	http://www.wpclipart.com	page 121
Knoxville area map	My adaptation	page 126
Battle clipart	http://www.wpclipart.com	page 128
Battle clipart	http://www.wpclipart.com	page 129
Battle clipart	http://www.wpclipart.com	page 129
Battle clipart	http://www.wpclipart.com	page 131
Battle clipart	www.ghead.awardspace.com/clipart/	page 135
Battle of Fort Saunders map	My adaptation	page 139
Battle of Fort Sanders clipart	http://www.wpclipart.com	page 144
Chapter 6 movements map	My adaptation	page 149
Battle clipart	www.ghead.awardspace.com/clipart/	page 154
Battle clipart	http://www.wpclipart.com	page 158
Battle of the wilderness map	My adaptation	page 160
Battle clipart	http://www.wpclipart.com	page 161
Battle clipart	http://www.wpclipart.com	page 162
Chapter 7 movements map	My adaptation	page 165

Archive record	National Archives and Record Service	page 166
Battle clipart	www.ghead.awardspace.com/clipart/	page 169
Siege of Petersburg map	My adaptation	page 171
Battle clipart	http://www.wpclipart.com	page 173
Battle clipart	www.ghead.awardspace.com/clipart/	page 180
Battle clipart	http://www.wpclipart.com	page 183
Battle of new market Heights map	My adaptation	page 187
Picture of Philip and Sophia Lenderking	Family photograph	page 191
Chapter 8 movements map	My adaptation	page 193
Civil War train and troops clipart	www.ghead.awardspace.com/clipart/	page 194
Archive record	National Archives and Record Service	page 196
Harpers Ferry area map	My adaptation	page 211
Battle clipart	http://www.wpclipart.com	page 214
Union Eagle	www.jewish-history.com/clipartgallery/illus.html	page 219
Archive record	National Archives and Record Service	page 220
Official Document of Citizenship	Family record	page 221
My family tree	Family record	page 231

Bibliography

2nd Michigan Org., history, *2nd Michigan Volunteer Infantry, "E" Company 1861 – 1865*, http://2ndmichigan.org/history.htm Accessed February 12, 2011

48ovvi.org, 2008, *Siege of Jackson (July 5, 1863 – July 28, 1863)*, http://www.48ovvi.org/oh48hd8.html Accessed June 1, 2011

72 PVI, *Civil War Zouave History*, 72nd Pennsylvania Volunteer Infantry, www.philazov.home.mindspring.com/page7.html Accessed March 21, 2011

A&E Television Network, 2011, History.com, Civil War, June 14, 1863 Battle of Second Winchester, www.history.com/this-day-in-history/battle-of-second-winchester Accessed March 4, 2011

Acton (1887)/ Pitt (1770), *Finder, The Phrase* www.phrases.org.uk/meanings/absolute-power-corrups-absolutely.html Accessed, August 4, 2011

American Civil War.com, *The Vicksburg Campaign May 1863 American Civil War*, http://americancivilwar.com/vicks.html Accessed February 2, 2011

Andrews, J. W., *Col. John W Andrews Official Reports.* (1864) Antietam on the web, www.antietam.aotw.org/exhibit.php?exhibit_id=31 Accessed, August 4, 2011

Archives, *Frederick Lenderking, Fremont Bodyguard*, Microcopy No. 405, roll 293, The National Archives and Record Service, Washington, DC, Accessed June, 2010

Archives, *Frederick Lenderking*, The 181st Ohio infantry, 1074, The National Archives and Record Service, Washington, DC, Accessed March, 2011

Archives, *George Lenderking, 27th Michigan infantry*,1796, The National Archives and Record Service, Washington, DC, Accessed June, 2010

Archives, *Rudolph Lenderking, 2nd Michigan infantry*, 1833, The National Archives and Record Service, Washington, DC, Accessed June, 2010

Archives, *Louis Lenderking*, The 12th Maryland infantry,(100 days, 1864), A– Th, Microcopy No. 384, roll 184, The National Archives and Record Service, Washington, DC, Accessed June, 2010

Archives, *Philip Lenderking*, The 5th Maryland infantry, Ke – Li, Microcopy No. 384, roll 142, The National Archives and Record Service, Washington, DC, Accessed June, 2010

Archives, *Tougart Snyder*, The 12th Pennsylvania Cavalry, 3697, The National Archives and Record Service, Washington, DC, Accessed June, 2010

Aronson, Alan, *Strategic Supply of Civil War Armies*, www.members.cox.net/rb2307/content/STRATEGIC_SUPPLY_OF_CIVIL_WAR_ARMIES.htm Accessed May 7, 2011

Barnhart, Lorenzo D., *The Second Battle of Winchester, June 13 – 15, 1863*, The 110th Ohio Volunteer Infantry, www.frontierfamilies.net/family/2ndwintr.htm Accessed March 10, 2011

Bates, Samuel P., *Welcome to 12th Pennsylvania Cavalry, 12th Pennsylvania Cavalry,* http://12thpacavalry.8k.com/service.html Accessed January 9, 2011

Bayne, Greg, *Burnside Mud 'March'*, the American Civil War Roundtable UK, www.americancivilwar.org.uk/news_burnsides-mud-march_185.htm Accessed February 18, 2011

Billy Yank and Johnny Reb, Virginia Western.sdu, Civil War Soldiers, History 269 the Civil War and Reconstruction, www.virginiawestern.edu/faculty/vwhansd/his269/Soldiers.html Accessed may 24, 2011

Byington, C., *Major Cornelius Byington, November 22, 1863, 2nd Michigan Infantry*, Washington, D. C., National Archives, Official Reports, CHAPT. XLIII, Series I. Vol. 31. Part I, Reports. Serial No. 54, Page 365 – 54, Accessed June, 2010

Cannon, Jessica, *Riots, Baltimore, 1861 /the Baltimore Riots*, 2005, Maryland Online Encyclopedia, www.mdoe.org/riots_balt_1861.html last accessed May 21, 2011, also located at www.gmshistory.net/DocL_Baltimore%20RiotCV.pdf Accessed August 6, 2011

Cannon, John, *The Wilderness Campaign, May 1864*, Conshohocken, PA: Combined Books, Inc., 1993, 151 East 10th Avenue, Conshohocken, PA 19428

Clarity Digital Group, examiner.com, *Baltimore and Ohio Railroad (B&O) History*, www.examiner.com/military-history-in-baltimore/baltimore-and-ohio-railroad-b-o-history-during-the-later-part-of-the-civil-war Accessed June 4, 2011

Cleveland memory.org, *Chapter 2 of Hungarians and their Communities in – Cleveland Memory*, page 089, www.clevelandmemory.org/hungarians/pg089.htm Accessed August 5, 2011

Crews, Dick, *Mule-Drawn Wagon Trains*, 2008, The Cleveland Civil War Roundtable, www.clevelandcivilwarroundtable.com/articles/means/wagon_trains.htm Accessed August 5, 2011

Digital History Home, *Civil War Casualties and Costs of the Civil War*, www.digitalhistory.uh.edu/historyonline/us20.cfm Accessed March 23, 2011

DWL and VLC, 1995, *Second Winchester (13 – 15 June 1863)*, www.nps.gov/hps/abpp/shenandoah/svs3-7.html Accessed March 4, 2011

East, Civil War in the, *2nd Michigan Infantry Regiment*, www.civilwarintheeast.com/USA/MI/2MI.php Accessed February 16, 2011

East, Civil War in the, *5th Maryland Infantry Regiment*, www.civilwarintheeast.com/USA/MD/5MD.php Accessed February 16, 2011

East, Civil War in the, *12th Maryland Infantry Regiment*, www.civilwarintheeast.com/USA/MD/12MD.php Accessed February 16, 2011

East, Civil War in the, *12th Pennsylvania Cavalry Regiment*, www.civilwarintheeast.com/USA/PA/PA12cav.php Accessed June 3, 2011

East, Civil War in the, *27th Michigan Infantry Regiment*, www.civilwarintheeast.com/USA/MI/27MI.php Accessed February 16, 2011

eBooks On Disk.Com, *Campbell's Station, Civil War Reference*, 2010, www.civilwarreference.com/battles/detail.php?battlesID=427 Accessed January 16, 2011

eBooks On Disk.Com, *Knoxville Siege, Civil War Reference*, 2011, www.civilwarreference.com/battles/detail.php?battlesID=94 Accessed January 16, 2011

eBooks On Disk.Com, *Lenoir's Station, Civil War Reference*, 2011, www.civilwarreference.com/battles/detail.php?battlesID=783 Accessed January 16, 2011

Elliott, Henry P., *"First Manassas (or Bull Run), July 21, 1861." Blue and Gray*, 150th Anniversary, Volume XXVII, Issue 5, 2011

Elrod, Mark and Garofalo, Robert, Civil War Bands, www.civilwarpoetry.org/music/bands.html Accessed January 11, 2011

Enoch Pratt Free Library, Baltimore, MD, *Marilyn Regiments*, www.pratt.library.org/locations/maryland/index.ospx?id=5244 Accessed May 15, 2011

Famento, Inc., 2009, US Civil War /The Battle of Wilmington February 11, 1865 – February 22, 1865, www.xtimeline.com/evt/view.aspx?id=29685 Accessed may 27 2011

French, W.H., *Brig. Gen. William H French's Official Report* (1862) Antietam on the web, www.antietam.aotw.org/exhibit.php?exhibit_id=54 Accessed, August 4, 2011

Furgurson, Ernest B., *Burnsides Mud March*, 2003, www.civilwarhome.com/mudmarch.htm Accessed February 18, 2011

Gayley, Alice J., *12th Pennsylvania Cavalry Pennsylvania Volunteers*, www.pa-roots.com/pacw/cavalry/12thcav/12thcavorg.html Accessed June 3, 2011

Gayley, Alice J., *Camp Parole, Annapolis, Maryland*, www.pa-roots.com/pacw/campparole.html Accessed March 11, 2011

Jordan, Brian Matthew, Encyclopedia Virginia, *Fort Monroe during the Civil War*, 2011, www.encyclopediavirginia.org/Fort_Monroe_During_the_Civil_War Accessed August 5, 2011

Harvey, Don and Lois Harvey, *2nd Regiment Michigan Volunteer Infantry*, www.michiganinthewar.org/infantry/2ndinf.htm Accessed August 5, 2011

Harvey, Don and Lois Harvey, *27th Regiment Michigan Volunteer Infantry*, www.michiganinthewar.org/infantry/27thinf.htm Accessed August 5, 2011

Heiser, John, the Civil War Soldier, *What was life as a soldier like in 1863?*, 1998, Gettysburg National Military Park, United States Department of the Interior – National Park Service, www.pennmanorus1.wikispaces.com/file/view/The+Civil+War+Soldiers+of+1863.pdf Accessed August 5, 2011

Historical Data Systems, *Regimental Casualty Analysis, The 2nd Michigan Infantry*, P.O. Box 35, Duxbury, MA 02331, Historical Data Systems, Inc. Accessed June, 2010

Historical Data Systems, *Regimental Casualty Analysis, The 5th Maryland infantry*, P.O. Box 35, Duxbury, MA 02331, Historical Data Systems, Inc. Accessed June, 2010

Historical Data Systems, *Regimental Casualty Analysis, The 12th Maryland Infantry*, P.O. Box 35, Duxbury, MA 02331, Historical Data Systems, Inc. Accessed June, 2010

Historical Data Systems, *Regimental Casualty Analysis, The 12th Pennsylvania Cavalry*, P.O. Box 35, Duxbury, MA 02331, Historical Data Systems, Inc. Accessed June, 2010

Historical Data Systems, *Regimental Casualty Analysis, The 27th Michigan Infantry*, P.O. Box 35, Duxbury, MA 02331, Historical Data Systems, Inc. Accessed June, 2010

Historical Data Systems, *Regimental Casualty Analysis, The 181st Ohio Infantry*, P.O. Box 35, Duxbury, MA 02331, Historical Data Systems, Inc. Accessed June, 2010

Historical Data Systems, *Regimental Casualty Analysis, Fremont Bodyguard*, P.O. Box 35, Duxbury, MA 02331, Historical Data Systems, Inc. Accessed June, 2010

Historical Data Systems, *Regimental Casualty Analysis, Knoxville, Tenn. (Siege of)Nov. 17th – Dec. 4th, 1863*, P.O. Box 35, Duxbury, MA 02331, Historical Data Systems, Inc., Union Army, vol. 6, Accessed June, 2010

Historical Data Systems, Battle History, *Springfield, Missouri, October 25, 1861,* The Union Army, Volume 6, P.O. Box 35, Duxbury, MA 02331, Historical Data Systems, Inc. Accessed June, 2010

Historical Data Systems, Battle History, *Wilderness, VA, May 5th – 7th, 1864,* The Union Army, Volume 6, P.O. Box 35, Duxbury, MA 02331, Historical Data Systems, Inc. Accessed June, 2010

Historical Preservation Services, CWSAC Battle Summaries, *Campbell Station, TN.*, CWSAC Referenced #: TN023, Preservation Priority: IV.2 (Class D) www.nps.gov/hps/abpp/battles/tn023.htm Access February 2, 2011

Historical Preservation Services, CWSAC Battle Summaries, *Fort Sanders, TN.*, CWSAC Referenced #: TN025, Preservation Priority: IV.2 (Class B) www.nps.gov/hps/abpp/battles/tn025.htm Access January 11, 2011

Historical Preservation Services, CWSAC Battle Summaries, *Oak Grove, VA.*, CWSAC Referenced #: VA015, Preservation Priority: IV.2 (Class D) www.nps.gov/hps/abpp/battles/va015.htm Accessed February 10, 2011

Historical Preservation Services, CWSAC Battle Summaries, *Springfield, MO.*, CWSAC Referenced #: M0008, Preservation Priority: IV.2 (Class D) www.nps.gov/hps/abpp/battles/mo008.htm Accessed January 16, 2011

Historical Preservation Services, CWSAC Battle Summaries, *Murfreesboro, TN.*, CWSAC Referenced #: TN037, Preservation Priority: II.4 (Class D) www.nps.gov/hps/abpp/battles/tn037.htm Accessed May 27, 2011

Historical Preservation Services, CWSAC Battle Summaries, *Vicksburg, MS.*, CWSAC Referenced #: MS011, Preservation Priority: I.2 (Class A) www.nps.gov/hps/abpp/battles/ms011.htm Accessed February 2, 2011

Holy Bible, *King James Reference Bible*, 2000, Zondervan, Grand Rapids, MI 49530 USA

How Stuff Works, Battle of Fair Oaks, www.howstuffworks.com/american-civil-war/battle-of-fair-oaks.htm Accessed January 15, 2011

Humphrey Wm., *Col. William Humphrey, The Jackson Campaign, 2nd Michigan Infantry*, Washington, D. C., National Archives, Official Reports, CHAPT. XXXVI, Series I. Vol. 24. Part II, Reports. Serial No. 37, Page 566 – 37, Accessed June 15, 2010

Hyslop, Stephen G. and Kagan, Neil, 2011, *Atlas of the Civil War*, National Geographic Society, Washington, D. C.

Kelly, Dorothy E., 1988, Knoxville Civil War Roundtable, *John Watkins: Battle of Fort Sanders*, www.discoveret.org/kcwrt/history/hw-text.htm Accessed January 9, 2011

Lamb, John, *Fifth Maryland Infantry*, US, alternate designations www.2ndmdinfantryus.org/usinf5.html Accessed February 28, 2011

Longley, Robert, *The Oath of US Citizenship and Allegiance to the U.S. Constitution*, About.com www.usgovinfo.about.com/od/immigrationnaturalizatio/a/oat hofcitizen.htm Accessed February 17, 2011

Mackie, B. and Lee, L. M., *Images of America, Fort Delaware*, 2010, Arcadia Publishing, Charleston SC, Chicago IL, Fort Smith NH, San Francisco CA, 2010 USA

Maier, Larry B., *Leather & Steel, the 12th Pennsylvania cavalry in the Civil War*, 1949, Burd Street Press publication, Beidel printing house, Inc., 63rd West Burd St., Shippensburg, PA 17257 – 0152 USA

McCarley, J. Britt, *Feeding Billy Yank: Union Rations between 1861 and 1865*, www.qmfound.com/feeding_billy_yank.htm Accessed August 7, 2011

McPherson, James M., *Immigrants in the Union and Confederate Army during the Civil War*, Louisiana State University Press, 1994, reprint of *"What They Fought for, 1861 - 1865,"* www.upa.pdx.edu/INS/currentprojects/TAHv3/Content/PDFs/Immigrant_Soldiers_Civil_War.pdf Accessed May 17, 2011

Memory Local Gov., *Civil War Band Music: The American Brass Band Movement*, The Civil War Bands, www.memory.loc.gov/ammem/cwmhtml/cwmpres07.html Accessed August 6, 2011

My Civil War.com, *The Battle of Springfield/ Zagonyi's Charge October 25, 1861 in Springfield, Missouri*, www.mycivilwar.com/battles/611025.htm Accessed January 9, 2011

New York Times, 1861, Affairs in Missouri; The Charge of Fremont Bodyguard, www.nytimes.com/1861/11/05/news/affairs-missouri-charge-fremont-s-body-guard-philidelphia-evening-bulletin.html Accessed August 7, 2011

Nosworthy, Brent, *"Roll Call to Destiny, The Soldiers Eye View of Civil War Battles,"* Basic Books, 2008, New York

Page, William Tyler, *The American's Creed*, 2011, www.ushistory.org/documents/creed.htm Accessed May 24, 2011

Pennsylvania Civil War Volunteers, Civil War Army Organization, www.pacivilwar.com/organization.html Accessed August 7, 2011

Pension records, *Frederick Lenderking, Fremont Bodyguard,* The National Archives and Record Service, Washington D.C., Accessed June, 2010

Pension records, *Philip Lenderking, 5th Maryland Infantry,* The National Archives and Record Service, Washington D.C., Accessed June, 2010

Ransom, John (Diary) and Hay, Brenda Smelser, *Belle Isle Civil War Prison*, 2008, www.censusdiggins.com/prison_bellisle.html Accessed April 25, 2011

Reno M. A., Col. Marcus a Reno's Operational Report, *Affair near Harpers Ferry*, source: Washington, D. C., National Archives, Official Reports, CHAPT. LVIII, Series I. Vol. 46. Part I, Reports. Serial No. 95, Page 455 – 95 Accessed June, 2010

Reno M. A., Col. Marcus a Reno's Operational Report, Pennsylvania cavalry, *of Operations March 20 – 25,* Washington, D. C., National Archives, Official Reports, CHAPT. LVIII, Series I. Vol. 46. Part I, Reports. Serial No. 95, Page 535 – 95 Accessed June, 2010

Richard, J. (27 August 2000), *Battle Bean's Station, 14 December 1863*, http://www.historyofwar.org/articles/battles_beans_station.html Accessed February 2, 2011

Richard, J. (16 May 2006), *Battle of Campbell's Station, 16 November 1863*, http://www.historyofwar.org/articles/battles_campbells_station.html Accessed August 6, 2011

Richard, J. (6 May 2006), *Battle of Knoxville, 29 November 1863*, http://www.historyofwar.org/articles/battles_knoxville.html Accessed August 6, 2011

Richard, J. (19 October 2006), *Battle of Oak Growth, 25 June 1862*, http://www.historyofwar.org/articles/battles_oak_grove.html Accessed May 10, 2011

Richard, J. (31 May 2007), *Second Battle of Winchester, 14 – 15 June 1863*, http://www.historyofwar.org/articles/battles_winchester2.html Accessed March 4, 2011

Rhodes, James Ford (1848 – 1927), *History of the Civil War, 1861 - 1865*, www.bartleby.com/252/pages/page132.html Accessed January 15, 2011

Ruehle, J. V.., *Capt. John V. Ruehle, November 24, 1863, 2nd Michigan Infantry*, Washington, D. C., National Archives, Official Reports, CHAPT. XLIII, Series I. Vol. 31. Part I, Reports. Serial No. 54, Page 365 – 54, Accessed June, 2010

Rule, G. E./Blair, Frank, *Fremont's Hundred Days in Missouri*, Atlantic monthly, Jan – Mar, 1862, Civil War St. Louis, 2004, www.civilwarstlouis.com/history2/fremont100pt2.htm Accessed August 5, 2011

Spartacus Educational, *Civil War: European Recruits*, www.spartacus.schoolnet.co.uk/USAcivilwarE.htm Accessed may 24th 2011

Schilling / Sellmeyer, Community and Conflict, (2009) "Zagonyi's Charge (Battle of

Springfield). www.ozarkscivilwar.org/archives/354 Accessed, August 4, 2011

Scriptoriumnovum.com, *Battle of Springfield Naughton's Irish Cavalry*, www.scriptoriumnovum.com/c/dragoons.html Accessed may 23rd 2011

Sears, Stephen W., *Landscape Turned Red, the Battle of Antietam*, 1983, First Mariner Books edition 2003, Houghton Mifflin Company, Boston, New York

Son of the South, Harpers weekly, *General Winfield Scott's Resignation*, www.sonofthesouth.net/leefoundation/civil-war/1861/november/scott-resignation.htm Accessed August 7, 2011

Stevens, L., *Fremont Bodyguard, Ohio, Civil War, 1995*, www.ohiocivilwar.com/fremont.html Accessed September, 2010

Stevens, L., *174th Ohio Infantry, 1995*, www.ohiocivilwar.com/cw174.html Accessed May 27, 2011

Stevens, L., *181st Ohio Infantry, 1995*, www.ohiocivilwar.com/cw181.html Accessed May 27, 2011

Stoddard, B. C. and Murphy, D. P. Ph.D., *Ethnic Makeup of the Civil War*, www.netplaces.com/american-civil-war/away-from-the-mainstream/ethnic-make-up-of-the-civil-war.htm Accessed August 5, 2011

Sesquicentennial, Missouri Civil War, *Springfield, First Battle of (Zagonyi's Charge)*, www.mocivilwar150.com/history/battle/185 Accessed August 5, 2011

Taylor, William, *Camp of First Division 9th A. C. Lenoir station, Tennessee Novr. 1, 1863*, https://digitalarchive.wm.edu/bitstream/10288/1517/1/Taylor 18631101.pdf Accessed January 16, 2011

Tuck, C.W. and Fairbanks, J., *Past and present of Greene County, Missouri*, Chapter 11 Military History, Part 5, *The*

Battle of Springfield 1861; Zagonyi's Charge,
www.thelibrary.org/lochist/history/paspres/ch11pt.html
Accessed August 5, 2011

Vosper R, *Capt. Richard Vosper, September 20, 1864, 27th Michigan Infantry*, Washington, D. C., National Archives, Official Reports, Wilderness, CHAPT. XLVIII, Series I. Vol. 36. Part I, Reports. Serial No. 67, Page 959 – 67, Accessed June, 2010

Walden, Geoff, First Kentucky "Orphan" Brigade, The Orphan Brigade At Jackson, Mississippi July 1863, www.rootsweb.ancestry.com/~orphanhm/jackson.htm
Accessed August 5, 2011

Waskie, Andy, foreign soldiers in the American Civil War, www.isc.temple.edu/awaskie/foreign_soldiers_civil_war.htm
Accessed August 5, 2011

Merriam, A., *Webster's Seventh New College Dictionary*, 1971, by G. And C. Merriam Com., Compositors: R. R. Donnelly and Son's Company, The Lakeside Press, Chicago Illinois, USA

Wikipedia, *"American's Creed,"* 2011, http://en.wikipedia.org/wiki/American's_Creed Accessed May 24th, 2011

Wikipedia, *"Battle of Antietam,"* 2011, http://en.wikipedia.org/wiki/Battle_of_Antietam Accessed March 4, 2011

Wikipedia, *"Battle of Bentonville,"* 2011, http://en.wikipedia.org/wiki/Battle_of_Bentonville Accessed May 27, 2011

Wikipedia, *"Battle of Blue Springs,"* 2010, http://en.wikipedia.org/wiki/Battle_of_Blue_Springs Accessed January 15, 2011

Wikipedia, *"Battle of Chaffin's Farm,"* 2011, http://en.wikipedia.org/wiki/Battle_of_Chaffin's_Farm Accessed March 8, 2011

Wikipedia, *"Battle of Chantilly,"* 2010, http://en.wikipedia.org/wiki/Battle_of_Chantilly Accessed January 15, 2011

Wikipedia," *Battle of Fredericksburg,"* 2011, http://en.wikipedia.org/wiki/Battle_of_Fredericksburg Accessed January 15, 2011

Wikipedia, *"Battle of Glendale,"* 2011, http://en.wikipedia.org/wiki/Battle_of_Glendale Accessed January 15, 2011

Wikipedia, *"Battle of Malvern Hill,"* 2011, http://en.wikipedia.org/wiki/Battle_of_Malvern_Hill Accessed January 15, 2011

Wikipedia," *Battle of the Wilderness,"* 2011, http://en.wikipedia.org/wiki/Battle_of_the_Wilderness Accessed January 9, 2011

Wikipedia, *"Battle of White Oak Swamp,"* 2011, http://en.wikipedia.org/wiki/Battle_of_White_Oak_Swamp last accessed January 15, 2011

Wikipedia, *'Battle of Williamsburg",* 2011, http://en.wikipedia.org/wiki/Battle_of_Williamsburg Accessed March 4, 2011

Wikipedia, *"Battle of Wilmington",* 2011, http://en.wikipedia.org/wiki/Battle_of_Wilmington Accessed May 27, 2011

Wikipedia, *"Carolinas Campaign,"* 2011, http://en.wikipedia.org/wiki/Carolinas_Campaign Accessed May 27, 2011

Wikipedia, *"First Battle of Springfield,"* 2011, http://en.wikipedia.org/wiki/First_Battle_of_Springfield Accessed August 5, 2011

Wikipedia, "*John Brown's raid on Harpers Ferry*," 2010, http://en.wikipedia.org/wiki/John_S._Mosby Accessed June 4, 2011

Wikipedia, "*Joseph E. Johnston*, 2011," http://en.wikipedia.org/wiki/Joseph_E._Johnston Accessed August 5, 2011

Wikipedia," *John S. Mosby*, 2011," http://en.wikipedia.org/wiki/John_S._Mosby Accessed August 5, 2011

Wikipedia, "*Knoxville Campaign*, 2010," http://en.wikipedia.org/wiki/Knoxville_Campaign Accessed January 9, 2011

Wikipedia, "*Oath of Allegiance (United States)*," 2010, http://en.wikipedia.org/wiki/Oath_of_Allegiance_(United_States) Accessed February 17, 2011

Wikipedia, "*Peninsula Campaign*," 2011, http://en.wikipedia.org/wiki/Peninsula_Campaign Accessed May 25th, 2011

Wikipedia, "*Second Battle of Bull Run*, 2011," http://en.wikipedia.org/wiki/Second_Battle_of_Bull_Run Accessed January 15, 2011

Wikipedia, "*The Second Battle of Winchester*," 2010, http://en.wikipedia.org/wiki/Battle_of_Winchester_II Accessed January 9, 2011

Wikipedia, "*Seven Days Battles*, 2011," http://en.wikipedia.org/wiki/Seven_Days_Battles Accessed may 25th, 2011

Wikipedia, "*Siege of Petersburg*, 2011," http://en.wikipedia.org/wiki/Siege_of_Petersburg Accessed January 16, 2011

Wikipedia, *"Siege of Yorktown (1862),"* 2011, http://en.wikipedia.org/wiki/Siege_of_Yorktown_(1862) Accessed January 15, 2011

Wikipedia, *"Third Battle of Murfreesboro,"* 2011, http://en.wikipedia.org/wiki/Third_Battle_of_Murfreesboro Accessed May 27, 2011

Wikipedia, *"Union Army,* 2011," http://en.wikipedia.org/wiki/Union_Army Accessed February 17, 2011

Wikipedia, *"Vicksburg Campaign,"* 2011, http://en.wikipedia.org/wiki/Vicksburg_Campaign Accessed January 15, 2011

Wormelle, R. L., Ruth Lenderking Wormelle, *The Lenderking Family, 19th Century,* 1969, self published

CPSIA information can be obtained at www.ICGtesting.com
Printed in the USA
BVOW031728260911

272117BV00001B/4/P